SHAPING
THE SELF

SHAPING THE SELF

Style and Technique in the Narrative

Herbert R. Coursen, Jr.

BOWDOIN COLLEGE

Harper & Row, Publishers
New York, Evanston, San Francisco, London

Sponsoring Editor: George A. Middendorf
Project Editor: Karla B. Philip
Designer: Jared Pratt
Production Supervisor: Will C. Jomarrón
Compositor: Maryland Linotype Composition Co., Inc.
Printer and Binder: The Murray Printing Company

SHAPING THE SELF:
Style and Technique in the Narrative

Library of Congress Cataloging in Publication Data

Coursen, Herbert R   comp.
    Shaping the self.

    1. College readers.   I.   Title.
PE1417.C665   808'.04275   74-31727
ISBN 0-06-041367-0

This book is dedicated to all young people trying to grow up in this less than perfect world we have bequeathed to them: particularly to Elizabeth, Leigh, Virginia, David, Tina, Jeff, Kimmy, Lee Ann, Paul, Oliver, and Mini-S, to the children of black and red America, and to the children of all Vietnam.

Acknowledgments

The following student-written selections originally appeared in *Quill: The Bowdoin College Literary Magazine*: John E. Cartland, "The Treehouse"; Paul B. Ross, "The Stillness and the Fury"; Richard Spear, "Gurry Bot 'Er"; Joe Dane, "The Man"; Nils-Arne Holmlid, "Memories of My Boyhood"; Lawrence G. O'Toole, "Vacation Bible School"; Michael Leonard, "Whale Hunt"; Chris Gahran, "Killing Cats"; John M. MacKenzie, "The Driftwood Stick"; Steve Sylvester, "Whitey"; and Aubrey Haffiz, "The Day of My Birth."

The following student selections originally appeared in *Growing Up in Maine* (1968) and *When Life is Young* (1969), anthologies of writing published by Bowdoin College Upward Bound Students: David Irish, "Barn"; Donna Van Tassell, "Home Thoughts"; Ray Begin, "We Wanna Go Fishing!"; Kenneth Hinkley, "To Get Away"; Phyllis Jalbert, "Jonah and the Whale"; and David Olmstead, "Let's Take a Ride into Tomorrow."

The remaining student selections were previously unpublished: Richard E. Fudge, "To Sing a Sad Song" (1972); Gregory McManus, "The Life of Harry Nelson" (1971); Kris Keller, "Riding High" (1971); Saranne Thomke, "The Dolphin" (1972); and Anonymous, "Who Was Really Responsible?" (1969).

Contents

Introduction: To the Teacher   xiii

Introduction: Discipline and Creativity   1

❀ Chapter 1

SUBJECT AND VIEWPOINT   7

John E. Cartland, The Treehouse   10
Anonymous, Who Was Really Responsible?   15
Gregory McManus, The Life of Harry Nelson   20
Paul B. Ross, The Stillness and the Fury   28
Maxim Gorki, Death and Life   30
Dylan Thomas, Reminiscences of Childhood   35
Summary   40
Exercise   40

❀ Chapter 2

DICTION AND SYNTAX   43

Richard Spear, "Gurry Bot 'Er"   45
Joe Dane, The Man   49
Richard E. Fudge, To Sing a Sad Song   50
Kris Keller, Riding High   52
James Baldwin, Notes of a Native Son   55
Katherine Butler Hathaway, The Disguise   73
Summary   80
Exercise   80

Chapter 3
IMAGERY AND CONTRAST 83

David Irish, *Barn* 84
Saranne Thomke, *The Dolphin* 88
Nils-Arne Holmlid, *Memories of My Boyhood* 93
Lawrence G. O'Toole, *Vacation Bible School* 95
Donna Van Tassell, *Home Thoughts* 97
Ray Begin, *We Wanna Go Fishing!* 100
Henry Adams, *A New England Boyhood* 102
Herbert R. Coursen, Jr., *The Son of Nick Massimo* 104
Summary 107
Exercise 107

Chapter 4
STRUCTURE AND DEVELOPMENT 109

Michael Leonard, *Whale Hunt* 110
Kenneth Hinkley, *To Get Away* 115
Chris Gahran, *Killing Cats* 122
William Gibson, *The Plot Where the Garden Lived* 128
Anne Moody, *Then What Was It?* 144
Summary 155
Exercise 156

Chapter 5
MEANING AND METAPHOR 157

John M. MacKenzie, *The Driftwood Stick* 159
Phyllis Jalbert, *Jonah and the Whale* 163
Steve Sylvester, *Whitey* 165
Aubrey Haffiz, *The Day of My Birth* 172
David Olmstead, *Let's Take a Ride into Tomorrow* 175
Lillian Smith, *When I Was a Child* 176
Frank Conroy, *White Days and Red Nights* 187
Summary 194
Exercise 195

✿ *Chapter 6*

CRITICISM AND REVISION

197

Original Version of *Riding High* 200
Earlier Version of *The Driftwood Stick* 204
Summary 207
Exercise 208

CONCLUSION

209

E. B. White, *Once More to the Lake* 210

Introduction:
To the Teacher

Teachers faced with some 25 to 35 students in each of two or more freshman writing classes often despair of the task before them. I have been and often am in that position. I assign eight to ten papers per semester, grade them diligently and promptly, discuss the principles of composition in the class, expand on my written comments for the guilty creature sitting before me at a conference, and wonder, a little vacantly, at semester's end just what I have accomplished. Maybe something. The students are now better able to cope with the written work that the upper reaches of the curriculum will demand of them. They are now slightly smoother components moving along the line that Henry Ford invented. But, while the students may have honed their compositional abilities to a certain sharpness under the cutting edge of my pen and voice, neither they nor I have achieved anything human. The process has been at best ahuman and at worst antihuman: the developing of a skill to be applied externally, not the probing into a life, the exploration which can allow that life to discover its premises.

But how can the latter—a presumably desirable goal—be accomplished within the seemingly impossible classroom format that presents itself to us, the mass of faces swimming before our sea-weary eyes? How can a teacher face a large class in writing without laying down the law, being arbiter and ultimate authority? Perhaps by taking the risk of allowing the class to assume a substantial portion of the role of critic-commentator, by allowing the class to judge the work usually exchanged only between the teacher and the individual student. I recognize that the individual student is seldom in a position to grade a critical essay. He does not know enough about writing skills (e.g., organization, content, technique) or about that poem by Keats, play by Shakespeare, story by Conrad. If, however, the subject of the essay were some portion of the life of a classmate, or if the student was writing about his or her

own life, a sudden expertise might emerge—not necessarily about writing per se, but certainly about subject matter. And because subject and style are related in some mysterious way, the student might have something to say about writing itself. He could often discern what doesn't work for him. And, I believe, his interest would quicken. It would no longer be the dull process of doing what is required to move on to the next higher level, and the next, and from thence into the world outside. The student might only be capable of a gut response to the sample writings he hears in class, but a valid gut response is probably the first thing any writer should hope for.

I envision a class (and have experienced many such in my 16 years of teaching) in which a student reads a narrative treating some aspect of his past life while his classmates hold copies of the piece before them. I envision response and rejoinder, healthy debate, with the teacher often a quiet, though hardly passive, element in the process—a final arbiter perhaps, but not an immediately imposed authority. Such a format, if format it be, can be accomplished in a large class. I recall a young colleague of mine, young enough to pass for an undergraduate, who wandered into his first class at a large university and sat down among the students, awaiting "the professor." "What do you think this guy will be like?" he asked the people sitting around him. He offered opinions and got others back, mostly clichés of course, stereotypic responses about college professors. My colleague was accomplishing several things. He got the class excited about the person who was coming and about why that person was coming. Just when it seemed that the professor was not going to show and that the class could leave after the passage of the necessary five minutes (my colleague was an instructor, not a professor, though that nuance made little difference to the assembled freshmen), he stood up and said, "Well, I'm it," and introduced himself. Instead of then marching to the podium, he asked the students to circle their chairs around while he remained within the circle. The class had already begun and it continued from there, successfully.

Most of us do not have the youth, personality, or inclination to accomplish what, for us, would be a tour de force. We can, however, create a class in which we ourselves become relaxed participants. Our role is harder at first, particularly with those compliant members of any class who *want* rules, whose need, seemingly, is to fill notebooks. Even when the class I envision veers off in wildly irrelevant directions, even when a student offers a seemingly invalid criticism of a fellow student's work, the teacher will often find the class applying an inner discipline, another student providing a corrective. Is it not better for a student to say, "Come on, let's get back to the point," than for the teacher to say so? Obviously, it takes time and skill to develop a positive dynamic within a group of 25 to 35 students. But is it not precisely such skill that we teachers of writing should develop once our formal training is completed? Admittedly, the process I envision takes more time than does a neat, concise lecture. But is creativity something to be measured by a time-study expert? (Time-study man on Shakespeare: "Wasted 5 minutes sharpening his goose quills, 5 more minutes scratching his head, wrote for 15 minutes, then wasted another 5 minutes reading aloud to himself from some old play.")

What a teacher says to a class, to be transcribed with inevitable inaccuracies into some notebook, is seldom as vital as what students can tell themselves when faced with a common creative or intellectual problem. Students talk and listen to each other. In the class I envision, students would also be ready to listen to the teacher when he or she has something to say. The teacher, the professional, can often summarize the more inchoate offerings of the students; he can usually weave the various threads of response into a fabric that is hopefully not pre-loomed, but rather a product of student attitudes and insights not totally available to the teacher, who is, after all, only one person. His students are many. I envision not a free-for-all, not the blind boxing match so perfectly realized in Ellison's *Invisible Man*, but a movement toward both creativity and discipline within a group, all of whose members are important. Important, though not equal. The teacher is more equal, in a sense, but must exercise his expertise with an almost infinite judiciousness. Some students, by dint of past training, innate ability, and/or fortunate circumstances, may also be more equal; but they may find that fortunate circumstances, be they those of the American middle class, are more of an inhibition than an advantage. No class is ever homogenized at the beginning, though it may be at the end. If a class in writing becomes homogenized, it has become a failure. Yet we, faced with 25 to 35 students several times a day, often force homogeneity on them. We should instead, I contend, encourage the variety latent within the group, not pretend it is not there.

The student-written essays in this book were inspired either by a direct assignment ("Select some significant moment in your past life and write about it"), or by the reading of good professional writing, as a kind of pump-primer. Some of the student writing, of course, was spurred by other student writing, usually after the class began and as students saw that their classmates were writing, and writing well, about their own lives. That most of the student pieces are by males and that many have the scent of Maine about them—wood smoke, salt fish, manure—is a product of my own career at a small college in Maine that has only recently, with my strong encouragement, gone coed. That many of the lives represented in the student selections reflect the style of living that Maine offers merely affirms what I say in the chapter entitled "Meaning and Metaphor." Much value pertains to our experiencing lives other than our own.

To achieve a balance between the student writing I have received and the smoggy, crowded world beyond this province, I have included within the professional writing more women and more blacks—not tokenism in either case, as the selections prove. These selections were also chosen to extend the scope of the readings to a wider range of geography and chronology than the student-written pieces can provide. The primary reason for incorporating professional writing into this book is, however, to allow students to recognize how more accomplished and more mature writers have solved the problems that often remain as problems in the student selections. The professional work demonstrates a fulfillment that much of the student writing merely hints at; but, that is what writing is all about.

The professional pieces also provide a way of looking at the political and social issues that most students perceive but have yet to realize as part of their lived experience. It takes awhile, for example, for some who were part of, say, the antiwar movement of the 1960s to assess their personal and unique involvement in what turned out to be, through some strange alchemy, a majority sentiment. Who knows of anyone, other than public officials on record, who was ever *for* the war? Lest I be accused of beating the dying horse of Vietnam, I should remind everyone that no students we will meet amid the continuing crises, real or manufactured, will cease to be shadowed by what Vietnam did to all of us or, more significantly, what we did to Vietnam. We cannot sweep these questions under our convenient carpets of hope and oblivion as was the presence of the bomb for those of us who reached some sort of maturity during the 1940s. The bomb is still with us, one of those subliminal factors that warp our lives on this insignificant planet we share with significant humans. Suffice it that the professional pieces are part of the challenge this book offers.

The modest proposals for assignments at the end of each chapter are intended as minimum requirements. I hope that this book will encourage far more than what its chapter endings suggest. While I hate apparatus, mine or anyone else's, the suggestions for writing at the end of each chapter are consistent with the goals intended for this book. But these goals are clearly ready to be transposed by whatever electricity an instructor and his class may transmit each to each and, perhaps, all to all. I have been neither a student in nor an instructor of the perfect class. Nor will I be. But somewhere, somehow, we can all do better. I hope the writing produced by a good writing class can be used, increasingly as the course develops, to contrast and compare with both the student and professional work contained in this book.

My initial format for this book made "subject" and "viewpoint" separate categories. I should have seen right away—having read both Henry James and Percy Lubbock—that subject, the experience selected for poem or story, and viewpoint, the author's attitude toward that subject or the way he chooses to project that subject to us, cannot be isolated from each other. Each can be discussed separately, but the first necessarily leads to the second. To impose a different format would be to lie to students, to suggest that once they have a good subject they can pause until they arrive at a section called "viewpoint" and then return to evaluate that subject. They cannot. The students' very selection of a subject involves their stance toward that subject. Indeed, the exploration of their attitudes toward the subject is an essential component in the process of transforming a good subject into an effective literary work. A student must examine his stance before he can know what his subject really is. If he is looking back to some past moment in his life, he may see that it means something quite different to him now than it did then. When it occurred, that past moment may have seemed a triumph or a defeat. He may have learned, however, as does Stephen Dedalus in Joyce's *Portrait of the Artist as a Young Man*, that seeming vindication may end in disappointment and apparent defeat may lead to personal arrival. To plunge into a subject without a defined viewpoint is to risk self-deception. Such a writer could develop the unconscious irony that might make a reader sneer, "Does he really believe this?" Such a writer might find himself being manipulated by rather than manipulating the clichés of his time or his characters. A character who lives within clichés can be an effective subject for a story, but only if the writer himself recognizes those clichés. A writer without a point of view cannot develop the controlled irony that allows readers to share, rather than reject, the writer's perceptions and the experience he brings before them.

This book is not intended as a set of neatly defined terms, obediently pursued by examples, but a pairing of elements of style and technique that belong together and involve the questions a writer must ask himself and the challenges he must meet if his writing is to communicate experience and meaning to his reader.

The student selections included in this book suggest that good writing is within the grasp of almost any student. Lest that claim seem farfetched, let me merely indicate that the range of both aptitude and ability represented by the student writers is extremely wide, some 400 points variation in that admittedly imperfect category called *verbal aptitude*. The selections run the gamut from those by students who love to write to those by students who responded in terror, surprise, or bewilderment at the suggestion that they try to write (many fell into the latter category). The cultural range is also wide, as the selections prove. The professional selections show a further level of achievement — beyond the grasp of most students, but nevertheless a level that can inform the student and toward which some students will aspire. After all, the professional writer was, and in many ways still is, a student.

The terms used as chapter titles are not intended as absolute and nonnegotiable categories to be captured within the strictness of some definition; they are intended to be flexible concepts, as living words always are, providing a vocabulary that allows us to discuss the selections in the book and the writing done by students who use the book. Hopefully, my inclusion of student writing, incorporated within a modest frame of terms and discussion, will allow students to respond more positively than were they coerced into that deadly textbook atmosphere which often defeats them at the start.

The nondefinitive approach challenges the teacher, of course. He cannot relax into a format. He must be an accurate evaluator of the writing in the book and of his students' writing. The book is intended precisely for that teacher willing to accept the challenge it offers him and his students. A textbook, ideally, should encourage a student to recognize his own potential creativity and the ways that creativity can be shaped and realized. A textbook should not be a final solution, providing the answers to the questions it raises. Such a book would deny that the student and teacher have something to add and would thereby suggest that it hasn't really raised questions at all.

The pairing of terms in each chapter title suggests merely that certain activities of writing are best discussed together; for example, subject cannot be divorced from viewpoint. In the first chapter, the combined consideration of subject and viewpoint leads inevitably to a consideration of *irony.* To toss irony at a student in an opening chapter might seem to introduce a subtle distinction prior to the mastery of basics. It is preferable, however, for a student to understand immediately that his attitude toward his material imposes a built-in irony on that material. Irony, after all, is a discrepancy between points of view, between (1) what a character says and what he means (verbal irony), (2) what a character knows and what we know (dramatic irony), or (3) the actual situation and what would *seem* appropriate either to the character, the reader, or both (situational irony). Students work effectively with situational irony—in their perceptions of their lives and their society—and with verbal irony. Dramatic irony is virtually automatic in a student's assumption of a stance toward his past life—a stance which not only looks at it, but which perceives that that former self is not the same as the person looking back. A discussion of irony in the first chapter, then, seems necessary. The dangers of not raising the issue are that the student may be unconsciously ironic in his writing if he is not aware that he is manipulating a built-in discrepancy between himself then and himself now, or between his character and the stance he has assumed as creator of that character. The student must grasp, right away, the inevitability of his use of irony. It is built into the structure of his life and, if his life is his subject, it must necessarily be built into his narrative.

In the second chapter, a discussion of *diction* (choice of words) leads to a consideration of *syntax* (the ordering of words, the structuring of sentences). Syntax will be treated only briefly in this book, for it is a concept best considered within the unique context of a student's writing. This book does not pretend to be a grammar text, and therefore does not define the uses of and distinctions between, for example, complex and compound sentences. This is not to deny the importance of such distinctions, but to suggest that such distinctions are best made by a teacher with the work of his own student before him. Furthermore, the student's development of a good ear, a sense of his own prose rhythms, and an increasing aptitude for alternating rhythms effectively are more important than an understanding of the rules of grammar, whatever they may or may not be. The question of the ear is basic to the course format I suggest, implicit in the discussion of specific terms and techniques, and dealt with explicitly in the chapter on criticism and revision.

Imagery, the writer's appeal to the reader's sense, can depend on *similarity* or *contrast*. Similarity, or likeness, can often relate an unusual situation to one more familiar to the reader. My own feeling, however, is that such likeness can best be discussed under the topic of *metaphor*, which is often used by writers to achieve images within the reader's senses, but is hardly reserved exclusively for that purpose. I have combined imagery with contrast in Chapter 3 for several reasons. First, we often see or experience things against a background, or in contrast to elements of a quality distinct from what we wish the reader to experience. "I see them bend to left and right," says Frost of birch trees, "against the line of straighter, darker trees." The whiteness and flexibility of the birches are seen and felt because of the contrasting background of oak and maple. Second, contrast often involves attitude. Many of the readings in this book suggest the contrast between what young people understand and the attitudes of adults. Thus, contrast can become *conflict*. Since this book is organized around narrative techniques and is not a book about writing fiction, I have not elevated conflict to a separate category. Many of the personal experiences treated by the student writers have, however, evolved into fiction. Conflict, for many students, summons up images of violence. Yet few of the narratives in this book depend solely on an external conflict, with a character poised against some person or force outside of himself. The concept of contrast has an applicability wider than that of conflict; it plays a major role in all genres of imaginative writing. Finally, contrast can also be a structural element, a way of ordering material toward its maximum impact.

At the risk of seeming arbitrary, I have included a brief discussion of *dialogue* in the chapter on imagery and contrast. The spoken words of different characters balanced against each other constitute a kind of contrast. More important, dialogue is a kind of imagery. Good dialogue allows us not merely to hear voices, but to feel what is behind the voices, tone, or attitude of the speakers. If a writer considers dialogue a very special kind of imagery, he is more likely to create it effectively than if he merely considers it to be words spoken aloud.

Structure, as we see in Chapter 4, is the placement of components within a narrative so that each section comments effectively on the other; it is different from *development*, which involves not the arrangement of elements, but the recognition of them. Even a beautifully structured piece of writing may be merely an outline for a complete exploration of the events described. Development, then, is also a function of viewpoint. Raw experience must be sorted out, assessed for what is significant and what is insignificant, so the experience can be shaped into something that is not experience per se but which transmits experience more vividly to the reader. Structure and development may be interdependent, but they are distinct considerations. Too many discussions of prose have obliterated or blurred the distinctions.

Meaning and *metaphor* are the subjects of Chapter 5. Metaphor, like contrast, suggests another potential organizing device, either because the metaphor of a story might dictate a series of related images to be woven throughout the narrative fabric or, more basically, because the story might have a further level of interpretation, either allegorically or symbolically. The narrative might be a story of initiation, reflecting in a specific way the universal experience of growing up, of encountering something new, exciting, or painful. The narrative might be more precisely allegorical, reflecting a single deeper element, the results of a character's pride or prejudice or innocence or false sense of sophistication. Metaphor, an implied comparison between two essentially unlike things, can be the writer's link between the specific elements of his story and what the story means. The best of writing seldom tells us directly what it means. In some cases it cannot, because the elements of the narrative are not reducible to some easy formula. Robert Frost once said that "poetry is what evaporates from all translations." *The Rime of the Ancient Mariner* means more than "He prayeth best, who loveth best, all things both great and small." The *experience* of the poem cannot be squeezed into an aphorism. The narrator should, above all, leave us with the feeling of experience and should allow us to find our way to the underlying meanings of that experience. Thus the metaphor often coalesces within the reader, within that "unlike thing"—another human—who perceives the comparison which metaphor enforces. A life totally unlike our own, if vividly recreated, can evoke resonances within us, the stirrings of universal human values, deeply shared hopes and fears. Metaphor, then, becomes a term for the allegory of human existence, which everyone shares, the magic bridge whereby we enter the lives of others and across which we return as our altered selves.

Criticism and revision, the subjects of Chapter 6, would seem to fit squarely under the rubrics of *discipline*; but revision in the light of careful reexamination of a piece of writing is often the final step toward true creativity. Such revision might involve the expansion of some sentences into paragraphs, the elimination of some details as irrelevant to the narrative thrust, the rearrangement of elements toward their maximum effect: in other words, the reconsideration of all the aspects discussed in this book. Above all, revision involves careful *listening*. Students should read their writing aloud to themselves and to their classmates. The latter experience can be traumatic, but once the class begins to listen to its prose, comment on it, debate it, develop an accurate critical vocabulary, and bring revised work forward, the process becomes accepted as if there were no other way to do it. The students become critics not only of their own prose but also of that of their classmates', whose work may trigger new ideas for the student's own work. Students who develop critical facility in class discussions are almost invariably more accurate critics of their own writing. No writer succeeds without the ability to accept criticism of his work or without the willingness to revise his writing toward that coherence Emerson defines when he talks of "prose that bleeds."

The terms heading each chapter, then, are not meant to be defined. Definition often circles back to the word itself and excludes the projection of that word into a context where it functions as something more than itself, as process, as principle. The terms are to be understood as ways of talking about what writers do and as ways of understanding how student writers can do the same things.

The use of personal experience has always been a good way of starting students off, of tricking them, perhaps, toward the analytical essay. But it is a valid genre, as many great writers have shown, and a way whereby good, average, nonverbal, marginal, and turned-off students can use language that is not merely effective, but human for both the writer and his audience.

Before students can write "sociology," "economics," "history," or "literary criticism," they should attain some preliminary sense of what has happened to them, of their own sociological and economic stance, of their own position within the pressure of history, of their own awareness that literature emerges from the center of lived experience and is not some mystery reproduced in anthologies. Writing about what one has seen, heard, and felt, about what has moved one toward perception, is potentially much more than a starting point for a composition course. The student who writes about his experience rather than about himself (and immediately we sense the relationship between subject and viewpoint), about what happened to him and how he responded and how he responds now, rather than about how he feels about things, may well discover that he has revealed more than he realizes. Once he recognizes what he has suggested about himself, he may also recognize the futility of the deceptions he practices upon himself and his world.

Many of today's students claim for themselves a greater honesty and self-awareness than that of prior generations, a greater desire "to get my head into something meaningful, something real." These students may be right to suggest that much of our curricula inhibit their drive toward this goal. To allow them to explore the curve of their own experience, its limitations, biases, and strengths is to allow them not only to move outward from a personal center but also more deeply into it—another metaphor of a bridge lengthening in two directions at once. A student writer can involve his readers in the multiplicity of images and responses that only he can recreate. Only he has been there, in the center of his consciousness ringed by the swing of his experience. The ultimate goal of the writing process is hardly that the student "find" himself in a static platonic sense. Rather, the goal is for the student to begin the process of creating a self in the dynamic existential sense, to discover not what his experience has meant, but what it means and will mean. The backward look can be the impulse forward, disciplined by deeper perceptions about the self that is shaping.

Everything that is to be
And all to which you aspire
Is within you to recall . . .

Lines found in the water closet
of the Turtle Cafe,
Cambridge, Massachusetts

Introduction:
Discipline
and
Creativity

Creativity, Fernald said, must be stressed in education. Let discipline come later, maybe in college. "Find a guy who wants to write poetry and let him write poetry. Then tell him he's got to learn the discipline."

"It's like saying get into my car and have as many crashes as you like," Bullock said to Fernald," and then I'll tell you what you do wrong."

"Creativity in itself is worth nothing," Potterveld said. "Creativity can be chaos."

"I'm all for creativity," Bullock said, "but I'm for discipline first."

This debate, excerpted from Peter S. Prescott's fascinating book about The Choate School, A World of Our Own, focuses on one of the central issues of education: Are we imposing discipline or are we encouraging creativity? To stand firmly on one side of the question or the other is to be both right and wrong. In writing, as in most other activities, discipline and creativity are simultaneous energies expended within a single event. Noncreative discipline is perhaps a kind of death, death at an early age, as many critics of our schools have suggested. Yet undisciplined creativity is impossible. The creative impulse must shape itself into form—on canvas, in stone, in words. Creativity and discipline cannot be separated, as the Choate masters tend to separate them.

Robert Frost once said that he would "as soon write poetry without rhyme as play tennis with the net down." Frost takes too restrictive a view of free verse, which can be highly disciplined, organizing itself around what a metaphor may dictate or deny; but he has a point. "Stopping by Woods on a Snowy Evening" is the supreme example of that point. Part of the poem's success depends on Frost's escape from the seemingly impossible rhyme scheme he has set for himself. Creativity bursts past discipline, but that creativity—Frost's decision to repeat the third line of the last stanza—could only emerge from the highly disciplined context of the series of rhymed quatrains he wrote. Why does Frost use the tennis analogy? Tennis involves hitting a ball over a net and into a zone within the sidelines and under or on the baseline. The players reveal skill within the dimensions set for them. As Frost suggests, if you play tennis without a net, without any lines, and allow as many bounces as necessary for the player to reach the ball, then you have no game—exercise and perhaps a free-form creativity, but no game. No shape, no form, no final cause. Two people beginning without limits would soon realize that to achieve meaning they would have to impose rules. Until that time, they would have no chance to be creative. What good is your perfect dropshot if your opponent can dawdle up to it, take it on the third bounce, and drive it back one foot off the ground? Creativity can define itself only within discipline.

By creating limits, by imposing form upon their initial creative impulse, those who developed tennis were also being creative. The creative impulse could realize itself only through a further series of creative acts—the invention of lines and a net, the stipulation of no more than one bounce—that have become the disciplined medium into which still more creativity flows. The superb poet Gerard Manley Hopkins took the inherited form of the Italian sonnet and achieved something new within the structure of the sonnet. He liberated it from the stricter rhythms of iambic pentameter, writing poetry that sounds unique—perhaps most notably in "The Windhover." Yet the form was there for him to work variations on, challenging him to achieve differences within its discipline. He overcame the challenge partly because he was a brilliant innovator, but also because it was there, latent within the inherited form.

The player who hits a brilliant—and intentional—shot, a lob volley over his net-crowding opponent's head, can do so only after he has mastered all the techniques of the racket and has attuned himself to the instant calculation of myriad data: How fast is his shot coming? Where is he? Where am I? What did I do in this situation last time? Did it work? Will it work now? What is he expecting? Can I do something different? Obviously, he cannot think of all these things within that instant when the ball presents itself for decision. Yet he does. He has disciplined himself toward that split second of creativity. The motivation that made him pick up a racket in the first place has been honed by hitting thousands of tennis balls millions of times, until initial impulse is fulfilled in that great shot. Writing gives its practitioner more time to chose the right word, but it demands the same instinct for the one word that will work at the moment it is needed. And that word is not the gift of some muse sitting on the writer's shoulder; the word will come only if the writer·has acquired the discipline needed to find it.

When I began planning this book, I separated it into two main sections, discipline and creativity. This separation seemed as logical to me as it did to some of the Choate masters quoted earlier. It may have seemed logical, but I soon became convinced that it excluded more truth than it contained. Few writers begin by saying to themselves, "I'll jot down some free-flowing ideas, then I'll come back and shape them into something" or "I'll write in a very tight form, then I'll come back and free it up." Without denying the importance of a writer's getting his ideas flowing, perhaps even randomly into a tape recorder, I suggest that the ideas would gradually flow toward *form*. The corollary to this suggestion is that the writer already has a sense of what form is, of the potential genre or media within which his ideas will find themselves. The tennis player warming up is not overly worried about where his shots go. He is getting his eye on the ball, loosening up his arms and legs, attempting to establish a rhythm that will move him effectively into that moment when the placement of his shots will be reflected in the score of a game, a set, and a match.

The writer moving into the rhythms of his ideas may recognize, for example, that the character he is thinking about, perhaps himself, is involved in a conflict. If he is a poet, he might move his idea toward the sonnet form, specifically a sonnet that would allow him to develop a structure of thesis and antithesis, statement and counterstatement. The conflict may not be resolved, but it may be explored effectively. If the writer works primarily in fiction, his ideas might flow toward a short story and all of the possibilities that form offers. Conversely, of course, the writer might sit down intentionally to write a poem or a story and bring his ideas to focus on the medium he has set for himself. I am not attempting to isolate the mysterious and elusive factors involved in the making of literature. Rather, I am urging the fusion of the twin processes of creativity and discipline.

The difference between what so many of our schools and colleges do to our students and the attitude advocated here is neatly captured in *Gestalt Therapy*:*

When one fears contact with actuality—with flesh-and-blood people and with one's own sensations and feelings—words are interposed as a screen both between the verbalizer and his environment and his own organism.

* Frederick Perls, Ralph Hefferline, and Paul Goodman, *Gestalt Therapy: Excitement and Growth in the Human Personality*, New York: Julian, 1969.

*The person attempts to live on words—and then wonders vaguely why
something is amiss! . . . He attempts in compulsive and obsessive ways to
"be objective" about his personal experience. [Thus] he avoids contact with
the feeling, the drama, the actual situations. He lives the substitute life of
words, isolated from the rest of his personality.*

I am not pleading for rampant subjectivity, but rather for a human
response to literature before that response is defined by a discipline
called "literary criticism." One of the finest teachers of writing I know,
C. B. Hudson, insists that when students respond to the work of their
classmates, "No criticism of form or technique is allowed until each
critic has given a gut reaction—has responded to the work on an
emotional level."

The exploration of personal experience may be a way of probing
beneath "how I feel" or "what's it all about?" or "what the hell
difference does it make?" to discover that which is at once unique and
universal within a student's life, that which he alone can communicate
to his audience. To encourage a student to prove that he has been
alive and is alive is to allow him to escape from the cliché world of
deplorings and platitudes that have become a too familiar litany in the
prose we often read. Furthermore, it will help him overcome whatever
forces he conceives to be threatening him or render them as irrelevant
as possible. This process cannot occur if his "education" gradually
detaches him from the experiential and emotional content of the life he
is leading.

The existence of a man and the words he uses to express his
existence are not only inseparable, but mutually controlling elements.
A student will recognize this as he replaces the clichés he has unwit-
tingly used with fresher language, language that is more his own
because expressive of his lived experience, language capturing a life,
not reflecting the graveyard of dead phrases. He will replace the passive
"could be heard" and "was seen" with the mutter and growl, the leap
and shimmer, the sights and sounds that hit his ears and eyes; he will
exchange the generalization for the image, the abstraction for the
concrete word.

The process of revision, combined with the criticisms of the writer's
classmates and teacher, will create in the writer a sense of the reader's
expectations. Such expectations exist not merely to be neatly fulfilled,
but often to be refuted, particularly since expectations often emerge
from the cliché: the happy ending with the protagonist victorious or
the sadder but wiser ending with the protagonist slightly bloody but not
likely to bow again to the same error of judgment. Such endings can be
valid, but the writer aware of convention can choose to defy it, as
Emily Brontë does in the final meeting this side of death between

Heathcliff and Catherine. Instead of swearing undying devotion and manfully clenching back his tears as he hearkens to the last faint endearments of the dying Catherine, Heathcliff excoriates her. The power of the scene derives partially from its refusal to reiterate the patterns of so many other scenes in so many novels, far more popular in their time than *Wuthering Heights* but now well lost in the darkness of time. Hemingway's Catherine Barkley and Frederick Henry escape from war to the safety of Switzerland, where they should live happily ever after. But Catherine dies anyway. Partly because *Wuthering Heights* and *A Farewell to Arms* reject the clichés they might embrace, they continue to be read, while the sentimentality of *A Catcher in the Rye* and the utter banality of *Love Story* drive these former best-sellers to oblivion. The more a writer senses his reader's expectations, the more he can challenge them, pushing his writing and his reader beyond the merely conventional. That iconoclasm which so many students claim for themselves can achieve meaning only in proportion to the student's awareness of the images he would break.

Clearly, this book calls for class participation, with one student reading his work aloud while the other students hold copies of the piece before them. In the discussion following the reading of each piece, the students should be encouraged to respond to each other rather than filter their responses through the authority figure behind the desk. Such redirection of the vectors of response and reply can mean participation beyond the lip-service involvement of a class whose format has been imposed, however covertly, by the teacher. Ideally, when the creativity of the class is encouraged, it will evolve toward discipline qua class. But the discipline will not be that imposed by an awesome or totalitarian teacher or even by a genial master of ceremonies. It will emerge from the class as its members recognize for themselves the importance and enjoyment of writing well. This is hardly to suggest the obsoleteness of the teacher. His skill and guidance, his orchestration of the materials and the members of the class will always be important. I hope, however, that this book will gradually become obsolete. The writings of the class should supersede that which has encouraged the creative action and discipline of the class and of each individual within it.

Finally, I suggest that language has a moral quality, an ethical dimension, which we ignore at our peril. If language is merely a tool, as we are so often told, then we discover that it is something apart from us—something alien and mechanical, something nonhuman at best. Consider those literate men who "designed" Vietnam, members of the Groton-St.Paul's-Choate-Harvard-Yale axis, Rhodes Scholars, elitely educated. Not once in those Pentagon Papers do they express any concern for human life, the many lives hinging on their decisions— the lives that would be lost, as those men had to know, once those decisions were implemented. They ask "Will it work?" or, more basically, "Can we sell it?" as if war were an automobile. For them language *is* a tool, the cutting edge of their careers and reputations, a way of avoiding their stake in mankind, not of expressing it and never of sharing it.

Language is a human creation. Used honestly it is a kind of self, a way of embracing our selfhood and our relation to our world. It is not something apart from ourselves—what I say is me. Used dishonestly, it is a way of divorcing ourselves from ourselves and, by extension, from our involvement in mankind. In the Elizabethan Age, the word *kind* meant, among other things, "of mankind." It expressed an awareness of oneness and union with our species, an ethical dimension that seems to have eroded as the word has come down to us. Now it seems to presuppose a certain arrogance: I am in a position of superiority and I can be patronizing or condescending; I can be kind, kind to animals, blacks, poor people, Vietnamese. The word *charity* has suffered a similar degradation. Charity was once synonymous with *love*. While these words cannot be reconstituted to their fuller meanings, writers must feel the words they use in their human context. Quite simply, words are the creations of men and, at their best, they appeal to what is deepest within the condition of mankind. If we do not insist that our language retain its central role as a human expression, we will learn only to lie. And in the process we will succeed in dehumanizing ourselves.

ONE

Subject
and
Viewpoint

Many people believe that a writer is someone blessed with an extraordinary imagination. A writer may have a fine imagination, just as some athletes seem to possess innate endurance. Marathon runners and boxers, however, gain endurance from training, including miles and miles of running. Most writers develop that elusive element "imagination" from training. The writer develops the ability to perceive the story in what is happening to him, to feel it in the words he hears or overhears, to see it in the faces he passes. The writer's imagination, then, is a product of conditioning, of facing each moment as if it were a potential story, poem, or play. He has a built-in point of view: "I am a writer and I relate experience to that fact." The painter sees each scene as a potential design on canvas and views details as potential blending of color, even as brushstrokes. Everything he sees, of course, does not become a painting, but his senses and mind are trained to translate automatically what he sees into his artistic medium. He enjoys what he observes as a potential painting, perhaps even something created in his mind's eye; when he sees the scene or face he *must* paint, he recognizes it. He has trained himself in the process of recognition, which is a large part of imagination.

The American painter Winslow Homer completed *Cannon Rock* on the coast of Maine—completed it, that is, with the exception of the single wave he felt his painting required. The canvas waited for two weeks until Homer saw precisely the wave he wanted breaking on the Atlantic a few hundred yards offshore. He captured it in his eye and rushed back to his studio to complete his painting. He could, of course, have painted in any wave and few would have been the wiser. But, for Homer, the painting would not have been right unless that wave were true to his experience. His uncompromising insistance on the actual is one of the elements that lend a feeling of authenticity to his paintings. We know that they emerge from an eye that has not merely glanced at the sea, but has really looked at it, studied it.

Robert Frost was asked by a college sophomore how he got the ideas for his poems. A sophomoric question (I know because I asked it), but Frost was in a benign mood that evening and answered in a metaphor, an allegory of the imagination: "The coming of an idea? . . . let's see . . . it's like this: You see your friend stumbling down the path toward you and you don't know what pleasantry you are going to inflict on him. But you know it will be something, and it grows on you as he approaches. Then, just as he passes, you turn and say the right thing." I did not know it at the time, but Frost was reflecting a decisive prior condition. You cannot "turn and say the right thing" unless you have trained yourself to recognize "the friend coming down the path"—that is, a possible poem approaching, an image caught in the eye, a fragment of language trapped in the ear—informed by an essential context: I am a poet and I relate experience to that fact.

Today, sitting in my kitchen in Brunswick, Maine, on a cold January evening, I listen to what I am saying and to the old electric clock behind me on the wall.

> The clock behind me rattles on the wall,
> Growing old, hands creaking as from works
> Congested with the winter's phelgm. The clock
> Has told the hours of a marriage in
> Another place, and taught the children time
> In what must seem to them another life,
> Recalling where all past years are. Somehow
> From all I've scattered in the wake of days,
> The clock survives to teach again the sweep
> And sequence of the question held somewhere
> Within the youth of love, the other face,
> The spring above an April's welling wish.
> The hands absorb the winter from the fall,
> The clock behind me trembles on the wall.

A half hour later, I return to this chapter, making no great claims for my poem, but possibly having illustrated a point. Writing demands that the writer assume the stance that says "I am a writer. I look at the world not merely as a usually dull, sometimes exciting, occasionally terrifying place where I serve out my time, but as a source, overwhelming in its richness of material, of all that I can shape into prose, poetry, drama." Obviously, too much material exists for any writer. But a life spent looking intently for that right wave, or watching for a friend to stumble down the path, or even listening for the first time to that old clock, is lived, not merely wandered through without comment.

If a student is willing to take that initial step, to say "Okay, what have I got to lose? It sounds strange, but 'I am a writer,'" he has mastered his first lesson in point of view. Now he must seek his subject, or allow it to seek him. Good subjects are abundant and can usually be found in the writer's past experience. Most students claim that "nothing much has ever happened to me," and possibly they are right. Nothing very exciting or dramatic seems to have happened to them. But good writing does not necessarily emerge from exciting events. The quieter things that have happened to us are often the most amenable to development. Excitement is not a product of external events, but instead a measure of the person living a life, a product of his vision, insight, and sense of humor. The claim that life is dull, the claim of Eliot's Mr. Prufrock and of many of us, says nothing about life; but it scores a telling point against the person making the statement. Conversely, truly exciting events often lose their excitement in the telling. One cannot write down an experience. Writing is an event, but it is not the event being written about. Reading is an experience, but it is not the experience being read about. *Actual experience* has to be carefully shaped, recreated through the control of a well-defined attitude, before it can simulate the impact of the *real experience*.

This book includes many narratives written by students and professionals. The class may wish, for starters, to read some of the essays aloud, perhaps even to have one member assume the role of the writer. He would be responsible for defending the essay in response to the critique of his classmates. This process might ease the transition to the student's presentation of his own work. Suffice it that the narratives in this book should be read aloud. Only then can their strengths and possible weaknesses be grasped.

The following essay was written by a college student.

❀ THE TREEHOUSE

John E. Cartland

The immediacy of a fourth grader's world is rarely breached, but as Roger Purvis was called to the school office, he was traveling to a place he had never been, into an adult world he only barely understood. He was relieved to find his mother there, and when he was told to get his coat and not to forget his books, he was more bewildered than frightened. As they walked out of the building, the echoing staccato of her heels told him not to say anything. She had the old car, the grey Dodge with the body rot and rust, whose field of action had been limited to errands around town. But as they drove out of town, the silence was still unbroken. He turned on the radio, and she just as firmly reversed the knob. She looked over at him and smiled, and then quickly stopped as if it had been a mistake. Her mouth moved once or twice as if she were trying for words that would not come, and then they came. He didn't understand all that she said. They were going to pick up his grandmother, and there was something about his aunt, his father's sister, being sick. He was confused about this. He tried to think of this aunt. She only lived a few miles away, but the most he could really remember was that it took an awfully long time to get there, but was much quicker on the way back. The person was much more vague—her house always smelled of something his mother said was nice, and there were a lot of china things on the tables, but since she didn't like children, he didn't see much of her. Anyway, something had happened to her and she was in the hospital being "observed." But why was his grandmother coming? She only came at Christmas with presents and she always had some candy which she shared with him in her room without the rest of the family knowing about it. But it wasn't Christmas. He remembered that earlier that day he had to write the date, May 3, on the board of his homeroom. And he was still more confused, but somehow agreed to the silence that continued after his mother stopped talking.

They had met his grandmother for lunch. But she hardly said hello to him, and he sat quietly trying to understand the talk between the two women. They had never really gotten along well, but now it seemed different; more talk of his aunt, and of the hospital and observations. He sat cut off from them, and didn't even know why he was there, and he thought of what would be going on in school. His grandmother turned once and asked him how school was, but as he was telling her about the baseball game that his homeroom was playing that afternoon, she seemed to lose interest and turned again to his mother.

The ride back to his house didn't go any more quickly than the one that morning. The back seat of the car held little of interest for him, and the world outside existed now without him. When they got home, his mother made a phone call to his father while he took his grandmother's suitcase up to her room. He stood around to see if she would come up and they could share some candy like they always did, but when she didn't, he decided to go outside and work on his treehouse. As he was going out the door, his mother called softly to him from the den, and he wondered what she wanted now. She sat him down and talked to him as she had that morning, but now her voice was softer, and more unlike the voice of his mother that he was used to.

"Your aunt has been very sick Roger, and that's why she was in the hospital. The doctors wanted to find out what was wrong with her—you see they thought she had a very bad disease. And the doctors were right, she had something called cancer. She died this afternoon, and this is something you must understand. Your father and grandmother are going to be very sad now, you see your aunt is no longer with us here on earth. She has gone to heaven, and she isn't sick any more or in pain, but she is gone from us, do you

see? So you could be a good boy and be very quiet, and do as
much as you can to make your father and grandmother happy, for
they are very sad now. If you want, go out and play, but try to be
quiet in the house." Though his mother had said this all slowly, he
didn't really understand, and was anxious to get out and play, and so he
only half-listened. He bounded out of the house, and as the screen
door repeated the slam of the kitchen door, he heard his mother's
voice sharply calling to him to be more considerate and quiet.

The treehouse was just as he had left it, and he noticed
on one of the lower branches his father's saw which he had been
told not to forget to bring in, and now it had rust on its edge. But
he didn't feel like building, he didn't think he should feel like
building. He was still confused, but he tried to make some sense as he
sat up in the half-finished house. He knew what heaven was from
Sunday School; well he didn't know really, but he thought of
happiness, with angels and harps and music, and no pain like his
mother said. But he wasn't sure how you got there—he didn't quite
know what his mother meant when she said that his aunt had died. He
wouldn't see her anymore. That didn't really bother him. He had
only seen her two or three times anyway that he could remember, and
now he wouldn't have to go into her smelly house. But there was
something else, something more that he couldn't think about
because he didn't know what it was. He didn't feel sad. Oh maybe
a little, because he saw how sad his mother was, but he couldn't
understand that either. And he didn't really know anything
except that he should be sad, be quiet. It seemed strange to him
up there in his treehouse as he looked down to where he lived. He
noticed that the shades in his grandmother's room had been drawn, but
then he began to think about the treehouse. His mother had laughed
at it—it did look sort of funny with only a platform and one or
two boards going up which would eventually support the roof.
And though it didn't seem adequate to provide protection from the
many tribes of Indians that were always sneaking around the house to
attack him, he always managed to win, even after being mag-
nificently wounded two or three times. And soon he wasn't thinking
why he should be sad at all.

The next days were spent in the same limbo of confusion, with
no relief provided by either understanding or normality. Roger
unconsciously reached a compromise between his parents' grief and his
own non-understanding, through a mechanical observation of what
was demanded of him by his aunt's death. Being out of school
for three days was almost like a holiday. He spent much of his time
alone, in his treehouse. His parents were pretty busy now, and
his grandmother just stayed in her room by herself, and he wondered

if she was eating the candy by herself. But the oppressive silence of the house made him uneasy and so he left the house as often as possible.

On the morning of the third day that he had been home, he was told that he had to get dressed for the funeral that morning. As he was struggling for control over his tie, his mother came to his room and began to talk about what would go on at the funeral. She tried to explain the religious significance of the rite, and how that afterwards the casket, the box his aunt's body was in, would be buried in the ground. And again, she talked about her soul going to heaven, and happiness and no pain. And again Roger was confused, that because his aunt had found happiness and no pain, he had to assume a mask of sadness. By this time he could not even recall his aunt, and his only association with her had become the sadness and quiet which he had to maintain. The church service was pretty much the same as they always were, except for the shiny wooden box in the front. The box fascinated him, and he wanted to go up to it and rub his hand over its smooth surface that shone in the odd light of the church. But the training of the past few days made him sit motionless. The minister kept talking, or reading something, very solemnly, and Roger wondered when he was going to finish. The pew became uncomfortable, and as he squirmed in the stuffy warmth of the room, a black glove rested on his elbow. His mother whispered that he had been a good boy, and that she knew how hard it was for him, and that it would soon be over. After the service he lost his parents in the crowd of people that came up to them, and he went to the parking lot where he had seen a hop-scotch game scratched on the asphalt.

He didn't go to the cemetery with his parents and some of the others, but was taken home by a friend of his mother's. By the time his parents came home, he was out in his treehouse again, the last survivor of a surprise attack by Geronimo. He had just killed the old chief when he first noticed that there were quite a few cars in the driveway and in front of the house. He wondered if all these people could be quiet too, the way they were supposed to be. He remembered that he was hungry, and that he hadn't eaten since that snack he had after he came home from church. He jumped down from the tree and shot a few more Indians, just to make sure it was safe. He wandered in the back door and into the kitchen. Alma, the girl who came in sometimes to help his mother, was there. She was bending over a tray of sandwiches so that she was startled when a hand reached around and grabbed one from in front of her. She turned around and said nothing for what seemed the longest time, and then murmured something about "you poor boy." Roger wasn't

sure why she was here, but then he wasn't sure what she had said
either, so he just left the room and went up the back stairs. He
wandered down the hall to where the front stairs met the second
floor, and sat down to listen to the people below. Their noise
was familiar to him, and he thought back to the other times when
his parents had had parties, and he was allowed to come and pass plates
of things around. The brittle sounds of swirling ice on wafts of smoke
came up the stairs to him, and he heard a muffled laugh, or more
rarely, a quiet tear being let go, and again and still he was
confused.

He went down the back stairs, and out to his treehouse
again. He took up some lumber and started to put up a wall for
more protection from the Indians. Just as he finished his house he
began to wonder about the events of the past few days, and
thought how much fun he had had being out of school and working
up in the tree.

❋   ❋   ❋   ❋

In "The Treehouse" we have nothing very dramatic. A fourth-grader
encounters death for the first time and he meets it in his own way—
bewildered, not able to comprehend adult attitudes—as he follows the
code he thinks is expected of him. He is finally quite happy to escape
to his treehouse. The treehouse is his world and he receives an unexpected bonus of time in which to enjoy that world. The story conveys
a truth: No matter what death may be, life goes on for the survivors.
They still eat, drink, and sleep. And, if they are children, they play. But
the story does not say this in so many words. It demonstrates its truth
by projecting us into the world of Roger Purvis as he is pulled from
his school and into the strange adult world of grief, soft voices, and
"arrangements." The story emerges from the child's point of view. We
know only what he knows, we see only what he sees, but we infer
much more because we are not children and because the writer uses
very mature language, recreating the world of the fourth-grader in
words obviously not available to the young boy. To use mature language to capture the experience of immaturity is valid. We have only to
recognize how impossible it would be for the fourth-grader to capture
his story in his own idiom. He can tell his story only with the aid of
that mature observer who can show us what he sees and feels and thus
allows us to know what he does not see. True, a great writer, a Mark
Twain or a William Faulkner, can accomplish the same effect by using
the voice of the youthful narrator; but a student can judge the difficulty
of that feat by recasting Roger Purvis's story into the language of a
fourth-grader. We have in "The Treehouse," as in most good auto-

biographical writing, a double vision: the world of the boy informed by the voice of the mature writer.

John Cartland establishes a further separation between the experience per se and the voice describing it by naming his character, changing from "I" to "Roger Purvis." This allows the writer to view his character as someone separate from himself. Even writers working from the materials of their own experience sometimes find it helpful to create an alter ego who can be observed with more detachment than an "I," the person the writer once was. The transfer to a named character also allows the writer to shape a narrative rather than merely report "what happened next." As André Malraux suggests, "Memory does not recreate a life in its original sequence." Nor does narrative. Narrative is informed by themes and patterns and a point of view only latent within the raw material of the experience from which the narrative is crafted.

An immediate question a writer must ask is: Who is telling the story? Here it is not the young boy, but a voice that restricts itself to only what the boy can see and know and frees itself of the restrictions of the boy's meager vocabulary. In the original draft of "The Treehouse," John Cartland wrote "but he sort of thought of happiness, with angels and harps and music." John cut "sort of" because he felt he had slipped into something like Roger Purvis's language and had thus blurred the distinction between the experience of the boy and the voice describing that experience. A basic question, of course, is whether the mature language detracts from or assists in the creation of a childhood experience. Other questions that may help suggest "*how* the story means" are: What details does Roger notice about the world he is drawn into and about the adults who inhabit it? Could a fourth-grader be expected to notice such things? Is it important that Roger was only vaguely acquainted with the aunt who died?

The following is a story written by a college freshman who chooses to remain anonymous for reasons the story makes clear.

❀ WHO WAS REALLY RESPONSIBLE?

Anonymous

Sunday afternoons, for an eight-year-old, promise nothing but boredom. I was eight years old, it was a Sunday afternoon, and I was sitting on the back stairs hearing the faint strains of church music coming from the radio, and was utterly bored. A full stomach, the faint taste of split pea soup in my mouth, and a "Spy 13" comic book on the stairs next to me. The perfect scene for relaxation and eventual sleep, but I was neither relaxed nor sleepy, and I knew that if I hung around much longer, my father would appear and order me to give the dog a bath. The bathing of the dog, like the split pea soup for lunch, had become a Sunday ritual. Fighting that vicious creature for two hours to make *him* clean and ending up smelling like him, was the last thing I wanted to do then. Revelation came. I decided to seek out Orin Richards and find out if he had anything going. I didn't really care for Orin's company, but I couldn't think of anyone else who would be allowed out on a Sunday afternoon in our staunchly Christian neighborhood.

I found him, and he did have something up. He had observed, while in church that morning, that the jamoon (a soft, purple, tropical fruit, somewhat like a grape) tree outside was loaded with ripe fruit, and we unanimously decided that, since the English Vicar did not particularly care for jamoons, it was our Christian duty to relieve the poor tree of its burden. Arming ourselves with two large plastic bags, we headed for the church yard, and I thought of the stinking dog, and my father's anger when he found out that I had skipped yard, and laughed to myself. I should have stayed at home, for little did I realize that a bathing battle with a dog would have been welcome compared to the mental agony I was to endure for weeks after that fateful Sunday.

An hour or so later, our bags were filled with ripe, purple fruit, but I knew that I couldn't return home yet, as there were still enough hours of sunlight left for the dog to dry himself after his bath. The church was set upon pillars about three feet high, and we crawled under the building to sit for awhile. Orin mentioned that he had a packet of Broadway cigarettes, and we sat on an old log, puffing away in the juvenile manner, the smoke never being inhaled, and reveling in the fact that we were pulling another one on the grown-up world, our bags of forbidden fruit next to our feet and the smoke from our forbidden cigarettes emitting from between our lips. Conversation soon died, and I began playing with matches, lighting one and putting it into my mouth without burning myself. An idea of a new kind of game grew and took root in my mind. Why not put some junk together, build a fire, just a small one, and sit around it, talking about what we would do when we became whatever we wanted to be in life? I gathered a bundle of old newspapers, covered it with a few sticks, and set a match to them. It was perfect! I spotted an empty paint can, moved it close to the fire, which was by now a mound of glowing ashes, and sat on it. I turned around to get some more wood, and in doing so, knocked over the can.

"Hey, look out man!" Orin shouted, but it was too late. The paint can was not empty, and as the flammable red stuff spread over the dying embers, they leaped into flame, catching into the can itself, and spreading to the pile of sticks I had accumulated nearby. I crawled out from under the building and ran to a pipe in the yard, but no bucket was in sight. I was confused and frightened. Things had gotten out of hand. It was a dumb idea to light the fire in the first place, and now we had to put it out before someone in the vicarage saw the smoke. I grabbed a piece of board and crawled back under the building, but Orin was nowhere to be seen. The fire was spreading rapidly, and I saw the two bags of jamoons enveloped in flame, the plastic disappearing with a hiss, spilling the fruit on the ground. The flames seemed to leap across to the pile of junk and I looked around and saw that the whole area was littered with flammable material. Smoke was choking me, and the yellow flames were licking at my face, making me gasp.

I crawled back outside, wondering what I should do, and where the hell was Orin. I leaned against the side of the building, shaking with fright and faced with two possible courses of action. I could run over to the vicarage and tell them, but they would call the fire brigade, and it would be discovered how the fire got started in the first place. I could run home, but suppose Orin talked? The agony of decision. I had to make up my mind soon, as I could see the flames eating hungrily at the floor of the church. Church! This was a house of God. What would happen to me if I were responsible for its destruction? But then again, they needn't find out. It wouldn't work, God saw everything, He would know. The picture painted by my Sunday school teacher and supplemented by my nanny was vivid before me. Eternal fire. I would burn for having burned. But if I saved the church, I would die of disgrace, if not from the beating I was sure to receive from my father. Why the hell hadn't I stayed at home to bathe the damn dog? And damn that Orin for running off and leaving me in this mess.

It is said that in situations like these, instinct governs human reason. Whatever the case may be, I decided that self-preservation in this world was my first concern and ran home as fast as I could go.

Noticing that no one was around, I took up my former position on the stairs, picked up the comic book, and waited for the inevitable reaction. It came. Ten minutes later, Mrs. Ross, our next-door neighbor, ran up our front stairs, pounded on the door, and said to my mother, "There's a fire down the street. They say it's the church!"

My father bounded down the back stairs, with a passing "Stay here, you" in my direction, and ran out to the street, where he joined a crowd of people headed in the direction of the church. Presently, I heard the sirens of the fire engines and went out to the gate. From two blocks away, I could see that the entire building was burning, with plumes of thick black smoke billowing upward. I felt sick. I wanted to become invisible, to stop living. I desperately hoped that it was all a dream, but if it was, I wasn't waking up. I saw Orin hurrying down the street, in my direction, away from the fire, and went out to meet him.

"Hey man . . ." he began.

"Look, boy," I said, "this shit is your fault too, and if you tell anybody, we both go to jail."

He looked at me, and I could see that he was as scared as I was.

"That's just what I was coming to tell you," he said. "You think they'll find out who did it?"

"I don't know, man, but I'm going home, and if you tell anybody, buddy, we both in jail."

It wasn't until the next day that I saw what damage my bright idea had caused. Where our church had stood was a mess of soggy, blackened charcoal beams and eight blackened concrete pillars. I remembered my nanny's favorite phrase, about the devil always finding work for idle hands, and decided that it was more the devil's fault than mine, since I hadn't intended to burn the church down.

The weeks that followed were constant agony, listening to my parents and their friends discuss the fire, and, even though the official verdict was that it was somehow accidental, neighborhood gossip did not rule out the possibility of arson. I believe that, in an effort to avoid going insane with guilt, which was not helped any by our household's refusal to drop the subject and constant wishing that "the vagabond who did the deed would burn in hell forever," I developed further my theory that it was the devil's fault, and not mine, since I was but a weak mortal and a mere tool in his diabolical plot.

Since the destruction of St. Sidwell's Church was the result of the devil's actions, and since, according to Mr. Best, my Sunday school teacher, the Good Lord had created the devil, then the blame for the fire must be shouldered by the Good Lord, for it was his fault to create the devil in the first place.

Even after having thus absolved myself of guilt, I continued to have steady nightmares in which I would be tied to a post, surrounded by licking flames, and the devil (strangely enough, he possessed my father's face) was poking me in the side with a trident of fire, and laughing. I was always scared the next day, but indignant too, for I fell back on my original reasoning. Why should I suffer because the Good Lord had goofed?

❉   ❉   ❉   ❉

In "Who Was Really Responsible?" we do have a dramatic event. We also have a first-person narrative. The subject, the burning down of a church, is unusual and exciting. But what makes the story work? The point of view is supposedly that of an eight-year-old. The writer, however, is looking back across the 10 years between himself and that eight-year-old. Even while the writer recreates the fear of damnation and the process of rationalization through which the boy passed, the writer is smiling at himself as he was then. Again, we sense the simultaneous involvement and detachment created by the contrast between what an eight-year-old sees, thinks, and feels and the way a more mature voice or attitude treats his youthful self. That smile must be felt underlying what we otherwise would label melodramatic clichés, like "the mental agony I was to endure for weeks after that fateful Sunday." That is intentionally overdone. The writer might have felt such agony when he was eight. Now the writer renders it amusing by overstating it. It is funny to him now, but the author is not sure what the statute of limitations is on burning down a church, so he chooses to remain anonymous. Although the event itself is dramatic, not only in itself but because the guilty party must hide his guilt, it comes at the reader couched in an amused tone. That tone does not make too much of the event per se, attributing "mental agony" in the context of an eight-year-old's ability to swing the world around to the most comfortable way of looking at it. The interaction between two times and two attitudes, the past in which the event occurred and the present from which the event is reviewed, is crucial to the narrative's effect.

Equally as important and perhaps obvious in both "The Treehouse" and "Who Was Really Responsible?" is that the world of each narrative is well known to the writer. He is not writing as an astronaut landing on the moon or as an adventurer into middle earth. Details like the rust and rot of the Dodge, the "china things" on the tables, the stinking dog, the odious Orin who alone would be allowed out on a Sunday, the mother of the one story and the father of the other are available not from the imagination, but from a memory that can select the details which will suggest for us "the way things were." Inherent in the selection of a subject is the necessity that the writer *know* his subject.

The following story was written by a college student.

❀ THE LIFE OF HARRY NELSON

Gregory McManus

Harry Nelson walked along the beach in the coolness of a late
autumn night. He had two more years at college and had no idea
what he was going to do when he graduated. Everybody he knew
seemed to be in that same sort of predicament, but then it
seemed fashionable to be in a state of indecision. A slight breeze
tossed his hair to the sky and then returned it to his head in a mass
of tangles.

Harry lived on an island some distance from the campus,
which seemed fashionable too. It was the trend for all bright men
seasoned with an awareness of the world to live off-campus
but trend or not, he enjoyed living where he did. He had wanted
to do it this way from the beginning. Yes, this was right. He liked the
outdoors, the clean ocean air, the tall pines that seemed to be everywhere, even on the campus, that sentinel of the lamp of knowledge
shining bright in the Northern sky, the last outpost of the little
ivy class of colleges.

The moon was peculiarly bright that night and shone its
smooth paleness upon the calm waters of the sea that stretched
interminably into the distance. And yes, Harry contemplated distance
and time and those other abstracts that young thinking college men
consider important and worthwhile. That was, of course, fashionable too.

But Harry was in love.

But not just with that crushing illusion of love or himself.
He had speculated often on that unfathomable force that seemed
to rule men's lives and also on the absence of it. But now he thought
he felt it and try as he might, he couldn't figure the damn thing out.
And Harry did love himself as much as anybody else loves themselves, maybe more. He could stand straight and tall and look
at himself in the mirror, straight in the eye, making sure his shoes
were scruffy enough, his blue jeans faded enough, and his hair and
moustache long and shaggy enough. He was a young man in
tune with the times, contented with those times, and quite
proud of his adaptability to his immediate environment.

Harry was a loner too, which might not seem so fashionable
in this day and age of if you can't be with the one you love, love the
one you're with. But he was well liked and politic and attempted to be
as honest as his pride would allow him to be. He rarely was involved
in an argument he could not diplomatically extricate himself from
with a few well chosen words. He had always seemed content

with himself and had few misgivings outside of the normal die of
philosophical slogans poured down his throat by the newspapers and
television which he regurgitated from time to time. But when
Harry was alone, he reveled in his aloneness until lately.
Harry had begun to crave. The craving gnawed at him constantly
and frustrated him. He wished at times that this feeling inside him were
caused by some physical object like a knife that he could easily take
from his side and then either bleed to death or relax and be cared
for in a hospital and heal totally and completely. At times he
managed to subdue and bury the craving either by becoming so
totally inebriated that he could no longer remain conscious or by
occupying himself with some diversion that meant nothing to him. But
still he craved constantly, almost malignantly.

He thought of her often, this girl he loved. And saw her often.
But it never seemed quite enough. He would dream spontaneously
and effortlessly of long nights filled with her gentle laughter,
the sweetness of her voice, and the vision of her love. At these times
he would try to shake himself into a state of reality where practical value
was the only value. He tried to remember the rational advice of
his friends and father before he had gone to college. Something
about these years being the best of his life and why waste himself
on one woman when there were so many just there for the taking.
What the hell, Harry.

But Harry couldn't bring himself to do that. He had no
desire to compromise himself, that self he was so proud of, by
succumbing to the urges of a sex machine that pumped for the
pleasures of a moment. It wasn't that he couldn't have led such an
existence, rather, he really didn't want to. He was a human sacrifice,
that martyr for love who pursued the tragic route of total involvement to that ecstatic destiny of being completely and utterly drained
of all passion and feeling and left to die, a worthless pulp, on
the shores of man's universe. And what doctor of the soul would tell
him, Harry Nelson, that this was not his true destiny?

He had to have her, that girl he loved. That girl he was so sure he
loved right from the very start.

The phone rang and rang and rang. These damn dorms, Harry thought
to himself, the damn phones are either always busy or no one's there
to answer them. Suddenly the ringing stopped and Harry was
greeted by bursts of laughter and giggles and finally a human
voice said hello.

"Susan Hanover, please."

"Just a minute," came the abrupt reply.

"Bitch," Harry thought to himself. A moment passed by.

"Hi."

"Hi. What's up?"

"Nothing much really. This dorm's in an uproar. I forgot you were going to call tonight but I'm glad you did."

"I'm glad too." A hint of a smile crossed his lips. "What have you been doing?"

"Oh, nothing much."

"Sure?"

"Well, really," the smooth voice answered, "I've got four dates lined up and I don't know what to do with them all."

"Get rid of 'em."

"Now, you know . . ."

"Yes, I know," he interrupted, smiling again to himself.

"Are you home now?"

"Yeah, got home this afternoon."

"How's your mother and father?"

"Pretty well. Ma's got laryngitis and Dad doesn't feel too well."

"Is he still going on the hunting trip?"

"As far as I know, yes." Why do all men go on hunting trips, she had asked before. To get away from their wives? He imagined some of them did and some of them didn't. Would he? No, not he.

"When did you say their anniversary was?"

"The eighth I think, I always get the dates mixed up."

"That's cause you're dumb, D-U-M-B."

"Well, not all the time."

"And when you're dumb, you're cute."

"Gee, t'anks a pantload."

"And when you're cute, you're dumb."

"Sounds like I've got a lot going for me."

"Oh, you do, you do. You're dumb and you're cute and you're cute and you're dumb."

"Fine, but tell me, what did you do all day?"

"Well . . ." She paused a moment and he envisioned her tapping her lower lip with her fingers, thoughtfully retracing the events of the day. "I went over to see Jane today. She was upset."

"Upset about what?"

"Well, she thinks she's pregnant. She's long overdue."

"How long?"

"Two months."

"Yeah?"

"She doesn't know what to do."

"What do you mean?"

"Well, she doesn't know . . . oh, I don't know. She doesn't know if she really likes this guy or not and she doesn't know if she

wants to have the baby or not and if she wanted to get an
abortion she doesn't know where she'd get the money."

"What do you mean, she doesn't know if she likes the guy or not.
Christ, if she doesn't know if she likes him or not, why'd she
do it with him?"

"She's just not sure."

"You mean she's not sure whether or not she wants to spend the
rest of her life with him?"

"I guess so. If that's what that means."

"Well, God, Susan, she made the decision."

"Oh, I know, I know. I don't want to talk about it any more."

His heart sank from the wall she had thrown up against
him. And what about you and I, he thought. Does that mean anything?
Are we so untouchable that something like that couldn't happen
to us? And what would you do then? But his mouth merely asked the
question, "What else did you do today?"

"I didn't get back from Jane's until late. This guy asked me
to go to a party at his fraternity house but I didn't want to. He had
already been here when I got back and there was a note on the
door to call him. So I did and I told him I had to get ready
for the workshop tomorrow and couldn't make it."

"Uh-huh." Good. Goddamn frat rat.

"But he asked me out for next weekend and I told him I
didn't know and that I'd let him know later on in the week."

"Why the hell don't you know?"

"Oh, Harry, do you always have to cross-examine me? You
know I can't say no."

"Yeah," he murmured dejectedly, "I know, I know." Only
too well.

"Oh, Harry, don't be hurt. I know I hurt you but I can't
help it. You know I love you."

"Yeah, I know." He sighed.

"Oh, Harry, now you're sighing. I'm not going to tell you
the truth any more. I've decided. I'm going to lie to you so I
won't hurt you."

"Don't you ever lie to me. I told you before that it would only
be worse. What in hell good would it do anyway?"

"No, Harry, I'm not going to tell you the truth. You know I
love you, don't you, Harry?"

He sighed again not knowing what to say.

"You don't think I do, do you?"

"Oh, well, yes I do, I know you do but . . ." And he paused
and sighed again. Damned cigarettes. His breathing always became
troubled in these situations.

"But what, Harry?"

"I just don't understand why, that's all. It doesn't make sense."

"But Harry, what sense would it make if I wasn't sure I loved you. I have to be sure, don't you think, Harry?"

"Yeah," he agreed halfheartedly. "Yeah, I suppose you're right."

Silence permeated the miles of telephone wire and nothing was said for some moments.

"Harry?"

"Yes?"

"I suppose we shouldn't listen to each other breathe over the phone. It's costing money."

"I don't care. I'd just as soon listen to you breathe. At least I know where you are."

"Damn it, Harry."

"Don't damn me, Susan, damn you. You know I love you."

"Yes, I know." Her voice twittered like a bird. His heart melted. God, how she controlled him.

"Am I going to give you a ride back to school on Sunday?"

"No, Harry. I have a ride already with a girlfriend."

"I want to take you back."

"No, Harry. It's out of your way and I don't like you driving on those dark country roads at night."

"I don't care if it's out of my way. It could be a thousand miles out of my way. Christ, I see little enough of you as it is."

"But it will cost you money for gas."

"I don't give a good goddamn about the money."

"I know you don't but if I don't, who is going to give a damn about it?"

"I'm taking you back."

"Well, all right." Her voice was soft, inviting. "If you want to."

"Well, I do."

"Okay, Harry."

"Are you going to call me tomorrow?"

"Yes, sometime when I get back."

"Okay. I'll talk to you then."

"Okay, Harry. I love you. Bye-bye."

"Uh-huh. Bye."

A faint click snapped the connection and Harry hung up the receiver. His parents had gone to bed and he walked around the silent house, smoking a cigarette and thinking.

If she's so damn unsure, why the hell is she so sure when she sleeps with me? Damned horse of a different color then. Christ, I don't know—I don't want to know. She sure as hell can be a bitch sometimes though.

Why did he have to think? It kept him awake nights, long
sleepless nights of sleeping alone and now he would have to go to
bed. There was nothing else he could do. And even if there
were, he probably wouldn't do it. He loved Susan. He knew he did.
But to what end he didn't know but he had to find out. There was
nothing else he could do. And even if there were, he probably
wouldn't do it.

❋   ❋   ❋   ❋

In "The Life of Harry Nelson" we have, again, a named character.
This character lives according to "the rules" as he perceives them, even
the rule dictating a mild nonconformity. The writer's point of view,
again, is not that of his character. The discrepancy between character
and writer here, however, is not that built in by the difference between
the past and the present. Greg McManus points out carefully that
Harry Nelson is a conformist and that such conformity, whatever its
rewards, can be dangerous. What happens when the clichés suddenly
don't work, as when Harry encounters a woman who refuses to abide
by his rules? Harry is in trouble because the code he has so easily
embraced no longer applies. Pain shatters the transparent shield he
has placed between himself and authenticity. Whether Harry's experience represents that of the author is, in this case, irrelevant. The author
has removed himself sufficiently from his character to allow himself to
suggest the elements Harry lacks and thus show why Harry cannot
cope with the problem that ultimately appears. Greg McManus takes
a step beyond that of John Cartland ("The Treehouse") or the author
of "Who Was Really Responsible?" In the last two stories a mature
attitude commented on an earlier event, but the child and the adult
were the same person at different moments of development. Harry
Nelson and his author are not the same person. They are contemporaries perhaps; but Harry is obviously less perceptive than his creator,
whose ironic detachment from Harry can be felt in his description of
Harry's fashionableness and the unreflective contentment it confers on
Harry. While the world of Harry Nelson is a product of the writer's
experience, either lived or observed, or both, the writer's stance
toward his material pushes it across the line from *autobiography* to
fiction. That does not mean it is not truth, but it is a different way
of formulating the truth. The same rule applies to an effective autobiographical narrative: It is not just what happened to me, but what
happened to someone, maybe me, maybe not me, observed from the
stance of a well-defined point of view.

The writer, then, must not only discover a subject, but he must ask
himself how he can treat that subject best. Will he create a character

who happens to be a younger self experiencing a past event, as in "The Treehouse"? Will he tell the story as the "I" of the narrative, even though he is writing in the idiom and with the awareness of the very different "I" of the present, as in "Who Was Really Responsible?" Or will he create a character who is not him, even though that character may have undergone experiences similar to the author's, as in "The Life of Harry Nelson"? I am not suggesting that these three approaches are the only ones available, but they are the most frequently used by beginning writers. Furthermore, while most good autobiographical writing impinges on the genre of the short story, an understanding of the three approaches helps the writer define the line between the autobiographical narrative and the short story.

When a writer looks back at himself as he was perhaps a decade before the moment at which he writes, when he reexamines a past moment from the more mature position of the present, he assumes an attitude toward that past self and that past experience. As L. P. Hartley says at the beginning of his superb novel, *The Go-Between,* "The past is a foreign country: they do things differently there." One cannot relive or even reconstruct his past; but he can reshape it. The writer cannot avoid the discrepancy between where he is now and where he was then. He must, instead, use that discrepancy between time and awareness, providing a mature viewpoint and mature language for an experience in which neither was available.

Differences of time and comprehension provide the writer with a built-in irony, an irony either implicit or consciously developed. Irony *means* discrepancy: between what is said and what is meant (verbal irony), between what is appropriate or anticipated and what actually happens (irony of situation), and between what a character knows and what we know as author or reader (dramatic irony). All of us indulge in verbal irony, but the last two types of irony are the ones we are most likely to use as writers. In "Who Was Really Responsible?" the young protagonist runs into that situational irony that so often traps us in real life. He escapes the odious dog, but in doing so he encounters a far worse situation; he burns down the local church. The young character in Hartley's novel goes off to spend a summer with a friend amid all the pleasures of an English country estate. But the idyll develops into a sequence of events that cripple the rest of his life. Huck Finn thinks he is helping Jim escape from slavery; but once the raft passes Cairo in the fog, it heads deeper into slave territory, toward the captivity imposed upon Jim by the Duke and the Dauphin and the Monte Cristo games Tom Sawyer plays with Jim.

Irony of situation involves contrasts between anticipation and result, hope and fulfillment. It is not merely a method of dealing with our material, but sometimes a way of discovering what it means, of finding the story in it. For many of the writers represented in this book, situational irony is a central component of *subject*. Harry Nelson has made all the right moves, but finds himself baffled by his infatuation for a woman who claims she loves him but acts as if she doesn't. The young man in the next narrative in this book must remove himself from the swirl of the street and sit immobile while his portrait is painted. In later narratives, a young boy invites a friend to play on a particular lawn, but never plays there again; an independent young woman hitchhikes into disaster; a young teacher finds himself controlled by his class; a boy goes down to the shore to empty the garbage and becomes a murderer; and a girl out for a swim discovers what it feels like to drown.

Dramatic irony is virtually a "given" of an autobiographical narrative. The writer looks back at that foreign country of the past across a distance formed of time and attitude. He may play the adult world against that of the child, as in "The Treehouse," allowing the attitude we share with the writer to remain implicit as his young character enjoys what we see as an irony of situation. A sad time for the adults becomes a happy time for him. The irony may be more explicit, as when we share with the author of "Who Was Really Responsible?" his attitude toward that former self who first suffers from a fear of damnation inculcated by religious training—enforced by the literal interpretation that young people tend to apply to such training—and then rationalizes his situation into one of God's blunders. We are meant to share the author's awareness that only a naive eight-year-old would accept hellfire as a literal consequence of his action. We are also asked to accept the eight-year-old's clever process of self-vindication. But that process is worked out within the religious context so that we do not feel too vivid an inconsistency in the movement from naiveté to sophistication.

Dramatic irony, then, involves our sharing with the reader awarenesses about the character in our narrative of which he is unaware, which he might even deny vigorously were he confronted with them. Although the writer's stance toward his material conveys a built-in irony, the irony does not necessarily become a condemnation of or even a criticism of the young or less-aware character. Strong criticism of the central character in "The Life of Harry Nelson" seems intended, but it is blended with real sympathy for the dilemma into which Harry unconsciously drifts. The eight-year-old character in "Who Was Really Responsible?" indulges in an obviously appalling process of self-justification. Since he is operating within a fundamentalist religious context, however, we and the author view him with a tolerant and amused eye. John Cartland neither criticizes nor defends his fourth-grader. He suggests that "this is the way things were, and are," and one value of the story is that it shows us a truth without the author's positive or negative judgment of his character.

The following example, for analysis of subject and point of view, was written by a college freshman.

✿ THE STILLNESS AND THE FURY

Paul B. Ross

Like jetsam tossed ashore by the night tide, hundreds of people just off the boat from Boston had inundated the single lane of shops and cottages. Summer always brought a surfeit of things, no less of people, and a fluid, chaotic crowd was engaged in nocturnal explorations and adventures. My family and I decided to join them. The fishing community was also an artists' retreat, and we were resolved to visit a number of their cells. Gliding our way through the maze of men and women, we headed for the open studios. How strange was the movement of the crowd, so much activity with so little being done! Old women and young men, Portuguese fishermen in worn clothing, and tourists in bright madras pushed and ran and talked. A giant Swede sauntered past. His face was masked in blond hair, and his eyes looked aimlessly about as he disappeared behind us. I felt as though I were in Dante's Limbo where the condemned rock and pitch in perpetual vertigo.

The fury of the streets poured into the shops in a rapid ebb and flow. The store lights, burning brightly, cast shadows into the crowd and revealed to it show windows stocked with the handiwork of men and the produce of the sea. White, spiraled enamel streaked with pink and grey clung to ancient netting. Idols of brass meditated mutely on the throngs outside, while goldfish, inattentive and erratic, swam within the confines of glass and water. Jewelry shone silver, blue, and gold, and mother-of-pearl cast its eerie light.

Of all these Circean grottos, only one tempted me to enter. It was a small bakery whose goods and confections paraded provocatively behind the glass. Jewish rye and Portuguese loaves lined the shelves. Sugar sparkled amidst cinnamon, caramel, mints, and toffee, while chocolate and peanut brittle vied for attention with pies and doughnuts. Quickly and involuntarily, fed by the imaginings of my mind, my body craved gratification. But we had set our goal, and it wasn't until we came to the portrait studios that we finally stopped.

My father motioned me indoors. The artist he had chosen
was an oriental whose small shop was arrayed with paintings in all
places and positions. Above me was a sunset, beyond it, a silent
sea. On the back wall I espied a maiden dressed in blue, her
hands folded in her lap, and her head bowed in thought. To my
right, a large Persian cat dozed about a ball of thread. I was seated by
my silent interrogator in a chair facing his easel. The shadows of the
street gave way to the heat and lucency of his floodlamps. Now,
only his hands and his eyes moved. The stillness was oppressive
and my imprisonment very real. I longed for freedom and
action, but because thought was the only diversion, my mind,
like the sea, raged, while my body, like the shore, was still. I worried
about my poise, my facial expression, and the artist's thoughts.
Were my features agreeable and did I challenge his skill? Were his
eyes sarcastic? How loudly did he laugh inside? Would I ever
be free of his gaze, and must I return it? No, I resolved. I would scan
the streets instead. And yet as I did so, faces loomed large behind him,
peering curiously at me, mimicking his scrutiny. While my mother
looked quizzically at the canvas, my younger brother clowned to
make me laugh. A small girl peeped through the glass and smiled. Other
strangers surveyed me with interest. My mental and bodily torment
eased and were replaced by modest self-consciousness. I was no
longer alone before my interrogator. He was now in my
place, perhaps. Anyway, his eyes could no more hold me rigid.
My torso relaxed, and the shadow of fear fled my face. I looked
about slowly seeing pictures that had not been there before. Near the
window were two sailboats racing, one slightly ahead. The other,
from whose deck the faster was seen, strained mightily to
take the lead. A matador was braving the wounded bull and alongside him, a woman, smiling gaily, loosed her purple bonnet. Her curls
were free, and laughing with their mistress, they teased and danced in
the autumn wind. The sea within me quieted, and as it did so, the
oriental rose, announcing the job was done. I was eager to
see myself with a Chinese mien, but I was also eager to leave
and rejoin the churning crowd. This we promptly and gladly did,
treasuring the still life on canvas but thankful for the moving life of the
street.

※   ※   ※   ※

The following selections by two great writers, Maxim Gorki and Dylan
Thomas, are very different. Gorki's is haunted by fear and death,
Thomas's is joyously overstated both in language and imagery. Yet each
essay combines craftsmanship and imagination to reproduce for us the

writer's childhood. While the point of view of each selection emerges
from an "I," notice that Thomas makes greater use of "we" than does
Gorki. The "we" is an index of the differences in tone and feeling
between the two essays.

❧ DEATH AND LIFE

Maxim Gorki

On the floor, under the window, in a small, shuttered room,
lay my father, dressed in a long white garment I had never seen
him in before. His feet were bare and the toes were strangely distended,
while the fingers of his hands, resting on his breast, were curled in.
The blackened disks of two copper coins covered his eyes, shutting
out their accustomed, cheerful gleam. All the light had gone
out of his still face. But what scared me most was the snarl his
open mouth showed with the teeth bared.

Beside him, on her knees, was my mother, in an undergarment.
She was combing his long, fine hair back from his forehead to the
nape of his neck. The comb she was using was the one with
which I scraped edible shreds from watermelon rinds. As she combed
away, she talked to him without stopping, through tears that fell
without stopping, until it seemed that they must finally flood
her eyes out of their sockets.

I saw all this holding on to the hand of my grandmother, whose
dark head and eyes and nose looked enormous—the nose shapeless
and pitted like a sponge—but a gentle, yet vividly interesting,
woman. She, too, wept with sobs that were like cadences to
my mother's. Shuddering herself, she pushed me toward my father,
but I was too terrified to let go and clung to her.

This was the first time I had ever seen grown-ups cry, and I
could not understand her repeated bidding, "Say good-by to your
father. You'll never see him again. He's dead before his time."

I, myself, was just out of sickbed after a long, hard illness. It was
still fresh in my mind how my father had done all he could to
amuse me; and then how his place at my bedside had suddenly been
taken by that old woman, then a stranger to me, my grandmother.

I asked her where she came from, using the verb form which
implies coming by foot.

"From up north, from Nizhny," she replied, "but I didn't

SOURCE: From *The Autobiography of Maxim Gorki*, translated by Isadore Schneider,
copyright 1949 by The Citadel Press.

walk it; I came down by boat. You don't walk on water, you
little scamp."

This made no sense to me at all. Upstairs there lived a gaily-
dressed Persian who wore a beard; and downstairs, in the cellar, there
lived a withered, yellow Kalmuck who dealt in sheepskins. And I got up
to one and down to the other by way of the banisters; and if I had a
fall, I just rolled down. But there was no place for water. So her
"down" from "up north" on water could not be true; but it was
a delightful muddle.

"Why do you call me a little scamp?" I asked.

"Because you make so much noise, that's why," she said, with a
laugh.

Her voice was sweet and her words were merry and I made
friends with her at once.

Now, clinging to her, all I wanted was for her to hurry and get
me out of the room.

My mother caught me to her with a burst of weeping and
moaning that frightened me. I had never seen her so before, this
strong, composed, reserved woman, always so glowing and neat,
strongly-framed like a horse and with tremendous power in her
arms. Now, quivering and puffy, she looked utterly stricken.
Her hair had shaken out of its gaily-trimmed cap and out of the
usual tidy coil around her head and was streaming over her shoulder, and the part of it that remained in braid tracked across my father's
still face. All this time she had not given me even a look, unable to
tear herself away from her grief-stricken combing of my father's
hair.

Then a policeman and some grave-diggers appeared at the door.
"Get a move on!" bellowed the policeman.

A draft had filled the shawl that curtained the window,
filled it like a sail. That picture came to me because my father
had taken me sailing, once, and the sail had filled out the same
way, in a sudden gust. With it had come a clap of thunder and my
father had pulled me to his knee to reassure me and, laughing,
had said, "It's nothing; don't let it frighten you."

All at once my mother dropped to the floor and immediately
turned over, her hair in the dirt. Her mouth came open on her
now-livid face so that her teeth were bared like my father's. In a
terrifying voice she ordered me out, and the door to be shut.

Pushing me aside, grandma rushed to the door crying out,
"Friends, there's nothing to be alarmed about; it's not the cholera; she's
giving birth. For the love of God, leave us! Good people, go away."

Hidden behind a big box in a corner I saw my mother moving
convulsively over the floor, panting through clenched teeth. Grandma

hovered over her with soothing, cheering words, "Patience, Barbara . . . Holy Mother of God, be her protection!"

I shook with fright. In their frantic movements they bumped against my father, they groaned and shrieked into his unmoved, even smiling, face. For a long time this thrashing about on the floor went on. And all through it, rolling in and out like a big, black woolly ball went grandma on her errands.

Suddenly there was a whimper of a child. "Thank God!" grandma called out, "it's a boy!" and got up to light a candle.

And at that point, I must have fallen asleep in the darkness behind the box, because that was all I remembered.

My next memory is a solitary spot in a cemetery, in the rain. Standing beside a muddy pile of earth, I looked down into the hole in which they had sunk my father in his coffin. Frogs splashed in the water that had seeped in, and two were perched on the yellow coffin lid. Beside me were grandma, the drenched sexton and a pair of grave-diggers with shovels.

The sexton ordered the grave to be filled and moved off. Grandma wailed into an end of her head-shawl. Bent nearly double, the grave-diggers shoveled lumps of earth over the coffin, kicking the frogs who were trying to hop out, back into the grave.

"Come, Alex," said grandma, her hand on my shoulder, but I was too absorbed and slipped away.

"What next, O Lord!" grandma complained, half to me, half to God, and stood there in silence, with a dejected droop of her head.

Not till after the grave had been filled and the diggers' shovels had clanged to the ground and a sudden scurry of breeze had spattered us with raindrops, did she stir. Then, leading me by the hand, she took me to a church some distance away, over a path bordered by occasional dim crosses.

As we left the graveyard, she asked me, "How is it you're not crying? You ought to."

"I don't want to," I replied.

"You don't? Well, you don't have to," she said, gently.

It was a surprise to me that I was expected to cry. My crying had been always more out of temper than sadness. Father had laughed my tears away and mother had forbidden them. "Don't you dare to cry!" And so I seldom cried.

Afterwards we rode down a broad, but filthy street in a drozhky between rows of houses all painted dark red. On the way I asked grandma, "Can those frogs ever get out?"

"Never, God bless them."

God came more frequently and familiarly into her conversation, it occurred to me then, than He ever did in my father's or mother's.

Several days later I found myself, together with mama and grandma, in a tiny steamboat cabin. On a table, in the corner, lay the corpse of my little brother, Maxim, in white trappings held together with red tape. The porthole had the appearance of a horse's eye; I climbed up our piled luggage to look through. All there was to see was muddy froth. It charged against the glass, at one moment, with such force that it splashed in, and I scrambled down to the floor.

"There's nothing can harm you," said grandma lightly, lifting me back upon the baggage in her caressing arms.

Gray and brooding over the water, the fog thinned, now and then, to let a distant bulk of the shore loom through like a shadow, only to be lost again in mist and spume. Everything seemed to be aquiver except mother. With her hands clasped behind her head she stood rigid against the wall, with a grim, iron-hard face. Mute and expressionless, she seemed far away from us, an utter stranger. Even her clothes looked unfamiliar.

Gently, now and then, grandma would say, "Barbara, have a bite to eat." Mama did not so much as stir.

To me grandma spoke in whispers; to mama she spoke aloud, but infrequently, and in a timorous manner. Her fear of my mother was something I understood and made me feel closer to grandma.

A sudden, harsh exclamation from mama startled both of us. "Saratov. Where's that sailor?"

Saratov. Sailor. New words to me.

The sailor turned out to be a broad-shouldered, gray-haired man in blue. He carried in a box in which grandma laid my brother's body. She could not get through the door with it, being too broad, and came to a perplexed and ludicrous halt.

"Oh, mama!" exclaimed mama angrily, and took the little coffin from her. Both disappeared and I was left with the man in blue.

"Well, matey," he said, "your little brother has left you."

"Who are you?"

"I'm a sailor."

"Who's Saratov?"

"Saratov's a city. You can see it through the porthole."

From the porthole, the land seemed to shimmer. Dim and crusty, as it steamed in the fog, it made me think of a slice of bread fresh off a hot loaf.

"Where's grandma?"

"She's gone out to bury the little fellow."

"In the ground?"

"That's right."

Then I told the sailor about the frogs that had been buried alive with my father.

Lifting me up he fondled me, "Poor kid, you don't understand. Pity your mother, not the frogs. You don't know what unhappiness is crushing her."

From above came a howl that I recognized as the voice of the ship, so I wasn't frightened. But the sailor put me down at once and left me, shouting, "I must be off!"

I had an impulse to get away. I looked out—the passageway was dark and empty. Nearby glittered the brass plates of steps. Looking up the stair, I saw passengers with valises and bundles, evidently leaving the boat. I thought this meant I must leave, too.

But, at the gangway, in the crowd of debarking peasants, I was met with yells, "Whose boy is he? Who do you belong to, boy?"

Nobody knew me, and I didn't know what to answer. I was hauled from hand to hand until the sailor came up, took hold of me and explained, "It's that Astrakhan boy, the one in the cabin."

He brought me back there, sat me on the baggage and went off threatening me with his forefinger and the words, "I'll give it to you."

The ship's voice, overhead, quieted down; the vibrations of the boat and its movements in the water stopped. Dripping walls opposite the porthole shut off the air and the light, and the cabin grew stifling and dark. The bundles among which I had been placed seemed to grow larger and harder, and I began to feel crushed by them. A fear that I had been left all alone and for good in the empty ship possessed me.

I tried the door, but the metal handle was unbudging. I picked up a bottle of milk and put all my strength in the blow I gave it to make it turn; but all I accomplished was to break the bottle and spill the milk, which splashed over me and trickled down my legs. Sobbing with exasperation, I cried myself to sleep on the bundles.

I woke to find the boat in motion and the porthole round and glowing like a sun. Beside me sat grandma, combing her hair back from her knitted brows and muttering to herself. Her blue-black hair was remarkable for its abundance. It came below her knees and even reached the ground. She had to hold it up with one hand while, with the other, she drew an almost toothless comb through the heavy mass. The strain made her lips purse and brought an exasperated sharpness to her eyes. There was something almost bitter in her expression; yet, when I asked why her hair was so long, it was in her usual melodious words and with her customary tender intonations that she answered, "God must have given it to me to punish me. It's combed out but look at it! When I was a girl I was proud of that mane but now I curse it. But sleep, child. It's early yet. The sun's barely up."

"I want to get up."

"Well then, get up," she said. As she braided her hair she glanced toward my mother who lay rigid on her bunk. "How did you happen to break that bottle? Tell me, but be quiet about it."

That was her way. Her words were like music and like flowers. They bloom in my memory like everlasting blossoms. I remember her smile as a dilation of her large eyes and a cheerful flash of her white teeth that gave her face an inexpressible charm. Despite her wrinkles and her weathered complexion she looked young and even glowing. All that spoiled her appearance was her bulbous red nose with its splayed-out nostrils, the result of a weakness for drink and her snuff-taking; her black snuff box was almost always in her hand. Outwardly she looked dark, but within burned a vigorous, inextinguishable flame of which the radiance in her eyes was a reflection. She was so stooped as to be almost hunchbacked, yet her motions were gliding and light like those of a great cat; and she was soft and caressing like a cat.

I felt that I had been asleep and in darkness until she came, and that then I woke and was led into the light. It was she who provided the threads with which my mind wove its multi-colored patterns. And by this she became my lifelong friend, the dearest and most understanding and the closest to my heart. Nourished by her wise love for every living thing, I gained the strength to face a hard life.

❀ REMINISCENCES OF CHILDHOOD

Dylan Thomas

I like very much people telling me about their childhood, but they'll have to be quick or else I'll be telling them about mine.

I was born in a large Welsh town at the beginning of the Great War—an ugly, lovely town (or so it was and is to me), crawling, sprawling by a long and splendid curving shore where truant boys and sandfield boys and old men from nowhere, beachcombed, idled and paddled, watched the dockbound ships or the ships steaming away into wonder and India, magic and China, countries bright with oranges and loud with lions; threw stones into the sea for the barking outcast dogs; made castles and forts and harbours and race tracks in the sand; and on Saturday summer afternoons listened to the

SOURCE: From *Quite Early One Morning* by Dylan Thomas. Copyright 1943, 1954 by New Directions Publishing Corporation. Reprinted by permission of New Directions Publishing Corporation, J. M. Dent & Sons, Ltd., and the Trustees for the Copyrights of the late Dylan Thomas.

brass band, watched the Punch and Judy, or hung about on the
fringes of the crowd to hear the fierce religious speakers who shouted
at the sea, as though it were wicked and wrong to roll in and out
like that, white-horsed and full of fishes.

One man, I remember, used to take off his hat and set fire to his
hair every now and then, but I do not remember what it proved,
if it proved anything at all, except that he was a very interesting man.

This sea-town was my world; outside a strange Wales, coal-
pitted, mountained, river-run, full, so far as I knew, of choirs and
football teams and sheep and storybook tall hats and red flannel petti-
coats, moved about its business which was none of mine.

Beyond that unknown Wales with its wild names like peals
of bells in the darkness, and its mountain men clothed in the
skins of animals perhaps and always singing, lay England which
was London and the country called the Front, from which many of
our neighbours never came back. It was a country to which only
young men travelled.

At the beginning, the only "front" I knew was the little lobby
before our front door. I could not understand how so many people
never returned from there, but later I grew to know more, though still
without understanding, and carried a wooden rifle in the park and
shot down the invisible unknown enemy like a flock of wild birds.
And the park itself was a world within the world of the sea-town.
Quite near where I lived, so near that on summer evenings I could
listen in my bed to the voices of older children playing ball on
the sloping paper-littered bank, the park was full of terrors and
treasures. Though it was only a little park, it held within its bor-
ders of old tall trees, notched with our names and shabby from our
climbing, as many secret places, caverns and forests, prairies and
deserts, as a country somewhere at the end of the sea.

And though we would explore it one day, armed and desperate,
from end to end, from the robbers' den to the pirates' cabin, the
highwayman's inn to the cattle ranch, or the hidden room in the
undergrowth, where we held beetle races, and lit the wood fires and
roasted potatoes and talked about Africa, and the makes of motor
cars, yet still the next day, it remained as unexplored as the Poles
—a country just born and always changing.

There were many secret societies but you could belong only
to one; and in blood or red ink, and a rusty pocketknife, with,
of course, an instrument to remove stones from horses' feet, you
signed your name at the foot of a terrible document, swore death to
all the other societies, crossed your heart that you would divulge no
secret and that if you did, you would consent to torture by slow fire,
and undertook to carry out by yourself a feat of either daring or

endurance. You could take your choice: would you climb to the top of
the tallest and most dangerous tree, and from there hurl stones and
insults at grown-up passers-by, especially postmen, or any other men
in uniform? Or would you ring every doorbell in the terrace, not
forgetting the doorbell of the man with the red face who kept
dogs and ran fast? Or would you swim in the reservoir, which was
forbidden and had angry swans, or would you eat a whole old jam
jar full of mud?

There were many more alternatives. I chose one of endurance
and for half an hour, it may have been longer or shorter, held up
off the ground a very heavy broken pram we had found in a bush.
I thought my back would break and the half hour felt like a day,
but I preferred it to braving the red face and the dogs, or to swallowing
tadpoles.

We knew every inhabitant of the park, every regular visitor, every
nursemaid, every gardener, every old man. We knew the hour when
the alarming retired policeman came in to look at the dahlias and
the hour when the old lady arrived in the Bath chair with six
Pekinese, and a pale girl to read aloud to her. I think she read the
newspaper, but we always said she read the *Wizard*. The face of the
old man who sat summer and winter on the bench looking over the
reservoir, I can see clearly now and I wrote a poem long long after I'd
left the park and the sea-town called:

The Hunchback in the Park

The hunchback in the park
A solitary mister
Propped between trees and water
From the opening of the garden lock
That lets the trees and water enter
Until the Sunday sombre bell at dark

Eating bread from a newspaper
Drinking water from the chained cup
That the children filled with gravel
In the fountain basin where I sailed my ship
Slept at night in a dog kennel
But nobody chained him up

Like the park birds he came early
Like the water he sat down
And Mister they called Hey mister
The truant boys from the town
Running when he had heard them clearly
On out of sound

Past lake and rockery
Laughing when he shook his paper
Hunchbacked in mockery
Through the loud zoo of the willow groves
Dodging the park-keeper
With his stick that picked up leaves

And the old dog sleeper
Alone between nurses and swans
While the boys among willows
Made the tigers jump out of their eyes
To roar on the rockery stones
And the groves were blue with sailors

Made all day until bell-time
A woman figure without fault
Straight as a young elm
Straight and tall from his crooked bones
That she might stand in the night
After the locks and the chains

All night in the unmade park
After the railings and shrubberies
The birds the grass the trees and the lake
And the wild boys innocent as strawberries
Had followed the hunchback
To his kennel in the dark

And that park grew up with me; that small world widened as I
learned its secrets and boundaries, as I discovered new refuges and
ambushes in its woods and jungles; hidden homes and lairs for
the multitudes of imagination, for cowboys and Indians, and the tall
terrible half-people who rode on nightmares through my bedroom.
But it was not the only world—that world of rockery, gravel path,
playbank, bowling green, bandstands, reservoir, dahlia garden,
where an ancient keeper, known as Smoky, was the whiskered snake
in the grass one must keep off. There was another world where
with my friends I used to dawdle on half holidays along the bent and
Devon-facing seashore, hoping for gold watches or the skull of a
sheep or a message in a bottle to be washed up with the tide; and
another where we used to wander whistling through the packed
streets, stale as station sandwiches, round the impressive gasworks
and the slaughter house, past by the blackened monuments and the
museum that should have been in a museum. Or we scratched at a
kind of cricket on the bald and cindery surface of the recreation
ground, or we took a tram that shook like an iron jelly down to

the gaunt pier, there to clamber under the pier, hanging perilously on its skeleton legs or to run along to the end where patient men with the seaward eyes of the dockside unemployed capped and muffled, dangling from their mouths pipes that had long gone out, angled over the edge for unpleasant tasting fish.

Never was there such a town as ours, I thought, as we fought on the sandhills with rough boys or dared each other to climb up the scaffolding of half-built houses soon to be called Laburnum Beaches. Never was there such a town, I thought, for the smell of fish and chips on Saturday evenings; for the Saturday afternoon cinema matinees where we shouted and hissed our threepences away; for the crowds in the streets with leeks in their hats on international nights; for the park, the inexhaustible and mysterious, bushy red-Indian hiding park where the hunchback sat alone and the groves were blue with sailors. The memories of childhood have no order, and so I remember that never was there such a dame school as ours, so firm and kind and smelling of galoshes, with the sweet and fumbled music of the piano lessons drifting down from upstairs to the lonely schoolroom, where only the sometimes tearful wicked sat over undone sums, or to repeat a little crime—the pulling of a girl's hair during geography, the sly shin kick under the table during English literature. Behind the school was a narrow lane where only the oldest and boldest threw pebbles at windows, scuffled and boasted, fibbed about their relations—

"My father's got a chauffeur."

"What's he want a chauffeur for? He hasn't got a car."

"My father's the richest man in the town."

"My father's the richest man in Wales."

"My father owns the world."

And swapped gob-stoppers for slings, old knives for marbles, kite strings for foreign stamps.

The lane was always the place to tell your secrets; if you did not have any, you invented them. Occasionally now I dream that I am turning out of school into the lane of confidences when I say to the boys of my class, "At last, I have a real secret."

"What is it—what is it?"

"I can fly."

And when they do not believe me, I flap my arms and slowly leave the ground only a few inches at first, then gaining air until I fly waving my cap level with the upper windows of the school, peering in until the mistress at the piano screams and the metronome falls to the ground and stops, and there is no more time.

And I fly over the trees and chimneys of my town, over the

dockyards skimming the masts and funnels, over Inkerman Street, Sebastopol Street, and the street where all the women wear men's caps, over the trees of the everlasting park, where a brass band shakes the leaves and sends them showering down on to the nurses and the children, the cripples and the idlers, and the gardeners, and the shouting boys: over the yellow seashore, and the stone-chasing dogs, and the old men, and the singing sea.

The memories of childhood have no order, and no end.

❊   ❊   ❊   ❊

SUMMARY

Most of the writers represented in this book had to search before they found the subject of their narrative. Some tried other subjects before they found the one that worked. Almost all of these who found a subject that worked for them quickly found other subjects from within their own experience and wrote other narratives, improving on their earlier efforts. Not only had their instinct for the right subject sharpened, but their skills in working with their material had also increased. They discovered that something to write about is not so much a product of imagination as of an ability to remember significant moments in their past lives. The narratives in this book will suggest possible subjects. So will your classmates as they uncover the richness of their own experiences. The writer himself, however, is the only person who can find the material about which he can write.

Once a writer discovers his subject, he must decide from what angle he wishes to transmit it to his reader. He will look back upon himself from the stance he has attained since the occurrance of the event selected as his subject. He may write as an "I," he can give himself another name, or he can treat his character as someone other than himself. The writer should choose the viewpoint that feels most comfortable to him. If he is at ease with the character he is working with, his narrative will reflect that ease. He must be aware that the assumption of a point of view presupposes some degree of ironic distance from his subject or character. The exercise that follows will help the writer make the best choice of point of view for him and for his material.

EXERCISE

Select a subject, something from your past experience, and write about it in three different paragraphs: In the first paragraph, give yourself a name other than your own; in the second, use the first person; and in the third, treat your character as if he were someone other than yourself. What are the strengths and limitations of each approach? Which approach seems to work best with the subject you have chosen? Does the assumption of a different point of view change the content and direction of the narrative?

Could each of the narratives included in this chapter be treated from other points of view? What would change? Suppose Roger Purvis, Harry Nelson, and the anonymous eight-year-old of "Who Was Really Responsible?" each told his story in the language and with the insights available to him at the time of the events narrated.

Your instructor will ask for additional writing from you beyond this initial exercise and beyond the minimum suggestions incorporated in the "Exercises" at the end of each chapter. The exercises, however, suggest ways in which any narrative writing you do can be improved. Apply the suggestions in each exercise to *all* the writing you are doing for this course. You may discover that your writing has anticipated the material presented in later chapters. Fine! Those chapters, however, suggest —primarily through the narratives of student and professional writers— how your own skills can be even further refined.

TWO
Diction
and
Syntax

Assuming that the writer has discovered a subject and has defined the point of view which most effectively projects the narrative to the reader, he must attend to the smallest components of the writing process: diction, the words he uses, and syntax, the order in which he uses them. John Cartland, for example, uses "staccato" to describe the sound of the heels of Roger's mother, a word that describes the sound itself and the silence surrounding the sound, and says something about the attitude of the person wearing the shoes. Roger's status during the days of mourning is described as a "limbo." He is neither within the adult world of decorum and arrangements nor within the childhood world of his fourth-grade contemporaries. His treehouse represents an escape from a very specific kind of limbo. The word has become a cliché for any indeterminate state, but when it is used precisely to describe a specific state of being neither here nor there, it is used accurately. Paul Ross writes of "Dante's Limbo," a slightly imprecise allusion to *The Inferno*, to the Vestibule on this side of the River Acheron, across which Limbo lies. On the Vestibule, neither heaven nor hell, those who made no allegiances, either for better or worse, aimlessly pursue a flag floating above them:

> And there I look, and see! an ensign borne
> On empty air, and spinning, twisting fled,
> To wrench a wretched multitude forlorn.
>
> Behind, in endless mobs they turned and sped,
> Pursuing nothing, as in life. I could
> Not think that time had made so many dead.

The writer, remembering the passage from Dante, finds his character in a similar situation—"perpetual vertigo." If we, as readers, remember the passage, it enhances our feeling for the street scene in which the young man finds himself and our feeling for the stillness he must soon assume. The bag of jamoons of our anonymous fire-setter evaporates with a "hiss," a word that tells us not only what happens but gives us the precise sound of that event—and perhaps conveys the Devil's commentary on the church he will be blamed for igniting.

The following narrative was written by a college freshman.

❀ "GURRY BOT 'ER"

Richard Spear

The dead fish lay stiff and inert. The glare of the afternoon sun was
fended off by a roadside lilac bush. Green-vested flies by turns hummed
their litany over the deceased. Otherwise, it was unnoticed. In a
parked car nearby, an elderly sage tilted three days of beard into the
air and snoozed. The other humans in the vicinity had withdrawn
a short distance onto the bridge over Winnegance Creek. There, as a
group of men and boys in rubber boots and shabby jackets, they
reclined at various angles against the parapet and squinted down at
the water. The corpse, a twelve-hours-dead alewife, was left in the
custody of the lilac and the insect mourners. The fact that the
fish was too old to retail was becoming increasingly evident. However,
the fish was not yet too disfigured to bring to mind how it had come
to be there.

A few days before, that alewife had joined company with the
great pilgrimage which swirled up the Kennebec River toward
the breeding grounds. At the stone wall of the Winnegance Bridge,
the fish school had been forced to halt the expedition and scout
the difficulty. A narrow chute of unpainted wood pitched at a
steep angle was perceived to be the sole route over this unexpected
dam; a rushing blanket of water shot out of it. The fish hesitated until
the tide ebbed, but on the flood tide preceding the dawn, they had
marshaled their numbers for the assault. With flailing fins, their
spasmodically contorting bodies had forced the chute in legions and
flashed ahead under the bridge and into the darkness of the level
section of the passage above the drop-off. There the obscurity of
deep shadows overflowed with constant sound. Water falling at the
steep end of the chute droned and lisped, creating a background for
smaller noises, which could be sensed but not truly heard in that
reverberating cavern. Water dripped, slapped, and chuckled all
around. A bobbing pulp-log nuzzled against the outside of the chute,
fishtails broke water, and still the alewives fled onward gliding somehow
against the current. They emerged from the black, sound-filled void
beneath the bridge and were undaunted by the softer gloom of
the stream under a night sky. Then, on an instant, the rush of black
phantoms was halted so abruptly that some alewives leaped clear
of the water. The leading fish had charged against a fine meshed screen
and the barrier blocked the attempts of the startled fish toward further progress. The alewives hovered in ranks behind the new
obstacle. Occasionally they rammed it head-on or slid back grace-

fully on the current. Secretive little splashes and suspicious eddies
gave their presence away to unseen eyes, straining above. Without
perceptible warning, the whole school sensed impending catastrophy.
A wave, a rolling tumult of individual splashes, surged back toward
the black shadows of the lower chute, the river, and safety. But
hardly had the school reached the bounds of the bridge's deeper
obscurity when they again caromed off a screen—a screen where there
had been none before—in the only avenue of escape! Trapped between
the two barriers, the fish panicked. Down from on high and into the
darting, kicking, leaping tumult, swept two nets. Up they struggled
overflowing, with a twisting, twitching burden. A frenzied surplus,
spewing back in breathless consternation, slapped the fish-churned
waters and was gone. The hapless remainder was hurled into a
wooden box. There, these fish beat out their lives smiting the resounding
planks, their gasping gills pulsating in the surfeit of air.

Presently, the then-subdued alewives were measured out in
bushel buckets. The gurry, that conglomerate of water, slime, and
secretions, rendered the alewives slippery and they slithered in the box,
fleeing the measuring net. But into the tin buckets they unwillingly
slipped, and the buckets were borne up the stony incline to the
causeway and a waiting truck. At this time that solitary fish must have
dropped, unheeded, from a bucket, to remain near a lilac for a day.

Now, it was late in the afternoon and the lobstermen had stopped
to buy alewives for bait. There were no fish here except for the old
one in the shade. The clump of men at the bridge suddenly
exploded. "Time to dip 'um," bellowed a small boy in a watch-cap. Two
boys rushed toward where the long-handled dip-nets leaned aslant
against a ledge while another boy vaulted over the fence and started
to drive a few straggling fish up the chute from the drop-off.
One of the lads eased along a staging out over the water toward the
chute. The thumping of the driver was audible from under the
bridge. Wavelets clapped against the sunlit, reflection-speckled cement
of the abutments. A sudden spurt of activity convulsed the surface
of the water below the screen. The boy on the scaffold forced
the second screen into place and the "bailing" out of alewives began.
Fish scales loosened in the struggle flashed high in the spring sun and
the air was dampened with their gurry.

As the boys lifted the first bucket of the "bait" into the back of
an immaculate Buick, they suggested that the fish gurry might
do damage to the car. "No trouble at all," grinned the now-wakeful
sage, "After all, gurry bot 'er!"

❋   ❋   ❋   ❋

In "Gurry Bot 'Er," (which, translated without the Maine accent means "gurry bought her") we immediately perceive yet another version of point of view. Here, whoever is describing the events is not a character in the narrative. Instead, the point of view is similar to that of a very selective camera, focusing first and last on an abandoned fish, panning over the alewives moving toward their spawning grounds, picking up sounds of fish and voices, but always remaining outside of the events themselves. This point of view is determined by the narrator's having no part in the story, except as observer. But notice that the voice telling the story is intimately acquainted with his subject. Like the painter who does not appear in his own picture, the author of "Gurry Bot 'Er" has been there and has carefully absorbed the imagery of the scene.

A narrator as character can be very important. Nick Carraway of Fitzgerald's *The Great Gatsby*, for example, is the only person who can tell the story as it is told. He has access to both worlds of the play, Tom Buchanan's and Jay Gatsby's. He is the only character in the novel who can both move easily within Buchanan's world and also recognize the validity of Gatsby's meretricious dream. The narrative is clearly affected by the point of view from which it emerges, as is the case in such different novels as *The Ambassadors*, *Lord Jim*, *All the King's Men*, and *One Flew Over the Cuckoo's Nest*. In the case of "Gurry Bot 'Er," no purpose would be served by a narrator who could merely say "next I saw" or "then I heard." When the narrator is not a character he can be erased. The event itself is the point of "Gurry Bot 'Er," and the event centers more on fish than people.

Precise observation and description are essential in "Gurry Bot 'Er." Such precision can emerge only in words, words carefully selected and arranged. The flies "hummed their litany"; a litany is a prayer in which a leader and a group alternate in statement and response. The fish is making his statement: that he is no longer marketable is becoming increasingly evident to the imagined nostrils that cross his wavelength. But the flies respond in their green vestments. A single word, litany, evokes a situation, not merely of a dead fish and a swarm of flies, but a reminder that death is subject to rituals, those of nature and those of formal religion. In his second sentence, Rick Spear introduces the colloquial "fended off." He might easily have said, "The fish lay in the shadow of a roadside lilac bush": an accurate enough statement. But two crucial elements of the narrative would have been blurred. "Fended off" not only suggests an ongoing process, as opposed to the static "shadow," but it introduces another kind of language to the narrative, a less elegant strain than that of litany, a strain which prepares us for the dialect of the sage who owns the slimy Buick and for the commercial reality of the scene into which our articulate camera projects us.

An example of syntax also helps us understand how the single sentences of a narrative capture its larger thrust: "The corpse, a twelve-hours-dead alewife, was left in the custody of the lilac and the insect mourners." Rick Spear might have said, "The corpse was a twelve-hours-dead alewife." That emphasis would have closed us in on the fish per se. But the fish is, like some detail introduced at the beginning of a film, merely the symbolic aftermath of a larger event, which we discover is going on right now. The precise nature of the fish is subordinated within a sentence that leaves him in "custody," and which leads to a consideration of how he came to be there. That, after all, is the point. The sentence begins with the fish, leaves him to the flies and lilac, moves to a sentence suggesting the evolving pervasiveness of the fish's smell, then moves to a more panoramic consideration of the single piece of evidence lying beneath the buzz and the blossoms. The ordering of the words suggests the importance of that single fish, but he is not the whole story.

Another example suggests why words must not only be selected carefully, but must be placed in a precise order. "Up they struggled" refers to the nets that have just enclosed a load of startled fish. The placement of "up" at the beginning of the clause, rather than at the end ("They struggled up") coerces us into a feeling of the upward direction of the net and of the inevitable fate of the fish. No matter how the net may struggle, we have no doubt where those fish are going—up and out of their element. The order in which words are placed is crucial to the effect of those words.

Compare these two sentences:

> His hair was tossed toward the sky by a slight breeze and was then returned to his head in a mass of tangles.

> A slight breeze tossed his hair to the sky and then returned it to his head in a mass of tangles.

The first sentence is passive: The subject of the sentence is acted upon, he is not the actor. The action of the sentence moves counter to the way the eye reads (e.g., "The ball was hit by John" versus "John hit the ball," which is active, the action moving across the sentence in the direction in which the eye reads). The passive might seem appropriate to oblivious and fashionable Harry Nelson. He is, after all, acted upon rather than actor, except in the roles that trends dictate. A passive construction might work stylistically to suggest his vulnerability. The passive voice, however, uses more words than the active, and, crucially for the story of Harry Nelson, the active force in the sentence is something outside Harry (the breeze) over which he has no control. The passive nature of Harry Nelson thus emerges in the active voice: He is acted upon. And as the story shows us, Harry, like his hair, will come back from his flight in a mass of tangles. A sentence with fewer words and cast in the active voice—so that the action moves across the sentence—is preferable, in narrative and almost any other writing, to any other syntactic structure. The active voice moves *with* the story, not against it.*

The following was written by a college student.

❊ THE MAN

Joe Dane

We lived in town, on a street crowded with old proud houses, and the yards were all small, very small except for one. Across the street lived "The Man" and beside his house, where he should have had a neighbor, was an empty lot. We never knew his real name but he loved his title and was addressed in no other manner. There were furrows carved into his brow, between his graying hair and his bright, glowing eyes, and he was always smiling, at least, as far as we were concerned he was, for we were always happy then and his joy came from us. He loved us, the kids who lived on his block, and he loved to have us play in his yard. He would watch us, maybe join us, and when any of us received a phonograph record on a birthday or Christmas, we would take it to him and he would lead us to his shed and play it on an old, hand-cranked victrola. His face would bear that smile and maybe he would tell us stories of Geronimo—an old friend of his. Certainly he knew Geronimo; he said he did. Besides, the time I dressed up as an Indian and crept over to his house, he could tell right away that I wasn't the old chief.

And then there was baseball and football and his sacred grass yielded to our insignificant weight. But it was only for us. No one outside our block was allowed on his grass. I suppose it was inevitable that I should make my mistake. A friend of mine from a few blocks away had come over to see me. It was summer and our own lawn was too small anyway. Tommy didn't want me to, but I couldn't see any reason for not asking The Man if he could play with me on the

---

* Perhaps the exception that proves the rule is Rick Spear's "The corpse, a twelve-hours-dead alewife, was left in the custody of the lilac and the insect mourners." Why or why not?

sacred lawn. The Man wore his glowing smile as I approached him. I
asked my question and the bright smile stole silently from his face.
He wasn't angry; rather, his expression denoted worry and disappointment. No he'd rather not . . . Please . . . Then finally, a
resigned "All right. Go ahead." He quickly turned away and I strode
jubilantly back to Tommy with the triumph on my lips. But Tommy
acted strangely. He decided he'd better not invade The Man's yard
after all. I hadn't really understood what I had done; I couldn't
understand The Man; and I couldn't understand Tommy's decision;
but I never played on The Man's lawn again.

The grass is gone now—covered up by a new house, and The
Man's house has long since been sold. Yet every once in a while, my
sister receives a postcard from some distant place signed "The
Man." No, The Man has never written me, but when he takes
his pen and addresses a card to my sister maybe he thinks of me, and
that expression that I remember so well returns to his wrinkled face.

❄   ❄   ❄   ❄

"The Man" incorporates many examples of precise diction and effective
syntax. The word "sacred" is repeated. Why? How does the single word
help us understand what the story means?

The following is a poem written by a college student.

❀ TO SING A SAD SONG

Richard E. Fudge

"What yo teacha callin' heah fo' you, boy?"
"I dunno, I didn't do nothin'!"
"That's just it, you *ain't* doin' nothin'!"
"But I am! I'm workin' on my studies!"
"Well, you ain't workin' enuff!"
She swung. I moved. She missed.
Couldn't see her left; too busy duckin' her right.
It came across my face like a mutha fucker—
"OOOOW!"
"I can't beat through dem pants. Take 'em off!"
"Pleease! Oh, Pleeease! I won't do it no more!"
Anything to stop this crazy lady—no use denyin' it,
Whatever "it" is I'm gettin' whipped fo'

"OOOOOW!"

"Shut up! You ain't hurt! Yo behind ain't even warm yet!"

"But I'm tryin' to learn, honest to God I am!"

"What yo talkin' 'bout, boy? What yo swearin' at God fo'?"

Another blow to my tuckered out ass.

Nothin' else to do now but lay here and get beat.

She don't hear me no how.

I guess she expects me to hurt out loud, but I don't feel nothin' now.

My behind feels like it fell off already.

"Get up! What's wrong wit you? You crazy, boy?"

"No mam."

"Then do yo work like Miss Pritches tells ya!"

"But Daddy says . . ."

(Smack!)

"Shut up! That nigguh don't know nothin'.

What you think I send you to school fo'?"

"Miss Priiitches, I'm ready to work now . . ."

❋   ❋   ❋   ❋

While this is not a book about writing poetry, "To Sing a Sad Song" is a kind of narrative and suggests that diction and syntax need not be *formal* or *grammatical* to be effective. Indeed, the words people use are the raw material out of which the writer recreates the feeling and sound of their use, as Richard Fudge does here. Through the words he expresses both a personal dilemma and a sociology. Replace the lines of the poem with proper and grammatical words and constructions, and then ask what happened to it. "Poetry is what evaporates from all translations," as Frost suggested. The words of the poem emerge from a specific situation. The words are ethnic, but no more so than those of Roger Purvis's mother: "but try to be quiet in the house." This sentence may seem more correct than the words of the mother in Richard Fudge's poem, but they merely emerge from a different social background—the American upper middle class, which, for better or worse, establishes standards of "correctness" for the rest of society. In some ways the words of Roger Purvis's mother are less "true" than those of the mother of Fudge's poem. The middle-class mother uses euphemisms, attempts to couch the unpleasant in favorable terms: "she had something called cancer. . . . She has gone to heaven, and she isn't sick anymore or in pain. . . ." The words of the "crazy lady" of Fudge's poem, whatever they may be, are hardly euphemisms. They are not evasions of whatever the truth may be.

"To Sing a Sad Song" does not suggest that any words may be used at any time. Quite the opposite: Only the words and the syntax appropriate to a particular situation will work effectively. Were the mother of the poem to speak as does the mother of "The Treehouse," we would have a "middle-class spanking" and a host of different associations. It is possible in the middle-class situation that punishment might be deferred "until your father gets home." The middle-class mother, however bitter toward her husband, would probably not say, "Your father doesn't know a damned thing!" Trained toward the importance of solidarity between husband and wife, she would have to be sorely provoked before shattering one of the rules of decorum of her social level. She might, but we can infer that her bitterness would spill out in other ways, not in a one-to-one confrontation with her erring son. Each writer, Jack Cartland and Richard Fudge, knows the sociology and decorum of the situation he treats. The rules of language, the choice of words, and the dictation of syntax flow from that knowledge.

The following example for analysis of diction and syntax was written by a freshman in college.

❀ *RIDING HIGH*

Kris Keller

By the age of fourteen I was invulnerable. I had witnessed the emaciating, year-long dying of a father-idol, and emerged from the experience feeling superior to my naive peers for the agony I'd known and the intensity they'd lacked. I had survived for two days and one sea-stormed night through what everyone had assumed to be my death by drowning. I had giggled my way through countless marijauna highs, jolted my way through a dozen acid trips, and learned, even, to stab that Methedrine-filled syringe into flexed veins. Other people, I knew, were forced under by the weight of their own living. But I was invulnerable; I felt my weight to be equal to that of any that might press down on me—I believed my determination to be greater.

This day in that year, I was standing by the side of the road, thumb extended and trustworthy smile set, waiting to catch a ride. A highway patrol car pulled up and the patrolman, holstered hips swinging, strolled towards me.

"Why aren't you in school?"

"School! My God, do I seem *that* young?"

I convinced him that my driver's license had been carelessly for-

gotten in my bureau drawer and assured him that I, being legally
adult, was capable of making my own decisions as to the advisability of climbing in and out of strangers' automobiles. I had faith in
my competence and projected that faith to the Paternal Figure, who
strolled back to his ornamental vehicle with an admonition to be careful
and a resigned shake of his balding head.

My life had taught me that people act almost exclusively by reaction. Their response to me was dictated solely by my approach to
them. I recognized that people expected certain actions under certain
circumstances, and that by contradicting those expectations, I could
alter their perceptions. I'd attended formal gatherings and, experimentally, had behaved informally and then studied the others
present reassessing the social climate, then adjusting their behavior
to fit what they perceived to be a different, and now informal,
circumstance. So I had no real fear of unfamiliar persons, of the dangerous men I'd been warned throughout my childhood to "never get
into cars with." I believed I could control anyone's behavioral reactions, be they polite social acquaintance or psychotic rapist. I was
the supreme manipulator. I was invulnerable.

A dingy-grey Chevy pulled up beside me. I opened the car door
and peered in at the driver, assessing his greasy black hair, middle-
age, and T-shirted, paunchy torso. Then, judging him unattractive but
not threatening, I slid onto the seat beside him and with a reflexive
"thank you," slammed the door.

We exchanged trivial conversation and he offered to travel fifteen
miles out of his way to deliver me straight to my destination. I knew
he expected an abashed, "Oh—you don't have to bother!" and I
gave him one. But he insisted, as I assumed he would, so I settled
back in the seat and congratulated myself once again on how
aptly I'd handled that highway patrolman. We traveled in silence
for a few minutes and the hum of the wheels, the heat of the Indian
Summer, left me drowsy. I slept.

I awakened to a change in the rhythm of that wheel humming. By
the sharp jolting of the seat beneath me, I knew we were moving
over unpaved surface. I straightened and looked out to acres of
orchard and a twilight sky. It seemed that a moment ago it had been
midday in a city of homes, of people, of familiarity. Where was I now?
My thoughts, my efforts to assess and clarify the circumstances, were
too vague to be panicky. I turned to question the driver, the car
slowed, he switched off the ignition and turned to me. My thoughts
were clarified—my hand reached for the door handle.

Instantaneously, the calm that had come with the stilling of the
motor was broken, replaced by the man's tight grip on my wrist and his
incoherent, throaty raspings. I strained to recall all I'd been taught

about defense against the rapist's attempts, but no recollection could come clear. There was no time to consider an analysis of his psyche while I struggled against his rough thick arms enclosing me, his sweating, reddened, contorted face pressing towards me.

A scream, beyond the range of my voice and the strength of my lungs, reverberated. His hand clamped over my mouth, I heard his short breaths, tasted the salt of his flesh, and my teeth clenched over fingers. My cheek was burned with the impact of his slap. His other hand groped over my thigh and my body recoiled. The fear I'd known a few seconds before vanished, replaced by only rage, hatred, hatred and rage for the despicable hand, the sticky, urgent, fondless touch of the aggressor.

I did not ask myself what to do. Legs knew to kick out, arms knew to slug and strike, voice knew to wail. Mind lost control over Body. Mind was not required.

I was out of his hold, out of his car. The man, sweating and swearing profusely, not stopping to slam the car door I'd managed to open, sped off into the orchard, leaving a wave of dust, a row of tire tracks, and a young girl racing frantically towards some well-traveled road, towards homes, towards people, towards anywhere familiar. Though he'd driven out of sight, I ran with the terror of the victim of pursuit—the hound's rabbit, the lion's gazelle. Anticipating meeting him any moment face to face, I turned my head constantly in every direction, ready to change the course of escape, ready to take any direction to lose the pursuer.

I tripped over a stone, tasted the dust, and heard my torn dress rip even wider. The orchard path seemed endless, and I imagined myself, rat on a metal wheel, running forever, running towards nothing, sobbing and sweating.

I came to a paved road. On the far side stood a staid, white Victorian home. A familiar suppertime aroma drifted from it. The scent brought to mind the dusks of my childhood when Mama would call me in to set the table and I'd hurry to finish the chore in time to greet my father as he came in from the day's work. I wanted to cross the road, to tell the strangers there of that fear, that rage, that struggle. But the home projected an aura of such placidity I knew my presence would be a disruption. A single car approached from farther down the roadway. I rearranged my twisted clothing, dabbed at the tears, and stuck out my thumb.

❊   ❊   ❊   ❊

The following selections, by James Baldwin and Katherine Butler Hathaway, explore two very different situations, that of a bitter young black and that of a handicapped young woman. Diction and syntax are used superbly in each essay to bring the reader, regardless of his race, gender, or physical condition, into the experience described.

✿ NOTES OF A NATIVE SON

James Baldwin

On the 29th of July, in 1943, my father died. On the same day, a few hours later, his last child was born. Over a month before this, while all our energies were concentrated in waiting for these events, there had been, in Detroit, one of the bloodiest race riots of the century. A few hours after my father's funeral, while he lay in state in the undertaker's chapel, a race riot broke out in Harlem. On the morning of the 3rd of August, we drove my father to the graveyard through a wilderness of smashed plate glass.

The day of my father's funeral had also been my nineteenth birthday. As we drove him to the graveyard, the spoils of injustice, anarchy, discontent, and hatred were all around us. It seemed to me that God himself had devised, to mark my father's end, the most sustained and brutally dissonant of codas. And it seemed to me, too, that the violence which rose all about us as my father left the world had been devised as a corrective for the pride of his eldest son. I had declined to believe in that apocalypse which had been central to my father's vision; very well, life seemed to be saying, here is something that will certainly pass for an apocalypse until the real thing comes along. I had inclined to be contemptuous of my father for the conditions of his life, for the conditions of our lives. When his life had ended I began to wonder about that life and also, in a new way, to be apprehensive about my own.

I had not known my father very well. We had got on badly, partly because we shared, in our different fashions, the vice of stubborn pride. When he was dead I realized that I had hardly ever spoken to him. When he had been dead a long time I began to wish I had. It seems to be typical of life in America, where opportunities, real and fancied, are thicker than anywhere else on the globe, that the

SOURCE: From *Notes of a Native Son* by James Baldwin. Copyright © 1955 by James Baldwin. Reprinted by permission of Beacon Press.

second generation has no time to talk to the first. No one, including
my father, seems to have known exactly how old he was, but his
mother had been born during slavery. He was of the first generation of free men. He, along with thousands of other Negroes,
came North after 1919 and I was part of that generation which had
never seen the landscape of what Negroes sometimes call the
Old Country.

He had been born in New Orleans and had been a quite young
man there during the time that Louis Armstrong, a boy, was running
errands for the dives and honky-tonks of what was always presented
to me as one of the most wicked of cities—to this day, whenever
I think of New Orleans, I also helplessly think of Sodom and
Gomorrah. My father never mentioned Louis Armstrong, except
to forbid us to play his records; but there was a picture of him on our
wall for a long time. One of my father's strong-willed female relatives
had placed it there and forbade my father to take it down. He never
did, but he eventually maneuvered her out of the house and when,
some years later, she was in trouble and near death, he refused to
do anything to help her.

He was, I think, very handsome. I gather this from photographs
and from my own memories of him, dressed in his Sunday best
and on his way to preach a sermon somewhere, when I was
little. Handsome, proud, and ingrown, "like a toe-nail," somebody
said. But he looked to me, as I grew older, like pictures I had seen
of African tribal chieftains: he really should have been naked, with
war-paint on the barbaric mementos, standing among spears. He
could be chilling in the pulpit and indescribably cruel in his personal life
and he was certainly the most bitter man I have ever met; yet it must
be said that there was something else in him, buried in him, which
lent him his tremendous power and, even, a rather crushing charm.
It had something to do with his blackness, I think—he was very
black—with his blackness and his beauty, and with the fact that
he knew that he was black but did not know that he was
beautiful. He claimed to be proud of his blackness but it had also
been the cause of much humiliation and it had fixed bleak boundaries
to his life. He was not a young man when we were growing up and
he had already suffered many kinds of ruin; in his outrageously
demanding and protective way he loved his children, who were
black like him and menaced, like him; and all these things sometimes
showed in his face when he tried, never to my knowledge with any
success, to establish contact with any of us. When he took one
of his children on his knee to play, the child always became fretful
and began to cry; when he tried to help one of us with our homework
the absolutely unabating tension which emanated from him caused

our minds and our tongues to become paralyzed, so that he,
scarcely knowing why, flew into a rage and the child, not knowing
why, was punished. If it ever entered his head to bring a surprise home
for his children, it was, almost unfailingly, the wrong surprise and
even the big watermelons he often brought home on his back in
the summertime led to the most appalling scenes. I do not
remember, in all those years, that one of his children was ever
glad to see him come home. From what I was able to gather of his
early life, it seemed that this inability to establish contact with other
people had always marked him and had been one of the things
which had driven him out of New Orleans. There was something in
him, therefore, groping and tentative, which was never expressed and
which was buried with him. One saw it most clearly when he was
facing new people and hoping to impress them. But he never
did, not for long. We went from church to smaller and more
improbable church, he found himself in less and less demand as a
minister, and by the time he died none of his friends had come to
see him for a long time. He had lived and died in an intolerable
bitterness of spirit and it frightened me, as we drove him to the
graveyard through those unquiet, ruined streets, to see how
powerful and overflowing this bitterness could be and to realize
that this bitterness now was mine.

When he died I had been away from home for a little over a year.
In that year I had had time to become aware of the meaning of all
my father's bitter warnings, had discovered the secret of his proudly
pursed lips and rigid carriage: I had discovered the weight of
white people in the world. I saw that this had been for my ancestors
and now would be for me an awful thing to live with and that the
bitterness which had helped to kill my father could also kill me.

He had been ill a long time—in the mind, as we now
realized, reliving instances of his fantastic intransigence in the new
light of his affliction and endeavoring to feel a sorrow for him which
never, quite, came true. We had not known that he was being
eaten up by paranoia, and the discovery that his cruelty, to our bodies
and our minds, had been one of the symptoms of his illness was
not, then, enough to enable us to forgive him. The younger
children felt, quite simply, relief that he would not be coming
home any more. My mother's observation that it was he, after all,
who had kept them alive all these years meant nothing because the
problems of keeping children alive are not real for children. The older
children felt, with my father gone, that they could invite their friends
to the house without fear that their friends would be insulted or,
as had sometimes happened with me, being told that their friends were
in league with the devil and intended to rob our family of everything

we owned. (I didn't fail to wonder, and it made me hate him, what on earth we owned that anybody else would want.)

His illness was beyond all hope of healing before anyone realized that he was ill. He had always been so strange and had lived, like a prophet, in such unimaginably close communion with the Lord that his long silences which were punctuated by moans and hallelujahs and snatches of old songs while he sat at the living-room window never seemed odd to us. It was not until he refused to eat because, he said, his family was trying to poison him that my mother was forced to accept as a fact what had, until then, been only an unwilling suspicion. When he was committed, it was discovered that he had tuberculosis and, as it turned out, the disease of his mind allowed the disease of his body to destroy him. For the doctors could not force him to eat, either, and, though he was fed intravenously, it was clear from the beginning that there was no hope for him.

In my mind's eye I could see him, sitting at the window, locked up in his terrors; hating and fearing every living soul including his children who had betrayed him, too, by reaching toward the world which had despised him. There were nine of us. I began to wonder what it could have felt like for such a man to have had nine children whom he could barely feed. He used to make little jokes about our poverty, which never, of course, seemed very funny to us; they could not have seemed very funny to him, either, or else our all too feeble response to them would never have caused such rages. He spent great energy and achieved, to our chagrin, no small amount of success in keeping us away from the people who surrounded us, people who had all-night rent parties to which we listened when we should have been sleeping, people who cursed and drank and flashed razor blades on Lenox Avenue. He could not understand why, if they had so much energy to spare, they could not use it to make their lives better. He treated almost everybody on our block with a most uncharitable asperity and neither they, nor, of course, their children were slow to reciprocate.

The only white people who came to our house were welfare workers and bill collectors. It was almost always my mother who dealt with them, for my father's temper, which was at the mercy of his pride, was never to be trusted. It was clear that he felt their very presence in his home to be a violation: this was conveyed by his carriage, almost ludicrously stiff, and by his voice, harsh and vindictively polite. When I was around nine or ten I wrote a play which was directed by a young, white schoolteacher, a woman, who then took an interest in me, and gave me books to read and, in order to corroborate my theatrical bent, decided to take me to see what

she somewhat tactlessly referred to as "real" plays. Theatergoing was
forbidden in our house, but, with the really cruel intuitiveness of
a child, I suspected that the color of this woman's skin would
carry the day for me. When, at school, she suggested taking me to the
theater, I did not, as I might have done if she had been a
Negro, find a way of discouraging her, but agreed that she should
pick me up at my house one evening. I then, very cleverly, left
all the rest to my mother, who suggested to my father, as I knew she
would, that it would not be very nice to let such a kind woman make
the trip for nothing. Also, since it was a schoolteacher, I imagine
that my mother countered the idea of sin with the idea of
"education," which word, even with my father, carried a kind of
bitter weight.

Before the teacher came my father took me aside to ask *why* she
was coming, what *interest* she could possibly have in our house, in a
boy like me. I said I didn't know but I, too, suggested that it
had something to do with education. And I understood that my
father was waiting for me to say something—I didn't quite
know what; perhaps that I wanted his protection against this
teacher and her "education." I said none of these things and the
teacher came and we went out. It was clear, during the brief interview
in our living room, that my father was agreeing very much against his
will and that he would have refused permission if he had dared.
The fact that he did not dare caused me to despise him: I had
no way of knowing that he was facing in that living room a
wholly unprecedented and frightening situation.

Later, when my father had been laid off from his job, this
woman became very important to us. She was really a very sweet
and generous woman and went to a great deal of trouble to be of
help to us, particularly during one awful winter. My mother called her
by the highest name she knew: she said she was a "christian." My
father could scarcely disagree but during the four or five years of
our relatively close association he never trusted her and was always
trying to surprise in her open, Midwestern face the genuine, cunningly
hidden, and hideous motivation. In later years, particularly when it
began to be clear that this "education" of mine was going to lead
me to perdition, he became more explicit and warned me that
my white friends in high school were not really my friends and that
I would see, when I was older, how white people would do anything
to keep a Negro down. Some of them could be nice, he admitted,
but none of them were to be trusted and most of them were
not even nice. The best thing was to have as little to do with them
as possible. I did not feel this way and I was certain, in my
innocence, that I never would.

But the year which preceded my father's death had made a
great change in my life. I had been living in New Jersey, working in
defense plants, working and living among southerners, white and
black. I knew about the south, of course, and about how southerners
treated Negroes and how they expected them to behave, but it had
never entered my mind that anyone would look at me and expect
me to behave that way. I learned in New Jersey that to be a Negro
meant, precisely, that one was never looked at but was simply at the
mercy of the reflexes the color of one's skin caused in other people.
I acted in New Jersey as I had always acted, that is as though
I thought a great deal of myself—I had to *act* that way—with results that
were, simply, unbelievable. I had scarcely arrived before I had
earned the enmity, which was extraordinarily ingenious, of all
my superiors and nearly all my co-workers. In the beginning, to
make matters worse, I simply did not know what was happening. I
did not know what I had done, and I shortly began to wonder what
anyone could possibly do, to bring about such unanimous, active, and
unbearably vocal hostility. I knew about jim-crow but I had never
experienced it. I went to the same self-service restaurant three times
and stood with all the Princeton boys before the counter, waiting
for a hamburger and coffee; it was always an extraordinarily long
time before anything was set before me; but it was not until
the fourth visit that I learned that, in fact, nothing had ever been
set before me: I had simply picked something up. Negroes were not
served there, I was told, and they had been waiting for me to realize
that I was always the only Negro present. Once I was told this,
I determined to go there all the time. But now they were ready for
me and, though some dreadful scenes were subsequently enacted in that
restaurant, I never ate there again.

It was the same story all over New Jersey, in bars, bowling
alleys, diners, places to live. I was always being forced to leave,
silently, or with mutual imprecations. I very shortly became notorious
and children giggled behind me when I passed and their elders
whispered or shouted—they really believed that I was mad. And it did
begin to work on my mind, of course; I began to be afraid to go
anywhere and to compensate for this I went places to which I
really should not have gone and where, God knows, I had no desire
to be. My reputation in town naturally enhanced my reputation
at work and my working day became one long series of acrobatics
designed to keep me out of trouble. I cannot say that these acrobatics
succeeded. It began to seem that the machinery of the organization I
worked for was turning over, day and night, with but one aim: to
eject me. I was fired once, and contrived, with the aid of a friend from
New York, to get back on the payroll; was fired again, and bounced

back again. It took a while to fire me for the third time, but the third time took. There were no loopholes anywhere. There was not even any way of getting back inside the gates.

That year in New Jersey lives in my mind as though it were the year during which, having an unsuspected predilection for it, I first contracted some dread, chronic disease, the unfailing symptom of which is a kind of blind fever, a pounding in the skull and fire in the bowels. Once this disease is contracted, one can never be really carefree again, for the fever, without an instant's warning, can recur at any moment. It can wreck more important things than race relations. There is not a Negro alive who does not have this rage in his blood—one has the choice, merely, of living with it consciously or surrendering to it. As for me, this fever has recurred in me, and does, and will until the day I die.

My last night in New Jersey, a white friend from New York took me to the nearest big town, Trenton, to go to the movies and have a few drinks. As it turned out, he also saved me from, at the very least, a violent whipping. Almost every detail of that night stands out very clearly in my memory. I even remember the name of the movie we saw because it impressed me as being so patly ironical. It was a movie about the German occupation of France, starring Maureen O'Hara and Charles Laughton and called *This Land Is Mine*. I remember the name of the diner we walked into when the movie ended: it was the "American Diner." When we walked in the counterman asked what we wanted and I remember answering with the casual sharpness which had become my habit: "We want a hamburger and a cup of coffee, what do you think we want?" I do not know why, after a year of such rebuffs, I so completely failed to anticipate his answer, which was, of course, "We don't serve Negroes here." This reply failed to discompose me, at least for the moment. I made some sardonic comment about the name of the diner and we walked out into the streets.

This was the time of what was called the "brownout," when the lights in all American cities were very dim. When we re-entered the streets something happened to me which had the force of an optical illusion, or a nightmare. The streets were very crowded and I was facing north. People were moving in every direction but it seemed to me, in that instant, that all of the people I could see, and many more than that, were moving toward me, against me, and that everyone was white. I remember how their faces gleamed. And I felt, like a physical sensation, a *click* at the nape of my neck as though some interior string connecting my head to my body had been cut. I began to walk. I heard my friend call after me, but I ignored him. Heaven only knows what was going on in his

mind, but he had the good sense not to touch me—I don't know
what would have happened if he had—and to keep me in sight.
I don't know what was going on in my mind, either; I certainly had no
conscious plan. I wanted to do something to crush these white faces,
which were crushing me. I walked for perhaps a block or two until I
came to an enormous, glittering, and fashionable restaurant in
which I knew not even the intercession of the Virgin would cause
me to be served. I pushed through the doors and took the first vacant
seat I saw, at a table for two, and waited.

I do not know how long I waited and I rather wonder, until
today, what I could possibly have looked like. Whatever I looked like,
I frightened the waitress who shortly appeared, and the moment she
appeared all of my fury flowed toward her. I hated her for her white
face, and for her great, astounded, frightened eyes. I felt that if
she found a black man so frightening I would make her fright
worth-while.

She did not ask me what I wanted, but repeated, as though she
had learned it somewhere, "We don't serve Negroes here." She did
not say it with the blunt derisive hostility to which I had grown
so accustomed, but, rather, with a note of apology in her voice, and
fear. This made me colder and more murderous than ever. I felt I had
to do something with my hands. I wanted her to come close enough
for me to get her neck between my hands.

So I pretended not to have understood her, hoping to draw her
closer. And she did step a very short step closer, with her pencil
poised incongruously over her pad, and repeated the formula:
". . . don't serve Negroes here."

Somehow, with the repetition of that phrase, which was already
ringing in my head like a thousand bells of a nightmare, I realized
that she would never come any closer and that I would have to
strike from a distance. There was nothing on the table but an
ordinary water-mug half full of water, and I picked this up and
hurled it with all my strength at her. She ducked and it missed her
and shattered against the mirror behind the bar. And, with that sound,
my frozen blood abruptly thawed, I returned from wherever I had
been, I *saw*, for the first time, the restaurant, the people with their
mouths open, already, as it seemed to me, rising as one man, and
I realized what I had done, and where I was, and I was frightened. I
rose and began running for the door. A round, potbellied man
grabbed me by the nape of the neck just as I reached the
doors and began to beat me about the face. I kicked him and got
loose and ran into the streets. My friend whispered, *"Run!"* and I ran.

My friend stayed outside the restaurant long enough to misdirect
my pursuers and the police, who arrived, he told me, at once. I do

not know what I said to him when he came to my room that
night. I could not have said much. I felt, in the oddest, most awful
way, that I had somehow betrayed him. I lived it over and over and
over again, the way one relives an automobile accident after it has
happened and one finds oneself alone and safe. I could not get
over two facts, both equally difficult for the imagination to
grasp, and one was that I could have been murdered. But the
other was that I had been ready to commit murder. I saw nothing
very clearly but I did see this: that my life, my *real* life, was in danger,
and not from anything other people might do but from the hatred
I carried in my own heart.

I had returned home around the second week in June—in great haste
because it seemed that my father's death and my mother's confinement
were both a matter of hours. In the case of my mother, it soon became
clear that she had simply made a miscalculation. This had always
been her tendency and I don't believe that a single one of us
arrived in the world, or has since arrived anywhere else, on time.
But none of us dawdled so intolerably about the business of being
born as did my baby sister. We sometimes amused ourselves, during
those endless, stifling weeks, by picturing the baby sitting within
the safe, warm dark, bitterly regretting the necessity of becoming
a part of our chaos and stubbornly putting it off as long as possible. I
understood her perfectly and congratulated her on showing such
good sense so soon. Death, however, sat as purposefully at my
father's bedside as life stirred within my mother's womb and it was
harder to understand why he so lingered in that long shadow. It
seemed that he had bent, and for a long time, too, all of his energies
toward dying. Now death was ready for him but my father held back.
   All of Harlem, indeed, seemed to be infected by waiting. I had
never before known it to be so violently still. Racial tensions
throughout this country were exacerbated during the early years
of the war, partly because the labor market brought together
hundreds of thousands of ill-prepared people and partly because
Negro soldiers, regardless of where they were born, received their mili-
tary training in the south. What happened in defense plants and army
camps had repercussions, naturally, in every Negro ghetto. The
situation in Harlem had grown bad enough for clergymen, policemen,
educators, politicians, and social workers to assert in one breath that
there was no "crime wave" and to offer, in the very next breath,
suggestions as to how to combat it. These suggestions always
seemed to involve playgrounds, despite the fact that racial skirmishes
were occurring in the playgrounds, too. Playgrounds or not, crime
wave or not, the Harlem police force had been augmented in

March, and the unrest grew—perhaps, in fact, partly as a result of
the ghetto's instinctive hatred of policemen. Perhaps the most
revealing news item, out of the steady parade of reports of muggings,
stabbings, shootings, assaults, gang wars, and accusations of police
brutality, is the item concerning six Negro girls who set upon
a white girl in the subway because, as they all too accurately put it,
she was stepping on their toes. Indeed she was, all over the nation.

I had never before been so aware of policemen, on foot, on
horseback, on corners, everywhere, always two by two. Nor had I
ever been so aware of small knots of people. They were on stoops and
on corners and in doorways, and what was striking about them, I
think, was that they did not seem to be talking. Never, when I
passed these groups, did the usual sound of a curse or a laugh
ring out and neither did there seem to be any hum of gossip.
There was certainly, on the other hand, occurring between them
communication extraodinarily intense. Another thing that was
striking was the unexpected diversity of the people who made
up these groups. Usually, for example, one would see a group of
sharpies standing on the street corner, jiving the passing chicks; or a
group of older men, usually, for some reason, in the vicinity of a
barber shop, discussing baseball scores, or the numbers, or
making rather chilling observations about women they had known.
Women, in a general way, tended to be seen less often together—
unless they were church women, or very young girls, or prostitutes met
together for an unprofessional instant. But that summer I saw the
strangest combinations: large, respectable, churchly matrons standing
on the stoops or the corners with their hair tied up, together with
a girl in sleazy satin whose face bore the marks of gin and the
razor, or heavy-set, abrupt, no-nonsense older men, in company
with the most disreputable and fanatical "race" men, or these same
"race" men with the sharpies, or these sharpies with the churchly
women. Seventh Day Adventists and Methodists and Spiritualists
seemed to be hobnobbing with Holyrollers and they were all,
alike, entangled with the most flagrant disbelievers; something
heavy in their stance seemed to indicate that they had all, incred-
ibly, seen a common vision, and on each face there seemed to be
the same strange, bitter shadow.

The churchly women and the matter-of-fact, no-nonsense men
had children in the Army. The sleazy girls they talked to had lovers
there, the sharpies and the "race" men had friends and brothers there. It
would have demanded an unquestioning patriotism, happily as
uncommon in this country as it is undesirable, for these people
not to have been disturbed by the bitter letters they received, by the
newspaper stories they read, not to have been enraged by the posters,

then to be found all over New York, which described the Japanese
as "yellow-bellied Japs." It was only the "race" men, to be sure,
who spoke ceaselessly of being revenged—how this vengeance was to
be exacted was not clear—for the indignities and dangers suffered by
Negro boys in uniform; but everybody felt a directionless, hopeless
bitterness, as well as that panic which can scarcely be suppressed
when one knows that a human being one loves is beyond one's
reach, and in danger. This helplessness and this gnawing uneasiness
does something, at length, to even the toughest mind. Perhaps the
best way to sum all this up is to say that the people I knew,
felt, mainly, a peculiar kind of relief when they knew that their
boys were being shipped out of the south, to do battle overseas.
It was, perhaps, like feeling that the most dangerous part of a dangerous journey had been passed and that now, even if death should
come, it would come with honor and without the complicity of
their countrymen. Such a death would be, in short, a fact
with which one could hope to live.

It was on the 28th of July, which I believe was a Wednesday,
that I visited my father for the first time during his illness and
for the last time in his life. The moment I saw him I knew why I
had put off this visit so long. I had told my mother that I did
not want to see him because I hated him. But this was not true. It was
only that I *had* hated him and I wanted to hold on to this hatred. I
did not want to look on him as a ruin: it was not a ruin I had
hated. I imagine that one of the reasons people cling to their
hates so stubbornly is because they sense, once hate is gone, that
they will be forced to deal with pain.

We traveled out to him, his older sister and myself, to
what seemed to be the very end of a very Long Island. It was
hot and dusty and we wrangled, my aunt and I, all the way out, over
the fact that I had recently begun to smoke and, as she said,
to give myself airs. But I knew that she wrangled with me because
she could not bear to face the fact of her brother's dying. Neither could
I endure the reality of her despair, her unstated bafflement as to what
had happened to her brother's life, and her own. So we wrangled
and I smoked and from time to time she fell into a heavy reverie.
Covertly, I watched her face, which was the face of an old
woman; it had fallen in, the eyes were sunken and lightless; soon
she would be dying, too.

In my childhood—it had not been so long ago—I had thought
her beautiful. She had been quick-witted and quick-moving and
very generous with all the children and each of her visits had
been an event. At one time one of my brothers and myself had
thought of running away to live with her. Now she could no longer

produce out of her handbag some unexpected and yet familiar
delight. She made me feel pity and revulsion and fear. It was
awful to realize that she no longer caused me to feel affection. The
closer we came to the hospital the more querulous she became
and at the same time, naturally, grew more dependent on me.
Between pity and guilt and fear I began to feel that there was another
me trapped in my skull like a jack-in-the-box who might escape my
control at any moment and fill the air with screaming.

She began to cry the moment we entered the room and
she saw him lying there, all shriveled and still, like a little black
monkey. The great, gleaming apparatus which fed him and would
have compelled him to be still even if he had been able to move
brought to mind, not beneficence, but torture; the tubes entering his
arm made me think of pictures I had seen when a child, of Gulliver,
tied down by the pygmies on that island. My aunt wept and wept,
there was a whistling sound in my father's throat; nothing was
said; he could not speak. I wanted to take his hand, to say something.
But I do not know what I could have said, even if he could have heard
me. He was not really in that room with us, he had at last really
embarked on his journey; and though my aunt told me that he said he
was going to meet Jesus, I did not hear anything except that
whistling in his throat. The doctor came back and we left, into
that unbearable train again, and home. In the morning came
the telegram saying that he was dead. Then the house was suddenly
full of relatives, friends, hysteria, and confusion and I quickly left
my mother and the children to the care of those impressive
women, who, in Negro communities at least, automatically appear
at times of bereavement armed with lotions, proverbs, and patience,
and an ability to cook. I went downtown. By the time I returned,
later the same day, my mother had been carried to the hospital
and the baby had been born.

For my father's funeral I had nothing black to wear and this
posed a nagging problem all day long. It was one of those
problems, simple, or impossible of solution, to which the mind
insanely clings in order to avoid the mind's real trouble. I spent most
of that day at the downtown apartment of a girl I knew, celebrating
my birthday with whiskey and wondering what to wear that night.
When planning a birthday celebration one naturally does not
expect that it will be up against competition from a funeral and this
girl had anticipated taking me out that night, for a big dinner
and a night club afterwards. Sometime during the course of that
long day we decided that we would go out anyway, when my father's
funeral service was over. I imagine *I* decided it, since, as the funeral

hour approached, it became clearer and clearer to me that I would not know what to do with myself when it was over. The girl, stifling her very lively concern as to the possible effects of whiskey on one of my father's chief mourners, concentrated on being conciliatory and practically helpful. She found a black shirt for me somewhere and ironed it and, dressed in the darkest pants and jacket I owned, and slightly drunk, I made my way to my father's funeral.

The chapel was full, but not packed, and very quiet. There were, mainly, my father's relatives, and his children, and here and there I saw faces I had not seen since childhood, the faces of my father's one-time friends. They were very dark and solemn now, seeming somehow to suggest that they had known all along that something like this would happen. Chief among the mourners was my aunt, who had quarreled with my father all his life; by which I do not mean to suggest that her mourning was insincere or that she had not loved him. I suppose that she was one of the few people in the world who had, and their incessant quarreling proved precisely the strength of the tie that bound them. The only other person in the world, as far as I knew, whose relationship to my father rivaled my aunt's in depth was my mother, who was not there.

It seemed to me, of course, that it was a very long funeral. But it was, if anything, a rather shorter funeral than most, nor, since there were no overwhelming, uncontrollable expressions of grief, could it be called—if I dare to use the word—successful. The minister who preached my father's funeral sermon was one of the few my father had still been seeing as he neared his end. He presented to us in his sermon a man whom none of us had ever seen—a man thoughtful, patient, and forbearing, a Christian inspiration to all who knew him, and a model for his children. And no doubt the children, in their disturbed and guilty state, were almost ready to believe this; he had been remote enough to be anything and, anyway, the shock of the incontrovertible, that it was really our father lying up there in that casket, prepared the mind for anything. His sister moaned and this grief-stricken moaning was taken as corroboration. The other faces held a dark, non-committal thoughtfulness. This was not the man they had known, but they had scarcely expected to be confronted with *him*; this was, in a sense deeper than questions of fact, the man they had not known, and the man they had not known may have been the real one. The real man, whoever he had been, had suffered and now he was dead: this was all that was sure and all that mattered now. Every man in the chapel hoped that when his hour came he, too, would be eulogized, which is to say forgiven, and that all of his lapses, greeds, errors, and strayings from the truth would be invested with coherence and looked upon with charity. This was perhaps the last thing human beings could give each other and it was what they demanded, after all, of the Lord. Only the Lord saw the midnight tears, only He was present when one of His children, moaning and wringing hands, paced up and down the room. When one slapped one's child in anger the recoil in the heart reverberated through heaven and became part of the pain of the universe. And when the children were hungry and sullen and distrustful and one watched them, daily, growing wilder, and further away, and running headlong into danger, it was the Lord who knew what the charged heart endured as the strap was laid to the backside; the Lord alone who knew what one *would* have said if one had had, like the Lord, the gift of the living word. It was the Lord who knew of the impossibility every parent in that room faced: how to prepare the child for the day when the child would be despised and how to *create* in the child—by what means—a stronger antidote to this poison than one had found for oneself. The avenues, side streets, bars, billard halls, hospitals, police stations, and even the playgrounds of Harlem—not to mention the houses of correction, the jails, and the morgue—testified to the potency of the poison while remaining silent as to the efficacy of whatever antidote, irresistibly raising the question of whether or not such an antidote existed; raising, which was worse, the question of whether or not an antidote was desirable; perhaps poison should be fought with poison. With these several schisms in the mind and with more terrors in the heart than could be named, it was bettter not to judge the man who had gone down under an impossible burden. It was better to remember: *Thou knowest this man's fall; but thou knowest not his wrassling.*

While the preacher talked and I watched the children—years of changing their diapers, scrubbing them, slapping them, taking them to school, and scolding them had had the perhaps inevitable result of making me love them, though I am not sure I knew this then—my mind was busily breaking out with a rash of disconnected impressions. Snatches of popular songs, indecent jokes, bits of books I have read, movie sequences, faces, voices, political issues—I thought I was going mad; all these impressions suspended, as it were, in the solution of the faint nausea produced in me by the heat and liquor. For a moment I had the impression that my alcoholic breath, inefficiently disguised with chewing gum, filled the entire chapel. Then someone began singing one of my father's favorite songs and, abruptly, I was with him, sitting on his knee, in the hot, enormous, crowded church which was the first church we attended. It was the Abyssinian Baptist Church on 138th Street. We had

not gone there long. With this image, a host of others came. I
had forgotten, in the rage of my growing up, how proud my father
had been of me when I was little. Apparently, I had had a voice and
my father had liked to show me off before the members of the
church. I had forgotten what he had looked like when he
was pleased but now I remembered that he had always been
grinning with pleasure when my solos ended. I even remembered
certain expressions on his face when he teased my mother—had he
loved her? I would never know. And when had it all begun to
change? For now it seemed that he had not always been cruel. I
remembered being taken for a haircut and scraping my knee on the
footrest of the barber's chair and I remembered my father's face as he
soothed my crying and applied the stinging iodine. Then I
remembered our fights, fights which had been of the worst possible
kind because my technique had been silence.

I remembered the one time in all our life together when we
had really spoken to each other.

It was on a Sunday and it must have been shortly before I left
home. We were walking, just the two of us, in our usual silence, to
or from church. I was in high school and had been doing a lot of
writing and I was, at about this time, the editor of the high
school magazine. But I had also been a Young Minister and had
been preaching from the pulpit. Lately, I had been taking fewer
engagements and preached as rarely as possible. It was said in
the church, quite truthfully, that I was "cooling off."

My father asked me abruptly, "You'd rather write than preach,
wouldn't you?"

I was astonished at his question—because it was a real question. I
answered, "Yes."

That was all we said. It was awful to remember that that was
all we had *ever* said.

The casket now was opened and the mourners were being
led up the aisle to look for the last time on the deceased. The
assumption was that the family was too overcome with grief to be
allowed to make this journey alone and I watched while my aunt was
led to the casket and, muffled in black, and shaking, led back to her
seat. I disapproved of forcing the children to look on their dead
father, considering that the shock of his death, or, more truthfully, the
shock of death as a reality, was already a little more than a child
could bear, but my judgment in this matter had been overruled and
there they were, bewildered and frightened and very small, being led,
one by one, to the casket. But there is also something very gallant
about children at such moments. It has something to do with
their silence and gravity and with the fact that one cannot

help them. Their legs, somehow, seem *exposed*, so that it is at once incredible and terribly clear that their legs are all they have to hold them up.

I had not wanted to go to the casket myself and I certainly had not wished to be led there, but there was no way of avoiding either of these forms. One of the deacons led me up and I looked on my father's face. I cannot say that it looked like him at all. His blackness had been equivocated by powder and there was no suggestion in that casket of what his power had or could have been. He was simply an old man dead, and it was hard to believe that he had ever given anyone either joy or pain. Yet, his life filled that room. Further up the avenue his wife was holding his newborn child. Life and death so close together, and love and hatred, and right and wrong, said something to me which I did not want to hear concerning man, concerning the life of man.

After the funeral, while I was downtown desperately celebrating my birthday, a Negro soldier, in the lobby of the Hotel Braddock, got into a fight with a white policeman over a Negro girl. Negro girls, white policemen, in or out of uniform, and Negro males—in or out of uniform—were part of the furniture of the lobby of the Hotel Braddock and this was certainly not the first time such an incident had occurred. It was destined, however, to receive an unprecedented publicity, for the fight between the policeman and the soldier ended with the shooting of the soldier. Rumor, flowing immediately to the streets outside, stated that the soldier had been shot in the back, an instantaneous and revealing invention, and that the soldier had died protecting a Negro woman. The facts were somewhat different—for example, the soldier had not been shot in the back, and was not dead, and the girl seems to have been as dubious a symbol of womanhood as her white counterpart in Georgia usually is, but no one was interested in the facts. They preferred the invention because this invention expressed and corroborated their hates and fears so perfectly. It was just as well to remember that people are always doing this. Perhaps many of those legends, including Christianity, to which the world clings began their conquest of the world with just some such concerted surrender to distortion. The effect, in Harlem, of this particular legend was like the effect of a lit match in a tin of gasoline. The mob gathered before the doors of the Hotel Braddock simply began to swell and to spread in every direction, and Harlem exploded.

The mob did not cross the ghetto lines. It would have been easy, for example, to have gone over Morningside Park on the west side or to have crossed the Grand Central railroad tracks at 125th Street on the east side, to wreck havoc in white neighborhoods. The mob

seems to have been mainly interested in something more potent
and real than the white face, that is, in white power, and
the principal damage done during the riot of the summer of 1943
was to white business establishments in Harlem. It might have been
a far bloodier story, of course, if, at the hour the riot began, these
establishments had still been open. From the Hotel Braddock the mob
fanned out, east and west along 125th Street, and for the entire
length of Lenox, Seventh and Eighth avenues. Along each of
these avenues, and along each major side street—116th, 125th, 135th,
and so on—bars, stores, pawnshops, restaurants, even little luncheonettes
had been smashed open and entered and looted—looted, it might be
added, with more haste than efficiency. The shelves really looked as
though a bomb had struck them. Cans of beans and soup and dog
food, along with toilet paper, corn flakes, sardines and milk tumbled
every which way, and abandoned cash registers and cases of beer
leaned crazily out of the splintered windows and were strewn
along the avenues. Sheets, blankets, and clothing of every description formed a kind of path, as though people had dropped them
while running. I truly had not realized that Harlem *had* so many
stores until I saw them all smashed open; the first time the word
wealth ever entered my mind in relation to Harlem was when I saw it
scattered in the streets. But one's first, incongruous impression of
plenty was countered immediately by an impression of waste.
None of this was doing anybody any good. It would have
been better to have left the plate glass as it had been and the
goods lying in the stores.

It would have been better, but it would also have been intolerable, for Harlem had needed something to smash. To smash something
is the ghetto's chronic need. Most of the time it is the members
of the ghetto who smash each other, and themselves. But as long as
the ghetto walls are standing there will always come a moment
when these outlets do not work. That summer, for example, it was not
enough to get into a fight on Lenox Avenue, or curse out one's
cronies in the barber shops. If ever, indeed, the violence which fills
Harlem's churches, pool halls, and bars erupts outward in a more
direct fashion, Harlem and its citizens are likely to vanish in
an apocalyptic flood. That this is not likely to happen is due to a great
many reasons, most hidden and powerful among them the Negro's
real relation to the white American. This relation prohibits, simply,
anything as uncomplicated and satisfactory as pure hatred. In
order really to hate white people, one has to blot so much out of
the mind—and the heart—that this hatred itself becomes an exhausting
and self-destructive pose. But this does not mean, on the other hand,
that love comes easily: the white world is too powerful, too com-

placent, too ready with gratuitous humiliation, and, above all, too
ignorant and too innocent for that. One is absolutely forced to make
perpetual qualifications and one's own reactions are always cancelling
each other out. It is this, really, which has driven so many people
mad, both white and black. One is always in the position of having to
decide between amputation and gangrene. Amputation is swift
but time may prove that the amputation was not necessary—or one
may delay the amputation too long. Gangrene is slow, but it is
impossible to be sure that one is reading one's symptoms right. The
idea of going through life as a cripple is more than one can
bear, and equally unbearable is the risk of swelling up slowly, in
agony, with poison. And the trouble, finally, is that the risks are real
even if the choices do not exist.

"But as for me and my house," my father had said, "we will serve
the Lord." I wondered, as we drove him to his resting place, what
this line had meant to him. I had heard him preach it many
times. I had preached it once myself, proudly giving it an interpretation different from my father's. Now the whole thing came back to
me, as though my father and I were on our way to Sunday school
and I were memorizing the golden text: *And if it seem evil unto you*
to serve the Lord, choose you this day whom you will serve: whether
the gods which your fathers served that were on the other side of
the flood, or the gods of the Amorites, in whose land ye dwell:
but as for me and my house, we will serve the Lord. I suspected in
these familiar lines a meaning which had never been there for me
before. All of my father's texts and songs, which I had decided were
meaningless, were arranged before me at his death like empty bottles,
waiting to hold the meaning which life would give them for me.
This was his legacy: nothing is ever escaped. That bleakly memorable
morning I hated the unbelievable streets and the Negroes and
whites who had, equally, made them that way. But I knew that it was
folly, as my father would have said, this bitterness was folly. It was
necessary to hold on to the things that mattered. The dead man
mattered, the new life mattered; blackness and whiteness did not
matter; to believe that they did was to acquiesce in one's own
destruction. Hatred, which could destroy so much, never failed to
destroy the man who hated and this was an immutable law.

It began to seem that one would have to hold in the mind
forever two ideas which seemed to be in opposition. The first idea
was acceptance, the acceptance, totally without rancor, of life as it is,
and men as they are: in the light of this idea, it goes without saying
and injustice is a commonplace. But this did not mean that
one could be complacent, for the second idea was of equal power:
that one must never, in one's own life, accept these injustices as

commonplace but must fight them with all one's strength. This
fight begins, however, in the heart and it now had been laid to my
charge to keep my own heart free of hatred and despair.
This intimation made my heart heavy and, now that my father
was irrecoverable, I wished that he had been beside me so that I
could have searched his face for the answers which only the
future would give me now.

THE DISGUISE

Katherine Butler Hathaway

When I was fifteen this horizontal life of night and day was ended. In
that year I was pronounced cured; I was to get up at last and see
things from a perpendicular and movable point of view, after watching
them for so long from a horizontal and fixed one. Everything would
look different, of course. Also, I knew that I myself would look
different standing up from the way I had looked lying down. Why, at
the great age of fifteen I didn't even know how tall I was! And
I had begun to wonder secretly about my back. There was that
unknown territory between my shoulders where the tuberculosis had
lodged and burrowed for so long. How much it had disfigured
me I didn't know. As I had grown older there had been a baffling
silence in regard to that side of my illness, and I never dared to ask.
Nobody guessed that I was secretly worrying about it, and I could not
tell them. Nobody guessed, because, I suppose, I gave the impression of
being such a happy, humorous child. But when I was alone in the
room I sometimes slid my hand up under me to explore that
fateful part. But my hand always got strangely panic-stricken and came
hurrying back without making me any wiser than before. My hand
seemed to be mortally afraid of that place, which remained therefore
unknown, waiting for the day when I should get up and stand
plainly revealed.

Although my mother had so often told me, when I was little, how
lucky I was, as I grew older she never spoke of my being lucky. Instead,
quite a different feeling seemed to come over her whenever she or
anybody else spoke of my "trouble" as it was called. I must first explain
that when I was young my mother seemed to me dull and uninteresting

SOURCE: Reprinted by permission of Coward, McCann & Geoghegan, Inc.
from *The Little Locksmith* by Katherine Butler Hathaway. Copyright © 1943 by
Coward-McCann, Inc.; renewed © 1971 by Warren H. Butler.

compared with my father. He and I were conscious of each other, almost as lovers are. Everything he said held my attention, and was interesting and essential to me. In comparison, my mother seemed to have to think and talk about a lot of unessential things, and her real self, for me, was swamped and obscured by them. I had a feeling that she didn't like unessential things, but that she didn't quite know how to manage them easily and get them out of the way. So she labored awkwardly, directing the house and servants, and she worried, and had to go to bed with sick headaches. Sometimes I felt very maternal toward her, she had such a hard time doing things that I thought looked quite easy. My own hands were so much more skillful than hers, for instance, that if she tried to make a paper doll for me she seemed to me like a clumsy younger child. She was not an artist, or a craftsman, like the rest of us, and so she thought we were much more wonderful than we were. I never saw her eyes really shine with happiness as much as they did when she was admiring us as artists, and treasuring all the things we made. Then she made herself, in comparison, seem humble and unimportant. In matters of our conduct as human beings she was relentless, and we feared her as we feared God. We learned very young to be good and to obey and to respect our father and mother. But when she was admiring us as artists she gave us a feeling of absolute freedom from authority. We were all for weighing and criticizing each other's works. We knew to a hair's breadth which was better than another, and why. But she liked everything we did, our good things and also the ones we would have torn up and thrown away. She gathered them all together and kept and treasured them, and her eyes shone over us with a pride and a tenderness that I shall never see again.

Because of this humble uncritical attitude of hers toward art, I didn't notice her very much, and when I did I often wished that she were more exciting and knew how to do things herself. But once in a great while, when somebody spoke of my illness or she mentioned it herself, she was all changed. I couldn't very well not notice her then. A terrific wave of pain sprang up in her blue eyes, and it was evident suddenly that the pain was always there, controlled, inside her, like something terribly alive, always ready to leap up and hurt her all over again. She never cried, but her self-control was worse than crying.

"I ought never to have *let* it happen! It was wicked! Wicked!" she would burst out. And then, immediately after, I witnessed the silent and to me awful struggle as for some reason she fought against the physical symptoms of her grief. Not a tear ever succeeded in getting past the barrier of her will, and not a sob. But during those few seconds when she could not trust herself to speak, and her gentian-blue eyes were fiercely widened to prevent the tears from coming into them as she stared away from me, out of the window, anywhere, away from me, and swallowed back that great lump of sadness and forced it away down into the secret part of her being, I was awe-struck and shaken, much more than I would have been to see her yield to tears. Her secretive Spartan way made crying seem like an enemy that one must never submit to. The awesome struggle that it cost her affected me almost as if I had been forced to watch her from a distance struggling all alone with a savage animal and managing by sheer force of her will and character to keep it at bay.

When she was like that I could not very well not notice her or think she was uninteresting. Then her aliveness frightened me. And I loved her more than I could possibly have told. I felt a furious will to cherish her and protect her and never to let her suffer, when I got old enough to influence or control her. Yet I could not show her what I felt. Besides being inarticulate myself, I knew that I had seen something in her that she thought I was too young to see or even to know about, and I knew I must pretend I hadn't seen it. It was not her concern for me that made me love her so much then. It was because I saw her in the grip of essential things, and she became alive and fiery and very brave. I felt humble before her, for myself and for all the rest of us toward whom she had made herself seem unclever and unimportant.

Although I felt an almost unbearable tenderness and love for her in those moments, I felt hatred and rebellion too. I hated and rejected the idea that there was anything tragic about my illness, or that she was to blame. I was angry because when she battled with those terrible surging tears I had to battle too. Watching her, I felt a violent emotion suddenly throbbing against my throat, surging and aching in my chest. For she seemed to waken something in me that was a disgusting traitor to my conscious self, a sorrow over my own plight that leaped up out of the depth of me, and answered her with a grieving that seemed to understand and match her own. I could love her piteous sorrow for me, but I loathed and despised it in myself. And I pushed it away from me with an almost masculine strength and confidence in my own soundness and well-being. This rebellion made me appear hard and cold toward her, just at the moment when I loved her most.

Yet I always longed to know intimately and adore and caress that real fiery self of hers. Why did she hide it from her children and almost from herself? It seemed as if she thought that if she ever once let her emotion escape from under her control its poignancy would be unbearable, and would destroy her and destroy us all. Whatever the reason, when these moments arrived they passed in fierce silence and aloofness. The hearts of the mother and the child ached in pity for each other, each separate, stoical, and alone.

So, lying still and watching her, I was tense and fighting for her, helping her with all my might not to be overcome by the enemy that was trying to make us both cry and break out into sobs. I knew that if anything could make her lose the battle it would be to have me be anything except the happy unconscious child she thought I was. And besides, except when she acted like this, I *was* happy. After all, what was there so sad about me and my illness? It was a mystery to me. I thought my mother's sadness must be just a phenomenon of mother love, which exaggerates everything.

When I got up at last, fifteen years old, and had learned to walk again, one day I took a hand glass and went to a long mirror to look at myself, and I went alone. I didn't want anyone, my mother least of all, to know how I felt when I saw myself for the first time. But there was no noise, no outcry; I didn't scream with rage when I saw myself. I just felt numb. That person in the mirror *couldn't* be me. I felt inside like a healthy, ordinary, lucky person—oh, not like the one in the mirror! Yet when I turned my face to the mirror there were my own eyes looking back, hot with shame. I had turned out after all, like the little locksmith—oh, not so bad, nearly—but enough like the little locksmith to be called by that same word.

What I felt that day did not fit in with the pleasant cheerful atmosphere of our family, any more than my horrors had fitted in. There was no place for it among us. It was something in another language. It was in the same language as my mother's suppressed panic-stricken grief, and I would have died rather than let that come to the surface of our cheerful life, for her to see and endure in me. And so from that first moment, when I did not cry or make any sound, it became impossible that I should speak of it to anyone, and the confusion and the panic of my discovery were locked inside me then and there, to be faced alone, for a very long time to come.

Here then was the beginning of my predicament. A hideous disguise had been cast over me, as if by a wicked stepmother. And I now had ahead of me, although I didn't know it, the long, blind, wistful struggle of the fairy tales. I had to wander stupidly and blindly, searching for I didn't know what, following fantastically wrong clues, until at last I might hit upon a magic that could set me free.

At the very beginning it was lucky for me that I found my brother Warren. Three things had ended suddenly all at the same time—my illness and my childhood and my father's life. When one thing ends another must begin. As I have already written, at the end of my illness there began my ignorant and lonely struggle to adapt myself to what I had seen in the mirror. At this same time my childhood ended and a thrilling ferment of new consciousness had begun to go on inside me which made me feel myself turning wonderfully into a haughty and grand young lady. Although my body was impeded in its growth and I was bewildered by its misfortune, my mind was not impeded. My mind grew independently of my body and independently of the shape of my body. It grew and behaved at first as if nothing were wrong with me anywhere. I was even more concerned at first with extricating myself from the disgrace of being considered a child than I was concerned with the fearful fact of my deformity. Now that I was up and walking around at last, like the rest of the world, I seemed to feel a fierce revenge against my bed and my invalid life, and especially against the bright little girl who had accepted it all so sweetly and submissively. I suddenly hated my adorable microscopic world, and all the little arts out of which with painstaking care I had constructed my joys. I hated the loving admiration of the grownups for me and everything I did. I felt fierce and rebellious and strong and mad toward them and myself. Something new had come into my mind, and it was like a labor agitator who furiously tries to destroy the docile contentment of workers who have so long adapted themselves to a narrow life that they do not even realize it is narrow. Out of loyalty to the new values that were dawning in me and making me, as I believed, into an entirely new person, I had to do cruel violence to the contented little girl. I had to emphasize my separateness from her in every possible way because the grownups persisted in clinging to her with an absurd devotion and insisting she was me. Whereas I knew with every part of myself that she was not me any more. I was through with her. I was through because a wonderful thing had happened to me. I had found suddenly that I was not frightened any more by the abstract ideas that had frightened the little girl so terribly in her bed. I had begun to fall at first gingerly and then boldly in love with the mystery of the Universe. Instead of wanting to curl my mind up and tuck it away in some cozy little place where it could never think those terrifying thoughts of death and birth and time, my mind suddenly wanted to reach out and embrace fearlessly those mysteries and become a conscious, proud part of them. It seemed to me that I had suddenly grown so tall that my head was among the stars. Relieved, by some miracle, of my cosmic fears, I felt an almost drunken sense of liberation, as if I had been released from a most abject slavery and admitted to the free and fearless aristocracy of the mind.

At this crucial time my father died, and on the day I lost him, after a long illness that had made him grow remote from me, I found my brother Warren. We sat side by side on the piazza of our house on the strange April morning when we became fatherless.

We watched the undertakers coming up the steps into the house, and going busily back and forth between the house and their terrible high black carriage. I felt cruelly little sorrow, considering how very deeply my father had cherished and loved me, perhaps because his cultivating love had helped to create the little girl whom I was now intent on destroying. Instead, his death gave me an exultant happiness because it strengthened and intensified my new awareness and adoration of cosmic things. It made me feel mature and experienced and proud because I could see it in the radiance of the new daybreak that was in my mind. Death was another of the great and ordered mysteries of life, and, being so, it could never frighten me any more. In that revelation there was indescribable ecstasy and joy for the young mystic who was beginning to inhabit my mind and look out of my eyes.

Like every fifteen-year-old person, my mind was so new to thought, and I was consequently so naïve, that I examined everything that came before me with the feeling that it was an entirely new phenomenon and had never been examined by anybody before. And when I was struck that morning as we sat on the piazza by the thought that the noble mystery of death ought not to be intruded upon and degraded by these loathsome undertakers—officious, practical, busy little men like black ants running to and fro—I was thrilled and surprised by my own angry resentment. In my experience older people seemed to take everything for granted, and I found that I did not take the undertakers for granted; it also dawned on me that I must be a wild and revolutionary thinker. I thought I had hit upon a point of view that probably nobody else in the world had ever held before. It was a purifying, beautiful, joyous sensation of anger that I felt, and I knew for the first time that I could feel passionately about an idea. Something had blazed in me, and from the blaze I discovered a new element in myself, a combustible something that would always blaze again in defense of the mystery and sacredness in things, and against the queer, blind, blaspheming streak in human nature which instead of adoring, must vulgarize and exploit and insult life.

In my excitement I turned to my brother and burst out with some incoherent exclamation about how I hated the undertakers. To my astonishment he said that he knew how I felt, and that he hated them too. This was the first time that I had ever exchanged anything like an abstract idea with anyone, and I could feel my new self expand still more.

So my brother and I looked at each other that day with curiosity and surprise and each recognized in the other a new and unexpected friend. We had both deserted the two absorbed and happy children we had lately been, and in doing so we had lost each other. It was lucky for me that we met again at that moment, which, for me, would have been intolerably bewildering alone. We were just entering the period which is like a magic forest, into which nobody either older or younger than ourselves could possibly be admitted. We needed to escape from them, from all the others, because our turn had come. It was our precious turn to believe, deluded and untested as we were, that we and our generation were the elect—the only beings on earth whose vision of life was really pure and abstract, a mystic's vision. We had not yet allowed ourselves to be corrupted by any such despicable things as expediency or money. Our actions and plans were not yet crippled by any of the loathsome timidities and misrepresentations of common sense, or stifled altogether by the paralyzing fears by which children and old people are all degraded. From that time of awakening onward there was a wild enchantment crying and singing in my blood, the enchantment and excitement that come, by rights, with the flowering of the young human body and its short-lived perfection. My youthful singing blood did not seem to know the crazy fact that my body had stumbled against, and never could listen to it and learn it and take it in. My very joyous blood took it for granted that my body was unfolding simultaneously with my consciousness, and the song of my blood was so much a part of me that I forgot, over and over, and took it for granted too.

Over and over I forgot what I had seen in the mirror. It could not penetrate into the interior of my mind and become an integral part of me. I felt as if it had nothing to do with me; it was only a disguise. But it was not the kind of disguise which is put on voluntarily by the person who wears it, and which is intended to confuse other people as to one's identity. My disguise had been put on me without my consent or knowledge like the ones in fairy tales, and it was I myself who was confused by it, as to my own identity. I looked in the mirror, and was horror-struck because I did not recognize myself. In the place where I was standing, with that persistent romantic elation in me, as if I were a favored fortunate person to whom everything was possible, I saw a stranger, a little, pitiable, hideous figure, and a face that became, as I stared at it, painful and blushing with shame. It was only a disguise, but it was on me, for life. It was there, it was there, it was real. Every one of those encounters was like a blow on the head. They left me dazed and dumb and senseless every time, until slowly and stubbornly my robust persistent illusion of well-being and of personal beauty spread all through me again, and I forgot the irrelevant reality and was all unprepared and vulnerable again.

At this time of secret confusion it was lucky for me that I found my brother Warren. He acted as if he did not even see my disguise. He never mentioned it, he never explained how he felt. He merely treated me as if he saw in me the growing-up proud person that I felt myself to be.

❋   ❋   ❋   ❋

SUMMARY

Not a wide vocabulary, but an ability to select the best word is vital to the writer. The more words available the more possibilities can be focused toward a particular blank space on the page. "Big" words are useful only when really appropriate, like John Cartland's "compromise" and "oppressive," Rick Spear's "litany," or our anonymous author's "revelation." Greg McManus's "adaptability to his immediate environment" is a cliché, but it is the product of the consciousness of a character, not of the writer's ineptitude. Paul Ross uses "inundated" in his first sentence, not "crowded," because the former word leads into the "tidal" suggestions he uses in much of the rest of the narrative.

Words are placed in sentences to achieve their maximum impact. If "He is a man who is afraid," then "He is afraid" is a more concise and effective construction, unless the writer is emphasizing *man*: "He is a man, yet he is afraid." The last sentence makes its point more clearly than "He is a man who is afraid." "Up you come!" expresses the lifting of someone, with the stress, both physical and linguistic, on the first syllable. "You come up" might be an order, but it would seldom be spoken while lifting someone. Some expressions, particularly in music, simulate the rhythm of the work being done: sea chanteys and the songs of Chinese bargemen and Volga boatmen. Prose rhythms are designed primarily to appeal to the ear of the reader, but prose also imitates action. If "The man was slapped by Nancy," then surely "Nancy slapped the man." The latter is obviously the superior syntax. It uses the fewer words, and the sentence moves in the direction of the action, from subject to object. John Cartland says "But the oppressive silence of the house made him uneasy and so he left the house as often as possible," not "He left the house as often as possible because its oppressive silence made him uneasy." The thrust of the story is on Roger's getting out. The atmosphere of the house impels him toward his treehouse, and that is the action imitated by the structure of the sentence.

EXERCISE

Select three words you feel work well in any of the narratives you have read and try to find better words. Are they better? Select three words in the narratives that you feel could be improved. Can you improve them? Select three sentences that you feel work well in any of the narratives and recast them in a different order. Are your sentences better, worse, or merely different? Since many of the narratives in the book were written by students, don't believe that just because they appear in print they cannot be improved.

Now look back at the exercise you wrote at the end of Chapter 1. Can you make any improvements in diction and syntax? Rewrite that exercise to incorporate a more precise awareness of word choice and the placement of words in each sentence. If you do not feel that your subject is particularly good, you may, of course, select another.

Reread the pieces by Maxim Gorki and Dylan Thomas in the context of this chapter's discussion of diction and syntax.

THREE
Imagery
and
Contrast

Imagery means not merely an appeal to the visual senses, but to all the senses. A writer knows something basic about his reader: His reader has senses, can see, smell, hear, touch, and taste. When a writer *describes,* when he appeals to the senses of his readers, he makes his writing the experience of the reader. It is one thing to say "it was a beautiful day" and another to convey the imagery of that day to the reader's senses and through his senses into his mind and his emotions. It is one thing to say "some frogs sat on the bank"—that conveys information—but the verb "hunched," if substituted for "sat," would convey not only the way the frogs looked but how the observer and the reader feel as they perceive the position of the frogs. The fish beating "out their lives smiting the resounding planks, their gasping gills pulsating in the surfeit of air" of Rick Spear's description appeals to the senses of sound, sight, and to our own sense of breathing, which we take for granted but would not were we fish out of water or humans five fathoms deep. John Cartland's Roger Purvis wishes to go up to the wooden box at the front of the church "and rub his hand over its smooth surface that shone in the odd light of the church." Here the appeal is to our senses of touch and sight and, beyond that, to the strange human desire to reach out and touch something we should not touch or to do something in a restricted situation, like church, which is forbidden. The last two examples suggest that effective imagery can evoke responses from something beyond the senses.

Consider the following student-written essay.

 ## BARN

David Irish

My father leads a very strange life. In some ways it is very interesting and fun, and in other ways it is a very hard life.

On the days when he has to work in the barn, he has to get up at a most beautiful hour, three o'clock in the morning. The air is extremely cold, crisp, and fresh. There is usually a sort of dim light outside due to the attempts of the sun to come up. There is almost always a hazy mist there, which makes the cold even colder.

Dad always gets up at just the right time, and he never uses an alarm clock. After long years of working like this, he has sort of developed his own alarm clock. He gets up immediately, without stretching, and his eyes are already wide open and his mind is as keen as ever. He pulls on the smelly, dirty, faded pants and colored plaid workshirt. He keeps his shoes downstairs, so he tiptoes in his stockinged feet so as not to wake us up. I would feel extremely guilty if I let him know I was awake. It is as if this were his own private world, and no one should ever intrude, except maybe my mother.

I can hear him moving around downstairs, picking up clothes for Mom so that she won't have to work so hard during the day. He goes out and splits a pile of wood, making sharp cracking echoes that reverberate through the trees. I can almost see him smiling because his muscles are just waking up and he feels better. He picks up a whole pile at once, rearranging them with his right hand while holding them with his left arm. The snow crunches and the door squeaks on his way in. He drops the wood on the mat by the stove, making a clunking noise. The old stove bangs a lot while he is arranging paper, putting in kindling wood, and then putting in the heater wood. As soon as he lights it, I can hear the crackling of kindling and can smell the pungent odor of wood smoke. After he has finished he sits at the table and has some coffee and toast. When I smell that buttered toast, my stomach suddenly feels empty and I feel obliged to turn over and try to ignore it. He'll have a real breakfast later on, so he's just filling up what he calls the "lower cavity." Now Dad takes the kettle of hot water, no longer making any attempt to be quiet because, to him, his world has come alive; the sun is breaking up the mist and glaring off the crusted snow. He walks out to the car and pours the water on the ice on the windshield, using the windshield wiper to help clear it off. Now he starts up the car so that it will be nice and warm when he gets ready to leave.

If it wasn't for the fact that he sometimes gets me up to go to the barn to help him, I would probably never get to know any more about his morning. He comes in on these mornings and comes to the bottom of the stairs and says my name. "Come on Dave, y'gotta get up if you want to go with me." He says it so softly that I feel almost obliged to get up, so I just jump right up, "Comin' Dad, just get me some of that toast and coffee, huh?"

We drive off and head for the barn. He drives very slowly, and he even gets angry if I'm driving and I'm driving with any speed. It kind of startled me at first, but I soon found out why. I never knew before that there were so many small creatures still moving in the winter, but at this time in the morning they are active because they are trying to store up food for the day. We would pass by several creatures, each seeming to disregard us and just walking along beside us. They were so dulled by winter sleepiness that they were incapable of scurrying away. We saw animals like porcupine, muskrat, and others. Dad kept talking to me and pointing out little things about the animals he thought I should know. He'd point out their size to indicate how they were faring the winter or maybe if they were just collecting food for their families. He'd point out where they came out of the woods and where they went back in so that we would know where they lived when we needed to know. He'd also see how often a certain species appeared so that we would know how plentiful they were, in preparation for the hunting and trapping seasons, and he'd describe the tracks in detail and their habits in detail so that someday I'd be a competent hunter and trapper myself. He often lapses into verbal remembrances of times when he hunted such an animal and just what trick he used to catch it. He often likes to go off hunting, but Mom protests because there is always lots of work to do around the house. Dad says, "Women just don't know what it means to a man just to get away by himself in the woods." He is quite frank like that with my older brother and me. He is only brought back to immediate reality if he sees another animal or we reach the barn.

The barn is big and white, but always friendly at any time, night or day. It seems friendlier now because I know of the lighthearted talk, the great jokes, and the cursing of equipment and cattle that goes on inside. It was nice stepping from the frigidity of the outside world into the comfortable warmth of the inside created by the body heat of the cattle. Though my eyes are hardly ever fully awake at this time, or my stomach filled, it is a comforting feeling knowing that when we leave, we will have an hour to rest and plenty of food to eat.

Now the day is in full swing. I do the odd chores while Dad cleans the cows off and milks. I climb the mow, feeling like a little kid up there pushing bales of hay down with my feet. It is often damp and musty and so is repulsive, so I hurry with the chore and get down. I hay up the calves, playing with the smaller ones and just pushing the big ones around. It is about the only excuse they have during the winter months to use their leg muscles. Their legs act like rigor mortis has set in on a living creature. If they feel they're not getting enough attention while I'm shoveling the manure, they'll come up to my backside and gingerly nose me so that I will have to turn around and push them out of the way. About the only way I ever could get the chore done was to simply ignore them. They are visibly hurt after a while; the nosing becomes feeble, and they clumsily wander off, sniffing at the walls. Often they'll visit another stall and smell the nails. It is a strange thing to do, but they always end up there, smelling the nails.

Of all the jobs I do in the barn, the one I dislike most is putting the calves back in their dark, lonely stalls. I encourage us both by talking to them about the nice, fresh hay there, and how nice it will be to lie down in a dry bed, all the while aiming their noses at the entrance and pushing them from behind. They bawl and kick a lot, openly protesting the idea.

Sometimes, when I'm here alone with the calves enjoying these simplest of conversations, I lean ahead of the fork and think just how quiet and peaceful it is. I even wonder if maybe I'd like to live a life on the farm myself. But then I hear the milking machines Dad is handling, I hear the cows bellowing, I remember how heavy those machines are, I can visualize Dad's muscles flexing as he lifts them, the same way they're flexed and strained all of his life, and I remember what he's always told me, "You're goin' to school and make a better life for yourself." Suddenly the farm seems like a jail with its door all triggered and waiting for me. I can come to visit but I can never let the door close, because if it does I'll never have a chance to get out.

I drive out the manure-spreader and empty it down by the woods. The cold air refreshes me and I forget about my thoughts, imagining now a life of ease wherein I could maybe come and help Dad like now.

I have a special job to do. I milk the newly freshened cows and feed their milk to the newly born calves. I take the pail of milk to the calves, which wriggle and jump and bawl with anticipation. The only way they can drink is for me to sort of simulate their mother by inserting my hand into their mouths. They suck on the hand like they would their mother, and I shove their noses into the milk. When they have begun to drink without this aid, I take my hand out and let them finish drinking. I feel satisfied and proud as if I have just finished a parental task.

Usually, by the time I finish all my chores, Dad has finished milking, so we wash out the dishes and machines, putting them neatly on the racks when we're finished. Dad dips our milk jugs into the fresh milk, which has been cooled off by the cooler, and I go to say a temporary good-bye to the cows by turning off the barn lights.

"Are you hungry now?" Those are Dad's customary words, indicating that the work is finished and it's time to go home and have a good, hearty meal. We each pick up a jug of milk and head for the car.

✻   ✻   ✻   ✻

"Barn" is, in part, a character study of the father. Through his observation of his father, the boy "places himself." He admires his father, but he does not wish to live the life of a farmer. The narrative comes at us, however, not as a statement but as a series of experiences. We feel the father's muscles wake up as he chops wood, we hear the crunch of snow, and we smell the buttered toast wafting up to the drowsy boy. We learn, as the boy has, about the morning and about the barn, moving with him through a series of images that have been repeated often for him in the past and would be in the future if he remains on the farm. It is such a peaceful and pleasant world in so many ways that we, like the boy, are almost lulled into a romantic notion that it would be good to stay. That feeling is reinforced by its analogy, the earlier desire of the boy to stay in bed. But he gets up. And he will ultimately leave the farm. Like so many narratives in this book, the essay does not mean anything profound. Through its carefully observed details and precise choice of words to capture those details, we sense what it means that the boy is growing up and growing away from the life he has known and which his father will continue to live.

David Irish uses contrast effectively, particularly between coldness and warmth and between drowsiness and wakefulness. The latter contrast is essential to the way the narrative works. The boy awakens literally at the beginning, muses on the attractions of his father's farm as he leans dreamily on his pitchfork, then awakens to the possibility of those doors closing him in and to his desire for a life beyond the boundaries of that barn. Contrast has been essential to many of the preceding narratives: the swirling motion of the street in Paul Ross's story opposed to the stillness he must maintain while the Oriental completes the portrait; the contrast between the adult and childhood worlds in both "The Treehouse" and "Who Was Really Responsible?"; the contrast Kris Keller builds into a fourteen-year-old girl who assumes a maturity and an invulnerability that does not accord with the inexperience which draws her into danger, as well as the contrast at the end between the prim middle-class house and the disrupting nature of her own recent experience and present appearance.

The following story was written by a young woman auditing a college writing course.

THE DOLPHIN

Saranne Thomke

The swish of the scythe stopped, the gnome-like body unbent itself and leaned heavily on the handle, his chin jutted and his face gleamed like an oiled walnut.

"Ain't yer goin' ter see the whale, then?"

"Whale! What Whale? Where?"

Sonsie sat straight up on the back of the pony. She was sitting
facing the tail and had flopped forward so her cheek rested on
the round hind quarters and her arms dangled beside his hind legs.
The pony grazed, moving slowly in the grass. But now he flinched and
put his ears back. Sonsie leaned on her hands.

"Tell me, Forse, where?"

"Whale came up river last night, fair flounderin' around in Gover's
Pond 'e is."

"A whale! You're daft, Forse. Hey Paddy, there's a whale in
Gover's Pond!"

"Wot?"

"A whale, a whale, you goon, in Gover's Pond!"

"You're daft."

"I'm *not*. Forse said so. Let's go and see."

Sonsie heaved forward on her hands and slid down the pony's
tail. A boy clambered out of the stream and came slowly towards the
gnome-man and the girl. He was older than she, about twelve, with
shaggy brown hair. He was mostly covered in mud and carried a jam-jar
full of water and tiny, darting, silver streaks. He held it up by the
string tied round the top.

"Pike," he said, "baby pike. They'll grow about two feet long,
won't they, Forse?"

"Maybe, can do," said the gnome-man, nodding and grunting as
he turned to swing the scythe again. "Mind out!"

"Whales are bigger than that," said Sonsie. "Come on!"

"Alright, alright, I'm coming. Let me find a good place for the
fish, though."

He stowed the jar between two longs on the log bridge that crossed
the stream, and together they tramped off through the orchard. They
climbed the gate and crossed the lane into Gover's fields, always soggy
underfoot, even in summer, because of the river. The Test River ran
down into Southampton Water and here, so near the mouth, it
was wide and wild with tributaries, almost no banks. Often the cows
grazing in the meadows stood knee-deep in water. Willows wept into the
water even when they stood far from the banks; but salmon fishing
was superb, only better in the north of Scotland, where the mountain
streams ran deep and rapid; fishing was more exciting there, the
country rugged and undiscovered.

Here it was flat, interminably flat, with only the trees and river,
swift and black, with weird whirlpools and eddies: which made it
frightening. The reeds, like pine trees, writhed and struggled to tear
themselves up by the roots, yet they never lost their moorings, only the
branches reached and streamed with the flow. Sometimes Paddy and
Sonsie saw fish there, motionless, mouthing the water, only their

great tails moving to keep them from being washed to sea. Sonsie
would watch them, spangled, speckled, svelte, and would be filled with
loathing for the men who would snare them.

Sometimes, when she and Paddy rode in the water meadows, they
would see a sombre figure with ridiculous waders, staturesque on
the bank. They would shout and sing and throw pebbles into the river
to scare the salmon. Last year their father had a letter from the
gamekeeper: "Would his children kindly ride elsewhere as they were
hazardous to the fishing."

"Hazardous to the fishing, but not to the fish!" they yelled in
glee, and the price of salmon probably went up that season.

Now, leaping from hummock to hummock, Sonsie and Paddy
wove their way through Gover's field towards the river and the pond. It
was a small pond, about seventy feet across, the river running in at
sluice gates and away towards the sea at the other end. Often the sluice
was closed—a great place to swim!

A crowd circled round the pond, and the shouts grew louder as
Paddy and Sonsie came in reach. Sonsie was panting from keeping up,
but her heart thumped in anticipation of this monster.

"Wait, Paddy," she said, her voice cracking, unable to bear that he
should get there first, but also scared. He waited, and together they
pushed to the bank. The water heaved and slapped the sides of the pool,
sending fountains into the air. The noise was like a vast bath plug
being pulled out, a glorious gurgling as the glistening shape curved
above the water, arched and fell and rose again. Round and round the
swirling pool it went, sometimes a black half-moon, sometimes a
tail flailing the air, never disappearing for more than a few seconds,
always moving, churning, panicking. Sonsie watched entranced, then
stepped backwards.

"Do whales eat you?" she whispered.

"Naw, you nit, it's not even a whale."

"What's it?"

"Think it's a dolphin."

"Oh . . . it has a little face. Look at the eyes!"

The man next to Paddy had a rifle under his arm. He spat on the
ground.

"Bloody thing'll scare them fish for miles. If 'e ever gets outer 'ere,
there won't be no fish left."

"How did he get here?"

"Op from the sea, commed in through the docks all way through
Millbrook Meadows till 'e gets 'ere. Now daft thing can't get out,
bin goin' round and round like that 'e 'as for hours, jus' round and
round like a bloody top."

"Why can't he get out?"

"Can't find the way. Too narrer."

"He's so beautiful. I love him. Paddy, look at his face—like a mouse."

Sonsie tried to whisper to her brother, feeling that she, he, and the dolphin were the centre of animosity. The day was hot, and far away the towers of Fawley Oil Refinery struggled to be noticed through the haze.

"Gotter get 'im outter 'ere," said the man with the gun. He turned and loped off, spitting again on the grass.

"What will they do?"

"Dunno. I expect he'll swim around for a bit and then find the way back to the sea."

"Then he'll be alright?"

" 'Spect so. We'd better go."

They came back after lunch. The dolphin danced in the pool, but more slowly, tired but his terror no less.

"We'll come back later to show Daddy."

"Better 'urry op, 'e'll be gone by six," said someone.

"Gone where?"

" 'E's gotter go, can't 'ave them things around."

"Why are the men so horrible, it's only a beautiful animal?" asked Sonsie on the way home. "What will they do?"

"I don't know, Sonsie."

The weary afternoon grew ugly, as clouds obliterated the oil towers and crept inland.

"Don't go back to the pond," Paddy said. "Wait for Daddy."

"I want to go."

"Please don't, that's all."

Late in the afternoon, Sonsie put the bridle on her pony, scrambled up bareback, and trotted down the lane into the water meadows, towards the pond and the darkening sky. The pony snuffed the air and cantered willingly. Rounding the river bend, Sonsie could see the pond and three black shapes. Everyone else had gone. She jerked at the pony's mouth.

"Stop, Eve, stop!"

Only in nightmares had she ever felt so terrified, that cold lump of unknown clawing at her throat. The pony slowed to a walk, ears pricked. Sonsie's hands wound in its mane. She shuddered as large raindrops began to fall. Lightning streaked across the sky, and for a moment the oil towers flickered on the horizon.

The shot cracked, and another. The pony stopped dead, Sonsie stiff on its back. Another shot, and the rain fell heavily.

❊   ❊   ❊   ❊

The imagery in "The Dolphin" creates for us the feeling of the meadows below Southampton, England, as seen through the eyes of a young girl. Her attitude is contrasted with that of her older brother, who shares her sympathy for living things, but who knows more than she does about the ways of the world. Her attitude is in conflict with that of the men who snare fish and, specifically, with the attitude of the man with the rifle, who, characteristically, spits on the ground. Sonsie's attitude is obviously naive, yet love itself, at any age, renders the lover vulnerable.

Conflict lies at the heart of any story. It can be the conflict between the child and the woman within the character of "Riding High," which results in the physical conflict between the fourteen-year-old and the rapist. It can be the conflict between overstated guilt and egregious rationalization in "Who Was Really Responsible?" While the latter "wins," the victory is at the expense of at least one "truth": that the boy has been careless with matches and with that fatal can of paint. In "Barn" the conflict is implied: between the life on the farm which the narrator knows so well and that unknown world beyond the farm, the world of education and a good job to which the young narrator is moving. Since this is not a book dealing exclusively with the writing of fiction, I have subordinated conflict to *contrast*. While this may seem a completely arbitrary distinction, consider, for example, Paul Ross's "The Stillness and the Fury." We can perceive conflict there between the boy's desire to be swirling along with the crowd and the necessity of his sitting still. The overriding principle of the narrative is the contrast between action and activity, as the title suggests. Whether "The Stillness and the Fury" is a story or not is debatable, but it certainly fits the larger category of narrative, just as the term conflict fits within the subsuming term contrast. The teacher and the student can, if they wish, consider conflict a specialized form of contrast. Although most narratives convey at least an implicit sense of conflict, the narrative can exist on the level of its sensory appeal, on the level of sheer experience, of eyes, ears, and nostrils. And certainly the transition from narrative to short story involves the writer's development of that contrast in attitudes known as conflict.

In "The Dolphin," much of the contrast in attitudes emerges through dialogue, between the girl and her brother and between the girl and the man with the rifle. If the writer *listens* to the way people talk he can recreate not only the words but the attitude behind them. The attitude behind them is their tone. "Stay here, you," says the father of the boy who has just ignited the church. We not only hear him, we have no difficulty hearing his tone of voice. The tone of the father in "Barn" ("You're goin' to school and make a better life for yourself") and of the mother in "To Sing a Sad Song" ("That's just it, you *ain't* doin' nothin'") both express certainty, but with a difference.

The first conveys quiet confidence while the second shows frustration and anger. Part of our experience of many of these narratives is in our hearing not merely something called *dialogue*, but also the emotional coloration of the spoken words, like the awkward phone conversation in "The Life of Harry Nelson," particularly Harry's bitterness: "I'd just as soon listen to you breathe. At least I know where you are." Young writers can develop a sense of dialogue by listening to themselves and others, not merely hearing the meanings of the words, but listening to the tone, or attitude, behind them. Dialogue shaped to express tone becomes yet another kind of image that we hear and feel simultaneously. The writer should not merely record what he hears but must create dialogue that suggests the attitude behind the words, from boredom to rage, from resignation to determination. Good writers of dialogue—Boswell, Irwin Shaw, Faulkner, Capote, for example, seldom rely on phrases like "she said resignedly" or "he shouted angrily."

The following essay was written in English by a Swedish student taking a freshman English course in the United States.

❧ MEMORIES OF MY BOYHOOD

Nils-Arne Holmlid

Thoughts about my boyhood are always thoughts of summer. There were no winters in these years, it seems, or else they are buried too deep down under the snow in my memory to be easily recalled. The winter was the period of recollection of the happenings during the summer which had passed, or a period of planning for the summer which was to come. I thus measured everything with the summer as my yardstick, and mostly the things measured seemed to be disappointments as compared to the summer.

This was because I spent my summer vacations in a small fishing village on an island. And the stay in this hamlet meant a close relationship with the sea, a relationship which could cause insecurity and even fright, but which above all yielded pleasure.

Memories of sounds and light. . . . There are days when the sea is calm. These days I feel a strange happiness, a calm, strong happiness, because the water surface is smooth and the air smells soft. But there are days, too, when the whistling gale is tearing the sea apart. These days I feel insecure, watching small boats being tossed by the waves.

We have a boat ourselves, a boat with which we can conquer the sea. It is an old-styled, new-built boat, made out of wood and with a weak, simple engine. It is a world in itself. We use it sometimes to go fishing. If it is a nice evening, not too chilly, not too windy, we go by boat out into the archipelago, or else we stay near the fishing village. We cast anchor; it is calm; it is silent. We do some fishing; we want the sea to give away its riches. There are no fish for us; we just catch a few mackerels. The people in the other boats around us are more lucky. They brag; they show us baskets full of fish. We do not mind, since the sea is all around us and the setting sun is painting the water red. The sea gulls are crying. The sea is around me, within me, I close my eyes.

One day we are out fishing on a grey, windy afternoon. The wind is increasing. Our anchor is not heavy enough to keep the boat in place, or we weigh our anchor and the engine will not start. We are adrift, and are forced by the wind toward a small rocky islet. I am afraid. My mother is afraid, she does not trust the sea, she has had unpleasant experiences. She is afraid, she makes me scared. Nothing happens; we are not smashed against the rocks; but we return home in some way. The sea is grey, unfriendly, cold—it does not take care of me; I do not know it.

On sunny, warm days I go for a swim. . . . The water is clear and salt; when I happen to swallow a mouthful of it I feel a bitter, strong taste on my tongue. *The sea can carry me if I want it to.* I just stretch out my legs and close my eyes and I can float. The sea is surrounding me; it makes me disappear. I am nowhere; I do not know my name any longer, for what good would my name do me? The water is friendly; the sea will not hurt me. I am no one.

But the sea can hurt me; I can be drowned . . . my ears, my mouth, my lungs filled with water. I walk along the shore now; I smile at the sea, but I know I cannot trust it completely. Instead, I pick up shells and mussels and throw them back into the water. They came from the sea, they have got to return to the sea. I must not swim too far away from the shore.

Thus the sea was both a friend and an enemy. . . . A friend, a playmate, with fascinating forms and colors, the ground on which I built my world. But also an enemy, the potential threat to what I called mine. These feelings still overwhelm me any time I reach the coast, any time I hear the cries of the sea gulls or the sound of a fisherboat engine. I still feel the same satisfaction, the same fear when I can live by the sea. When I cannot live by the sea, I mourn. The summers of my boyhood are still within me; the sea is still within me.

❋   ❋   ❋   ❋

What are the basic images in "Memories of My Boyhood"? What is the basic contrast? Is there sufficient conflict here to make this a short story, or is it best termed a *descriptive essay*? If you find it an essay, as I do, what elements would be necessary to make it a story? The following was written by a college student.

❄ VACATION BIBLE SCHOOL

Lawrence G. O'Toole

This day was as hot as the last. Ten miles away the grass and the trees were soaking up wave after wave of luxurious warmth. Here, in the city, the sun was straining with all its useless energy against concrete, iron, and dust. No life came forth, only the barren reflection of heat and light. Outside the small stone church the sidewalk burned and glared. The street gave forth the clank and roar of metal machinery and the hum of rubber on asphalt. Outside the sun was overwhelming, inside it went unseen and unfelt.

In the dank, cavernous basement of this church floated a sea of children, city children, arranged in distinct but uneven waves. There were over a hundred kids, mostly small ones, with drastically decreasing numbers up through the eighth grade. All the faces were brown and harmonious with the exception of a startling few. These few belonged to taller people. Teachers. White, suburban, collegiate, "involved." In this place they wore their whiteness like refrigerated cadavers. The glare from the big, bald light bulbs, suspended from the ceiling in inverted bird cages, contributed to the sickly character of their paleness. The imprisoned bulbs irritated, but did not illuminate.

Richard Wells stood uneasily with his small seventh and eighth grade group while the younger classes were being pushed into straight lines. He half smiled at one of the eighth graders who half acknowledged Rich's existence in return. When it came time, Richard's class followed the others down the hallway. Their casual strolling was in marked contrast to the orderliness of the lower grades. As they ambled into their classroom, Richard asked himself once again how and why he was where he was. When he originally volunteered he had no idea that he would be assigned to a Bible teaching operation. He had the depressing feeling that he wasn't doing a very effective job. How could he say what had been said so often before and have it mean something? Well, at least it's only temporary.

They sat around a stained, paint-spattered Masonite table in creaky folding chairs. Richard took down seven worn Bibles from the shelf and passed them around the table. Then he opened his own copy, and his mouth, and uttered the Golden Truth.

"Well, the play this morning was the story of how God gave Moses the Ten Commandments. I guess we oughta read it over to make sure you all understand how it went. Marilyn, you read the narrator's part; Calvin, you can be Moses; and I guess I'll be God. Start at the beginning of chapter twenty, Marilyn."

"And God spack

"Spake!"

spake these words, saying . . .' "

"Calvin?"

"Do we hafta read this, Mista Ritchie? Why don't we have singing now?"

Richard hesitated and replied almost apologetically. "I guess there isn't much sense in repeating the whole thing, but we oughta talk about the meaning of the Commandments for a while. Gerry, what's the first one?"

"Uh, thou shalt not . . . uuh . . ."

"Mista Ritchie, the fifth grade is having singing now, I can hear 'em through the wall. Why can't we?"

"We can sing when we're through with the lesson. Now pay attention to what the rest of us are doing."

". . . thou . . . shalt . . . not . . . ummmm"

In his seat Calvin began chanting softly, rhythmically, to himself. The volume gradually increased. When Sharon and Gloria recognized the sound, they joined the hand-clapping response.

> Ah got that feelin'!
> oh yeah!
> It's in ma eyes—
> oh yeah!
> Ah caint see!
> oh yeah!

"Okay, you kids knock it off and listen. We're discussing something important. This whole idea of the Ten Commandments is probably the most important thing you'll get here. Now c'mon, Gerry, give us the first Commandment of God. You just got through hearing them ten minutes ago."

". . . shaaaalt not . . . thou shalt . . ."

> It's on the roof—
> oh yeah!
> A hundred proof!
> oh yeah!

"Look, if Miss Chase comes in now, she'll be really mad. Now I told you once already . . ."

It's in ma whisky—
oh yeah!
It makes me frisky!

"One of those Ten Commandments we happen to be studying demands obedience to the people in charge. If you three can't act like normal human beings, I'll have to tell Miss Chase, and she'll probably cancel your trip this week!"

It's in ma leg—
oh yeah!
Ah caint walk!

"Did you hear me?!"

It's between ma legs—

"Shut up, goddammit!"

oh *yeah!*

*   *   *   *

What are the basic images in "Vacation Bible School"? What is the basic contrast—or conflict? How does dialogue help develop it?

For further analysis of imagery and contrast, consider the following student-written story.

✿ HOME THOUGHTS

Donna Van Tassell

Half darkness gradually fading into dawn hung like fog in my room. If a pin dropped, I'd be its only witness. If a word was spoken, it was my own. The freshly starched white pillow on which I rested my head only accented my aloneness. I tossed and turned and retossed with self-pity.

Days came and left, leaving me silent. Each morning I awoke
sure of my next movement. My mother would be rolled in her
bed covers unaware that a new day had come and that the cat needed
to be let in from out back where my stepfather had chained him
according to his custom shortly before work. I freed the cat and hurried
to the greasiness of the kitchen to scramble eggs before it was too
late and I'd go hungry again. No breakfasts had been allowed
after seven-thirty ever since my mother's remarriage and I dared not
alter her rule. Besides, the school bus was due at eight and unless I
caught that I'd be trapped at home all day.

There was no mad rush to put on my coat, pick up my books, and
bang out the door, as one normally expects. I was much too eager
to leave not to be already on my mark and set to go.

A mile trip to school on rough and twisting road through the woods
only takes a few minutes. Often I arrived in class with the words
of my mother still ringing in my ears, "Aren't you ever going to get out
of here?" or even more often, "Where's that damn bus?"

By the end of the first class I had usually lost myself and my
problems in a book or a discussion and by the last class I secretly began
dreading the three o'clock bell. I didn't need a clock to tell me what
time it was, something inside of me forewarned me.

Kitchen smells rarely greeted me as I idled through the front
door but even less frequent was a word from anyone to assure me that
human existence wasn't altogether foreign to that house, that
surprisingly was by some few considered home. Perhaps the clatter
of tin plates and plastic ones, the ring that glasses make, and the
jingle jangle of silverware being sloshed in water was my welcome home
each night. Or perhaps the sound of one foot pressing upward always
ahead of the other as I climbed the stairs leading to my bedroom was
my only assurance that I was home.

Turning at a right angle from the stairs, walking mechanically to
the big wooden dresser near my bed, flinging my books down in a
nearby chair, and methodically changing my clothes were all ordinary
movements on my part. Sometimes I found myself wondering what I
would have done had someone rearranged those few pieces of furniture
to which I turned every night.

Before supper I usually sprawled out on my cot with a book.
And so I would read until either boredom or some particular words
within my book made me drift off into some distant memory.

"My Lord, I think I saw him yesternight."

"Saw? Who?"

"My Lord, the King your father."

"Where was my father," I wondered. "Was he working or was he
drunk somewhere." I looked down at my watch; it was five-thirty—

five-thirty—Just four years ago I would have known where he was. He'd
be home with mama and me up on the hill where we used to live.
We'd all be sitting around the kitchen table eating and talking.
It was always a good life back then before the divorce. I can't remember
having any real problems then but now . . . now it was all changed.
We never talked anymore; mama was always too busy or too tired.
My stepfather rarely spoke. It was almost like he was a complete
stranger and the only thing I really knew about him was his face. Each
night he came home from work, puttered with the familiar chores, sat
down in his wooden rocking chair with his pipe tucked in his teeth
and slept until supper. After supper he always returned to his chair or
else mama and he went up the road to visit with his mother. Even
there he slept. Rage and laughter looked bad on him. Whenever he
put them on, I felt uncomfortable because they seemed unreal.

What would life have been like if I didn't know this man, my
unwanted stepfather? If only things hadn't changed and my real father
was the man downstairs. But no, it was best not to think about it
and so I forced myself to think of other things. I looked again at my
book but my thoughts quickly returned to my family. I asked the
question—"What would it be like?" Before the divorce there was
carefreeness. I had a kitten for a pet and a back yard swing, and I'd
chased June bugs, caught tadpoles, and hunted wild flowers. I went
barefoot, picked berries, and rolled in clover that made my clothing
sweet with scent. Even now I can close my eyes and picture life as
it was. Now at twelve I wanted the things that twelve-year-olds are
supposed to have. I wanted pretty dresses, not hand-me-downs; curls in
my hair and jewelry just because everyone had them. I wanted to
invite friends over to my house after school or go to theirs. Maybe
even have a boyfriend.

A voice from my past urged me onward, to get up and conquer, to
be that twelve-year-old of my dreams. I started up, pressed down the
wrinkles from my clothing with my hands, started for the mirror to
comb my hair, got there, and as the comb took its first sweep, the
words of my mother came exploding in the air, "Get downstairs, supper's
ready." I dropped the comb, walked to the door, turned back for
just a moment, then went slowly down those stairs.

❈ ❈ ❈ ❈

For further analysis of dialogue, used both as image and as contrast,
consider the following student-written story. It might well be read
aloud by the class, with parts assigned for the three boys, the mother,
old Jack, and the narrator.

❀ WE WANNA GO FISHING!

Ray Begin

"Think she'll let you go?"

"Not tonight."

"But why not?"

"Because we still have to keep digging under the house."

"Dig for what? China?"

"Naw, we ain't going to dig that far. We might come out in Vietnam."

"Very funny. But what are you digging for?"

"It's a cellar, stupid, and I still have to get this hard clay dug out."

Ronnie threw another shovelful of clay out of the hole, narrowly missing my feet.

Before I could holler, Dana came running out of the house.

"Ron, Mom said we could quit now."

"Maybe she did, but did Dad?"

"No, but I'm not going to ask him."

"Well, if you don't we're not going to be able to quit."

"Okay, you want to wake him up?"

"Ron, quit arguing," I broke in, "and tell Dana what we were planning."

"I just hope it works."

"What? What?" asked Dana.

"Let's try to get your mother to let you guys go fishing tonight," I said. "We'll tell her we'll be extra careful, and won't get drowned, or get our feet wet, or catch a cold. And this time we'll clean the fish before we get home. I'm not for getting up at 6:30 again just to clean those slimy fish."

"Yeah, she sure didn't like the way they smelled up her kitchen," Dana said.

"And she didn't like the three million cats that came in from somewhere," Ronny added.

"Okay then," I said, "let's ask her. What have we got to lose?"

"Nothing," said Ronny, "except we'll get grounded if she's baking another cake."

"All right guys, when I count to three, let's go. One . . . Two . . . THREE."

"MOM, CAN WE GO FISHING TONIGHT?"

We waited a few seconds, everything was quiet. Then we heard a "No!"

"Well, that does it," Ron said. "Might as well keep digging in the hole."

"Cool it, you guys," I said, looking at the next house, "don't you guys know your own mother's voice?"

"Yeah," said Dana, "That was old Jack next door."

While I was laughing, I turned back toward the guys. My face , froze as I saw a figure standing in the doorway. Ron and Dana didn't say a word.

"What's all the noise out here? Don't you know your father's sleeping?"

"Gee, Mom, we just want to go fishing," Ron said.

"Please, Mom, please?" Dana implored.

"Forget it, boys, you know what the answer is. Remember that mess you left me with last time?"

"But Mom, we've reformed. New People! You know . . ."

"Yeah, yeah, I know. Just like the last time, eh?"

"We'll do anything you want, we'll clean the fish, we'll . . ."

"We'll even wear our jackets," Dana said.

"Don't listen to 'em, they're a bunch of cons," shouted old Jack next door.

"You keep your cool, Jack," she shouted back. "You ain't telling me nothing I don't know."

"So," she said, looking back at Ron and Dana, "again you think I was born yesterday. What you gonna fish for? Honnypout again?"

"You mean we can go?" Ron and Dana asked together.

"But I want you back earlier than last time."

"You mean nine o'clock?" Ron asked.

"We won't get there till nine o'clock," Dana complained.

"When you guys got back last time I lost three hours' sleep," Jack shouted from his rocking chair on the porch next door.

"Hey Jack, why don't you come with us. We'll even put bread crumbs on the ground so we won't lose our way this time," Dana said.

"Yeah," I said, "we'll try real hard to see that you don't fall in the brook." I winked at the others.

Old Jack laughed so hard his chair fell back against the wall and his arms and legs kicked, making him look like a bug on its back.

"Eleven o'clock. No later."

"Thanks, mom." Ron and Dana shouted. "Let's get ready!"

"All right, guys, now that I've sprung you, how about talking to my mother with me?"

"What do you mean?" Dana said.

"Now let's see if I can go."

"Ten to one says you can't," said Jack.

"You mean . . ." said Ron, advancing towards me with his right fist clenched.

"Let's not get emotional. I'm all set. Just got to get my pole."

"Okay! Let's get out of here before Jack decides to come," Dana said.

As we turned around, there was no one in his chair. But it was still rocking, so we ran down the hill as fast as we could.

*   *   *   *

The following selections, by Henry Adams and by me, attempt to appeal to the reader's senses so that the experiences described become experiences for the reader himself. Each essay uses several contrasts:—between the seasons and between places (town and country, the world of the newsreel and that of surburban New Jersey). In addition, each essay makes a contrast between different lives, the two lives lead by the young Henry Adams and the lives of those who live in suburban New Jersey and "foreigners."

A NEW ENGLAND BOYHOOD

Henry Adams

The chief charm of New England was harshness of contrasts and extremes of sensibility—a cold that froze the blood, and a heat that boiled it—so that the pleasure of hating—one's self if no better victim offered—was not its rarest amusement; but the charm was a true and natural child of the soil, not a cultivated weed of the ancients. The violence of the contrast was real and made the strongest motive of education. The double exterior nature gave life its relative values. Winter and summer, cold and heat, town and country, force and freedom, marked two modes of life and thought, balanced like lobes of the brain. Town was winter confinement, school, rule, discipline; straight, gloomy streets, piled with six feet of snow in the middle; frosts that made the snow sing under wheels or runners; thaws when the streets became dangerous to cross; society of uncles, aunts, and cousins who expected children to behave themselves, and who were not always gratified; above all else, winter represented the desire to escape and go free. Town was restraint, law, unity. Country, only seven miles away, was liberty, diversity, outlawry, the endless delight of mere sense impressions given by nature for nothing, and breathed by boys without knowing it.

SOURCE: From *The Education of Henry Adams: An Autobiography* by Henry Adams. Reprinted by permission of Houghton Mifflin Company.

Boys are wild animals, rich in the treasures of sense, but the New England boy had a wider range of emotions than boys of more equable climates. He felt his nature crudely, as it was meant. To the boy Henry Adams, summer was drunken. Among senses, smell was the strongest—smell of hot pine-woods and sweet-fern in the scorching summer noon; of new-mown hay; of ploughed earth; of box hedges; of peaches, lilacs, syringas; of stables, barns, cow-yards; of salt water and low tide on the marshes; nothing came amiss. Next to smell came taste, and the children knew the taste of everything they saw or touched, from pennyroyal and flagroot to the shell of a pignut and the letters of a spelling book—the taste of A-B, AB, suddenly revived on the boy's tongue sixty years afterwards. Light, line, and color as sensual pleasures, came later and were as crude as the rest. The New England light is glare, and the atmosphere harshens color. The boy was a full man before he ever knew what was meant by atmosphere; his idea of pleasure in light was the blaze of a New England sun. His idea of color was a peony, with the dew of early morning on its petals. The intense blue of the sea, as he saw it a mile or two away, from the Quincy hills; the cumuli in a June afternoon sky; the strong reds and greens and purples of colored prints and children's picture-books, as the American colors then ran; these were ideals. The opposites or antipathies, were the cold grays of November evenings, and the thick, muddy thaws of Boston winter. With such standards, the Bostonian could not but develop a double nature. Life was a double thing. After a January blizzard, the boy who could look with pleasure into the violent snow-glare of the cold white sunshine, with its intense light and shade, scarcely knew what was meant by tone. He could reach it only by education.

Winter and summer, then, were two hostile lives, and bred two separate natures. Winter was always the effort to live; summer was tropical license. Whether the children rolled in the grass, or waded in the brook, or swam in the salt ocean, or sailed in the bay, or fished for smelts in the creek, or netted minnows in the salt-marshes, or took to the pine-woods and the granite quarries, or chased muskrats and hunted snapping-turtles in the swamps, or mushrooms or nuts on the autumn hills, summer and country were always sensual living, while winter was always compulsory learning. Summer was the multiplicity of nature; winter was school.

The bearing of the two seasons on the education of Henry Adams was no fancy; it was the most decisive force he ever knew; it ran through life, and made the division between its perplexing, warring, irreconcilable problems, irreducible opposites, with growing emphasis to the last year of study. From earliest childhood the boy was accustomed to feel that, for him, life was double. Winter and summer, town and country, law and liberty, were hostile, and the man who pretended they were not, was in his eyes a schoolmaster—that is, a man employed to tell lies to little boys.

❀ THE SON OF NICK MASSIMO

Herbert R. Coursen, Jr.

Autumn, 1939, the suburbs of New Jersey—America drifts in a dream towards war with jag-helmeted Nazis, jack-booted Italians, and bandy-legged Japanese. They flicker at us from newsreels, these menacing foreigners. The grey domes of sky fill with the drone of bombers. People stand stock-still, look up, then scurry off, flicking glances over shoulders. Refugees flee from pillars of smoke, plodding and heavy beneath bundles and children, thick in peasant garments, huddled and ducking, as if avoiding invisible blows, behind crude wagons, moving too slowly, piled with bedding and other refuse that once had known a home. Hostages die with contemptuous stares, their women wringing hands and wailing. Children stare up at men swinging slowly—like dolls—from gallows. Cities crumble like castles of sand.

We play under the blue bowl of an almost endless August and return to school through crackle-leaf streets as our suburb dozes in the bask of Indian Summer, curls cozily into wrappings of pipe-smelling smoke woven from countless bonfires licking leaves in our cobbled gutters. Munich is far away and Japan appears only on the bottoms of the cheap toys cluttering the counters of the Five and Ten.

My brother and I have a few busy-work chores each Saturday morning—rubbing wax on the floors in the spaces between the oriental rugs, emptying the wastebaskets—chores which take time only because we evade them until a motherly voice grows peremptory. By 10:30 we are bounding from the house to trot the half mile to the grammar-school field, an eroding plain rutted like a miniature Colorado by the rains coursing from the hills above to the clogged sewer below. There we play baseball until September, football until snow. Or we may dash the 100 yards to the woods around the corner, filling now with urgency as darkening skies appear earlier and grow larger through the thinning trees. Hurry, snow is coming and the woods will close. Autumn is urgent.

Spring had been eager. We had run to the woods after school, long before the mud began to parch and crumble, early ferns tracing

SOURCE: From *The New England Review*, 1:3(1970).

along our bare legs, low mounds of grey snow lurking like animals in the
shadows of evergreens, eager we had run into the damp scented woods
to play hide-and-seek. I lie in a trench, absorbed in the smell of
generations of leaves layered beneath me, watching the boy who is "it"
pass by. I am warm with the knowledge that he will not find me. I
rise to all fours, push off like a sprinter, and rush towards the big tree
which is "home" and shout "homefree!" an instant before my
fingers touch the veins of bark. The woods have a stream with a rough
planked bridge over it—it had all been a farm once before trees stepped
back across its acres. One day I pick out the brightest pebbles in the
stream to take home to my mother. In a half hour they are uniformly
dull-brown. The next day I sprinkle them back into the stream where
they are bright again. The woods of spring say that something good
is coming. They sing of my immortality. But the fall woods are not the
same, and usually my brother and I go to the field for football.

One day we do something mean. A boy named Brian, new to the
neighborhood, joins our game.

"You're the ball carrier, Brian," I say, winking at everyone else.

"Great!" he says.

The ball is centered. Brian wraps his arms around its bulk and
charges forward. He is hit by everyone in the game—the three people on
his team and the four on the other. Down he goes beneath 400
pounds of little boys. His ancient leather helmet spins sideways on his
head, so that his nose protrudes from an ear-hole. We unpile. He sits up
and twists his helmet back in place and looks at us groggily.

"Great!" I say. "Brian, that was great!" The others join in.

"Gee, was it?" We tell him how great it was and he carries the
ball again. And again. Finally Brian decides that someone else should
carry the ball. In a little while it is time for him to go home. He never
plays with us again.

Every Saturday in the fall, "Nick Massimo—Landscape
Archetect" (so says the sign on his old pick-up truck) works over the
leaves on the McKell's lawn across the street, never looking up as we
sprint past. With him works his son, raking steadily towards the huge
piece of canvas in which Nick will bundle the leaves. The fathers of the
neighborhood burn their leaves in the gutters. Nick carries his off to
some unknown place. One day Nick takes a mattress we have left
for the garbage men and ties it to the back of his truck. I report this
theft excitedly to my mother.

"Well, I'm glad *someone* can use that old thing," she says.

"You mean someone's going to *sleep* on it?"

"Of course. You did, didn't you?"

The son of Nick Massimo is my age—eight or nine—but smaller,
with black hair that shines in the slanting light of autumn, wearing

always the same black sweater cut short at elbows and the same
dungarees faded pale and patched in red. His lustrous eyes follow us
even as his olive forearms move the rake. We know that he watches us.

One day as we issue forth, virtuous for the completion of our
chores, I say "Hi" to Nick Massimo's son. Soon we are exchanging a few
words at the end of the McKell's lawn—tentatively, because he
doesn't go to our school, doesn't play on our field or in our woods,
doesn't, we guess, collect baseball cards or listen to "Your Hit Parade"
on Saturday nights. But soon he has convinced us that we should spend
Saturday morning helping *him* on the lawn. He hints at the money
his father will pay us.

"You get *money* for this work," he says.

We rake furiously, hoping to gain the approving eye of the elder
Massimo working stolidly far across the expansive lawn. We move the
old rakes the boy has given us and envision the jovial noon—Nick,
smiling, with thick hands full of gleaming quarters, pressing one or two
into our rake-roughened palms. We pile the pungent leaves onto the
huge canvas and curry the lawn as if we are preening a prize stallion for
a show. On we toil, perspiring now in the direct sight of the sun,
until the lawn shines. We wait politely for our pay while Nick ties the
corners of the leaf bundle and plods bent-backed to his truck, looking
like a nightmare of St. Nicholas. Finally, he approaches, grasping
a new wooden rake by the throat and pointing at it with the jab of a
blunt finger.

"Looka dis," he cries. "Looka dis!" his grainy thumb points at a
missing tooth in the rake. "How you expec me to pay for dis? My new
raka ruin!"

We cower before his invincible foreignness. My brother's white face
reflects back my own. I hadn't used that rake. Had he? Will Nick
Massimo charge across the street brandishing the rake and demanding
payment from our parents? No—he moves his free hand up and down
the air and across the shattered implement, then turns towards his
leaf-burdened Chevrolet, where his dark-eyed son stares straight
ahead and waits to go home.

War comes. Nick and his son are seen no more.

"Probably got a job in a defense plant," my mother says. Our maid,
Sally, and, in fact, the entire colony of maids which had inhabited
the neighborhood and which had trooped down the streets on Thursday
mornings to take the train to Newark, had left for good—to take jobs
in defense plants.

My brother and I play on in the woods which change only with
the seasons. We play war games—always against the Japanese, who fall
obligingly before our voiced gun-shots. We charge forward invulnerable
and, tree by tree, reclaim our sacred woods from the invader.

But one spring our woods are full of real men, swart, with strange sounds on their tongues, carrying milk bottles full of water and eating dripping, dark sandwiches, the bread looking as if it encloses something alive. The men ride roaring machines and strew grainy sewer pipes over the ruined fields that had been our woods. And I am afraid of the men and do not know why.

⁜   ⁜   ⁜   ⁜

SUMMARY

Through imagery the writer activates his reader's senses, thus allowing the narrative to become part of the reader's experience. Dialogue is a kind of imagery because it allows us to hear words spoken and to feel the attitude behind the words. Although dialogue is often used sparingly in many of the student-written pieces in this book, it is often an essential component of narrative. It is hard to believe that "The Life of Harry Nelson," "The Dolphin," or "Vacation Bible School" could convey their experiences unless we heard the words and felt the attitudes behind the words of the various speakers. "We Wanna Go Fishing!" is composed almost exclusively of dialogue. Imagery—an appeal to the senses—is an absolutely basic ingredient of imaginative writing.

Contrast allows us to see more clearly and feel more profoundly. The contrast between warmth and coldness, for example, becomes a medium for sensing deeper contrasts: between a woman and a man, between different generations, or a contrast within a person (which almost invariably reflects the contrasts the character encounters outside of himself). Contrast of course, can evolve to conflict, but conflict is not essential to a description like that of Paul Ross's or Nils-Arne Holmlid's. Conflict, however, is basic to a story like "Riding High" or "The Dolphin."

EXERCISE

Which of the images of the narratives you have read so far made the most effective appeal to your senses? To what extent are those images indebted to precise diction and careful syntactic structuring?

Which of the pieces you have read are based primarily on contrast? In which does contrast develop toward conflict? How many different kinds of contrasts and conflicts can you find in each narrative?

Which of the narratives incorporate dialogue? Can you sense the tone of voice behind the words? Could some of the dialogue be translated into descriptive prose without loss?

Look again at the writing you have done so far. Do you find

opportunities to develop your imagery, to deepen your contrasts? If you did not use dialogue, are there places where you could? If you did use dialogue, can we hear the attitude behind the words spoken? Is there conflict in your narrative? It need not be there; but if it is latent in what you have written, it offers a line of development toward a short story. You may wish to consider some of these questions in the context of a subject other than that of whatever writing you have done so far.

Reread the pieces by Gorki, Thomas, Baldwin, and Hathaway in the context of this chapter's discussion of imagery and contrast.

FOUR
Structure
and
Development

Structure involves the way the writer chooses to shape his material. A straight chronological sequence may be the best way to organize the narrative, as shown in "The Dolphin" and "Riding High." Some writers, however, choose to rearrange the sequence of events in their narratives. Writing is not life, not a sequence of what happened next. It is a translation of actual experience into a different medium that makes demands on the writer radically different from those made by "reality." Nils-Arne Holmlid, for example, chooses to arrange his impressions and memories of the sea around the contrasting principles of "friend" and "enemy." Imaginative writing is a different way of encountering truth, using words in place of experience, words that recreate the experience within the senses, emotions, and imagination of the reader. A good photographer does not merely snap pictures randomly. He selects an angle from which to take his picture, taking into consideration light, shadow, and tonality. He selects the details he considers important and de-emphasizes those he feels unimportant. The photographer does not capture reality; he creates a composition, a version of the truth in front of his lens. He must decide how best to transmit what he sees there to the eye that will see the photograph.

The following story was written by a freshman in college.

❁ WHALE HUNT

Michael Leonard

It was the sound that brought me back to reality, a noise like hailstones or a hammer striking an iron roof. Then I knew that we were close to what we had been searching for the last few days. Being the lightest member of the crew, I had been given the mast watch. Now I began to search the horizon, my eyes making ever decreasing circles toward the boat.

The people who tell you whale hunting is gone forever and elaborate the dramatic side of the past should have been on the searing teak of the deck that day. The late part of Indian summer brought many things to the Maine coast. We had our harvest from the sea then in the form of lobsters and schools of fish that inhabited the

peaceful inlets and quiet pine-encased coves. The fishermen set out
seines to catch the vast schools of herring that leaped like silver flashes
and swam like precision units in the shallows. The problem was
that we were not the only ones after this catch. For weeks the
men had been plagued by a whale which ripped through the cordage
of their nets. The whale was only after food, and a captive meal
kept him marauding our seines and destroying thousands of dollars
worth of twine, and, in some cases, a man's chance to face the winter
with something more than beans and salt fish.

My father had banded the fishermen together in one of our boats;
it wasn't much to look at after ten months of work. The paint peeled off
in yellow-white chunks, but only to show the heavy oak planks
which are the symbol of Maine craftsmanship. Her insides weren't
much better, permeated by the oppressive smell of rotten bait and
decaying weed which none of us noticed but which made the tourists
hold their breath and turn away with inflated cheeks and red faces.
From the center of the cockpit rose the greasy Budda diesel. This
was the fisherman's hope and security miles offshore, where an engine
failure sometimes could mean a lonely death. We were in the second
day of our search for the whale and, so far, no luck. However, the
noise was as good as a sight, because we all knew it for a whale
breathing. When whales blow after surfacing, it isn't the storybook
spout; it's a breath of vapor like a man's on a cold day and it has to rank
among the world's worst smells: a cross between rotten eggs and
old outhouses. As I searched the sparkling water, much clearer now
that the summer boats were gone and the sand and weed had settled
again, I knew I would never see the spout; it would be too small among
the whitecaps, but turning to look at one of the many spruce-covered
islands, I saw a glint like a mirror in the waves. There was no need
to yell, even though I was about to burst from joy and excitement.
Rather, I leaned over the mast hoops and pointed off to port.
Suddenly the taciturn fisherman huddled around the engine were no
more. My father sprang to the windward shrouds and up the
mast. One man went forward, and two began to clear the harpoon line
on the after deck. When my father was satisfied that the glint
rolling along unaware was our target, he returned to the wheel and the
pulsating chug of the diesel turned into a head-shattering roar as
we came around and took up position behind the whale with the sun
off our beam. The reflection was no longer blinding. We could all see
the black head and dorsal fin rise rhythmically a few inches out of
the water. We all also knew that there were probably thirty tons
of living being under that spot.

The whale dove just then, perhaps scared by the engine. My father
gave up the wheel and went forward. In his right hand he held the

ten-foot pole with the sharp, malicious piece of metal at its tip.
A few coils of line dangled from his left hand and ran along the deck
like a sunburnt snake to the stern where the orange barrel with its
staff and profusion of flags was set. We cruised for several minutes
without seeing our quarry, then a shape like a giant black log rose from
the depths ahead of us.

We weren't in the 1950s anymore; we were back more than half a
century and there was a big man in sea boots and a navy wool jacket far
from the bow on the thin wooden bridge of the tuna pulpit. He
motioned slightly toward port; then toward himself. His commands,
though silent, were obeyed as if a whip were over the men; they all knew
that his word was law now. He slowly straightened up, his hands
over his head clasping the shiny pole. He motioned again to
the fight, then his hands drove down in front and we heard the chunk
of metal piercing unsuspecting blubber and bone. A thousand
things exploded at once; my father yelled and the man at the wheel
slammed the engine into full reverse. My father ducked behind the
protective iron grating to avoid the loose harpoon pole which
shot off to leeward like a javelin, and the man in the stern stepped back
and punted the barrel into the foaming turbulence. We all rushed
to the side as the bobbing orange blob started off toward Europe at a
full eight knots. My father walked back to the cockpit, took over
the wheel, and the men settled down, anticipating a long chase. After
what seemed like hours the barrel stopped moving and bobbed
peacefully in an ocean calmed by the approach of night. The men were
tense again. Someone went forward to bring out the sheepskin case
which held a .32 Winchester. This part was the most dangerous
of the whole chase. The whale, although small, could still take the
boat with him in his death flurry. His dark shape didn't seem as black
or large as he slowly surfaced beside us. His tail flopped slightly, and the
line which was wrapped around him disappeared in a circle of
foamy red into his back. My father took the rifle and knelt over
the gunwale. There was a crack; then the whale rolled fin up, dead.
In the settling night the falling sun was reflected in his skin; we
brought out ballast rocks and tied them to the line trailing from his
body. The men looked at each other as he was cast adrift and
disappeared in a swirling patch of milky red. They hated to kill anything
unless it was a necessity, especially something so powerful and almost
awesome.

The man with the rifle returned it carefully to its case, then took
the wheel and said, "Michael, better turn on the running lights;
we're going home."

*   *   *   *

The suppressed excitement in the early part of "Whale Hunt" is a product of structure, as well as precise diction and syntax and vivid imagery. Mike Leonard begins the story at the moment just before his young narrator sights the whale. Before the actual sighting, the narration returns to fill in the background happenings that have led to this moment. The background information then comes back to the opening moments of the story and moves on to the actual sighting. Such a technique is known as the *narrative hook,* which captures our interest immediately and allows the writer to fill in necessary background within the context of our already aroused excitement. Feeling the tug of the narrative hook, we are more willing to accept information than were it merely given us at the beginning of the story. Had the essay begun with the second paragraph, the logical starting point from a chronological standpoint, we would still have a good opening. The background section is vivid and detailed. But the element of suspense would be missing. Were the actual sighting to occur in the first paragraph, we would lose the sense of those eyes probing in "ever decreasing circles toward the boat," as we read the second paragraph. Mike stops the action of the first paragraph at precisely the moment that carries its tension across the next two paragraphs to its conclusion: "I saw a glint like a mirror in the waves." Chronology is altered for the sake of narrative interest.

Other elements worthy of notice in Mike Leonard's narrative include the quiet, matter-of-fact manner in which he tells where he is, what he sees, and why these Maine fishermen are out on the sea this afternoon. The tone conveys the businesslike atmosphere and, at the same time, allows the more exciting moments to emerge in contrast to the precision and detail of the narrative voice. This is, after all, not the quest of a mad Ahab, pursuing the white whale that has amputated his leg, but the work of fishermen hoping to have more than "beans and salt fish" to stave off the piercing and approaching winter. The matter-of-fact tone even debunks the "storybook spout" we have seen in paintings of nineteenth-century whale scenes. The narrator notices the greater clarity of the water "now that the summer boats were gone and the sand and weed had settled again," the kind of detail that only someone who has been there can provide. Some excitement is released when the whale is sighted, but the narrative builds again toward that moment when the harpoon strikes home. Then the narrator launches into some hyperbole, which is all the more effective because of the calm, observant attitude that has projected the story to us until the moment of the harpooning.

Other specific points worthy of observation:

1. The narrator's use of past and present: his evocation of the past in the second paragraph and his unexpected transition back to that

past in "We weren't in the 1950s anymore; . . ." We get a sense of the continuity of the fisherman's heritage, the concerns and dangers that have not changed with time.

2. The use of technical details that are kept enough in the background of the narrative so that, while they tell us that the narrator is an expert on the subject of boats, fish, and the sea, he does not demand that we be experts. The details give the narrative a density and a sense of the narrator's expertise without blocking the flow of the story for us landlubbers. We may not quite know what it means to take up "position behind the whale with the sun off our beam," but the next sentences makes things clear enough so that we too can see the whale: "The reflection was no longer blinding. We could all see the black head and dorsal fin rise rhythmically a few inches out of the water."

3. The narrator's mild contempt for tourists, whose pleasure boats churn up the seaweed and sand, but who cannot stand the smell of a working fishing boat. The narrator establishes himself as a native.

4. The quiet ending, not only reflecting the cessation of high excitement and danger, but also the men's awareness that what they have done, though necessary from their commercial standpoint, has been to destroy a great natural force. We aren't given the simple-minded "victory" of old war films, where William Bendix leads the cheers as a submarine filled with living men sinks out of sight.

5. The use of the final phases of the day, sunset and dusk, to echo the death of the whale. The end of day is noticed *through* the whale, still the primary concern of the fishermen even as they prepare the whale for his final trip to sea: "the falling sun was reflected in his skin."

6. The narrator's use of his father as a kind of "god figure:" he has organized the fishermen, and he controls the final moments of the chase, the boat and crew responding to his motions because "his word was law now." The father becomes very much like a character out of Conrad.

7. The use of a voice to end the narrative, not merely a "sun sinking slowly in the west." The voice, appropriately, addresses "Michael," the young man with whom the narrative begins. And the voice closes the narrative with an appropriately nautical command.

Consider the following student-written essay.

❋ TO GET AWAY

Kenneth Hinkley

As I passed through that process of suddenly realizing that the world is real, although dark, gray, and blurry, called awakening, I heard below me in the kitchen-dining room the muffled clang-clanging of pans and dishes made daily by my father as he prepared his usual morning meal of fried eggs and toast chased down by a cup of hot coffee into which he put a heaping teaspoon of sugar.

I rolled over onto my back, tangling myself into the folds and wrinkles of the blanket and light quilt that served as bed covers, to persuade myself that I was really awake and not still dreaming a gloomy dream where everything is colored in one shade of gray. I lay there staring at what I could see of the unfinished wooden ceiling above me and thought about the day to come and the things I had to do to make it complete. I thought with regret of the chores I had to do.

Since my mind could not focus itself on anything I enjoyed thinking about, except maybe the face of some girl I knew, I decided to rise and greet the day in my usual manner. I untangled myself from the jumble of quilt and blanket which seemed to be all edges and no corners. I found one and threw the covers off and swung my feet to the floor. There being an old carpet on the floor with about three inches of dust accumulated over a period of about six to eight months, I didn't mind standing on the floor, but the sub-zero weather chilled my bones through and through before I could even reach and get my cold-stiffened clothes on to hold in my body heat. It didn't usually take me more than a minute to get dressed in winter. I had a great urge to get near the stove.

At some point in this process, Dad finished his breakfast and put on his heavy outdoor wear and left for work in a neighboring town. He worked for a shoe company which makes high-heeled shoes for women. On some mornings the weather would be so cold the car wouldn't start and Dad would come back into the house cursing it and the weather.

"How many coals are there in that stove? That son-of-a-whore won't start."

He used the coals to put under the oil pan and warm the oil to make it flow more easily. But this didn't always work either and he would cuss and fume all the while he was trying to find out what the trouble was.

By the time I crossed the attic, descended the stairs, and crossed the cold linoleum of the floor of the room where we piled unused articles, I would be cold enough to make icicles if someone poured water over me.

Just before my father left (on mornings when there was no trouble), my mother would rise, throw on a housecoat, and busy herself with tidying up the kitchen—unless it was one of the many days that she didn't feel well. My mother has blood cancer, therefore she doesn't feel well a lot of the time. On such days, she would sit at the table and pour out her troubles upon me as I warmed myself beside the woodstove. I hardly ever listened, though, because I knew there wasn't anything I could do to help her.

The stove was an old cast-iron giant that seemed to spread itself into people's way when they tried to pass by. The oven door was left open when the oven wasn't in use and made a gaping red hole, like a giant yawning. One could see through the holes in the firebox wall into the fire. The heat it threw out, however, was hardly enough to heat the kitchen, to say nothing about the other four rooms downstairs or the attic. Once in a while we'd build a fire in the heater which squatted on the bricks of the false fireplace. The heat from this was a little more intense than that of the woodstove, but it didn't go any further. There were too many draft holes. Near any window or door one felt the wind driving through. Snow even blew onto the floor and, if it hadn't been swept up, would have set there for a week or more before it would melt.

We plugged the big draft holes with old rags or paper to keep the cold air out. Even though we did this, the heat from the stove or stoves could not warm the rooms. Many times we had to close the doors to the bedrooms on the ground floor to conserve heat for the kitchen and living room.

When I had thawed out by the woodstove, I would remove a bowl and a box of cereal from the cupboard and a spoon from the drawer and set them on the table at the spot nearest the stove. I would then fetch a pitcher of diluted canned milk from the cellarway (which was our only means of refrigeration, kept cool by the draft from the cellar below) and the sugar and sit down to eat.

I went through all this more by my sense of touch than sight, since the sun had not yet risen and the sky was only just beginning to lighten. The house was illuminated by two or three kerosene-wick lamps which were placed in any place which seemed convenient. The glass chimney on top of a kerosene lamp is the most delicate part. It is easily broken in moving a lamp or, if one isn't careful in washing the chimney, a quick change of temperature will shatter it.

Sometimes I would sit in that thin light and read the cereal box, just to waste time so my breakfast would last longer. The longer I stayed near the woodstove the longer it would be before I went out into

the cold. Some of the boxes would have information from different
parts of the world on them, while others might have things which would
only appeal to the mind of a youngster. There were at least two
things which could be found on every box, the list of ingredients and
the table of minimum daily requirements. I read them just to see if
I could get my tongue around some of the big words they used. I never
felt any more ready to face my chores after having all those important
things my body needed to get through the day.

Pouring frozen and diluted canned milk on dry cereal is a mess.
I would have to crack the ice with my spoon or, if it was too thick, I
would set the pitcher on the back of the stove to soften the ice.
Either way I would not wait for the ice to become completely dissolved
and remixed with the milk, so I would have lumps of ice in my cereal
where other people might have fruit. Finally, I would have to face my
chores.

The chores were divided among the three of us boys who were old
enough and strong enough to handle them. We had two other brothers,
but one was excused for being too young and the other for being an
almost complete cripple. The part of the chores that fell to me was one
I disliked very much, no matter what it was. We usually rotated them
among us, say, every week or so. On one week I would have to go out
into the cold and pull logs or old timbers from a collapsed barn, throw
them across a makeshift sawhorse or hard snowdrift (frozen solid by
melting and refreezing) and cut them into sections about a foot long and
carry them into the kitchen to fill the woodbox. I would always stop
by the stove and warm myself between armloads.

Another week I would have to work inside the shed which we
referred to as our "barn." We usually had one or two animals—a cow,
or calf, a pony, or a couple of goats. I would have to clean the frozen
manure from under the animal's feet, throw them some fresh hay, and
give them some grain if there was any (which was very seldom). Our
few chickens usually lived off our table scraps, which were very scanty.
Many of the chickens did not live out the winter.

On the third week I would have to fill two ten-quart buckets with
water from the well behind our house. This wasn't too bad a job except
once in a while after you'd filled the evening's quota of water and
settled as much as possible for the evening, someone would yell,
"Waterboy! We need some water!"

Still, it was easy. You took two ten-quart buckets out into the back
room where the well was, set them down, cranked down the bucket
hanging in the well, let it fill, cranked it back up, poured the water into
the pails, then carried them back into the kitchen. When the weather
was very cold, however, the well froze over, and if it was too solid to
be broken out with the bucket, I would grab the long stick, on the end

of which was a once-sharp ice chipper, lower it into the well, and hang over the edge and chip out a hole in the ice large enough to lower the pail through and let it fill. Sometimes it would be frozen extremely solid, and chipping it would take a long time.

Usually about three trips would take care of the water needed for one day. Washing days were exceptions. On washing day it took about twelve to fifteen bucketfuls to suffice. Washing day occurred only once a week, unless my mother had nothing better to do and decided she wanted to do a washing. She would wait until we started filling the drinking pails and then say, "I think I'll do a washing today. So bring in the tub and fill it up." We would then bring in a large round tub and set it on the back of the kitchen stove and fill it up. After it was full, we poured more water into a smaller tub as rinse-water. How the last load of clothes came clean in this water after the other loads had all gone through it, I don't know. That water got dirty after the first load and more and more so after each additional load. Sometimes when I drained the washer there would be a pile of dirt—literal dirt—lying in the bottom.

No matter which of the three chores were assigned to me, I did it because I had to, not because I liked it at all. Any one of the three would require me to put on my shaggy jacket and cap which I wore to try to protect myself, although I always knew that they didn't do that much good. My mittens were either full of holes or extremely thin (or both) and kept no cold away from my fingers. Many a time I have removed my mittens after being out-of-doors and found my fingers numb with cold. The boots I wore were hand-me-downs which were absolutely no good when I got them. Most of the time I wore old rubber boots with no lining and about four or five holes in each one ranging from the size of a matchhead to an enormous tear.

After completing my chores, I would usually have about five or ten minutes before the school bus came. During that period, I would sit around the kitchen as light rose in the room and talk with my brothers and sisters about what had happened at school during the past few days. It was mostly just gossip, but then what do children in grade school talk about that isn't gossip?

On some mornings, if it wasn't too cold out or if the wind wasn't blowing to make the cold seem more intense, I would stand out by the road to await the arrival of the small two-toned green paneled pickup used as a school bus. As I stood there, many thoughts raced through my mind. Many of these were just thoughts of temporary incidents, but there was one that kept recurring to me—I would be so glad to get away from this place. Sometimes I would stand there and look at the weather-beaten old run-down farmhouse which once had had a coat of white paint applied to it, but has not received one since we have lived there and wonder what I did to deserve to live in such a place as that. The shingles on the roof had all rotted and the snow and rain fell down through the house during a storm. There have been lots of mornings when I have awakened to find a small pile of snow either on the floor at the foot of my bed or on the bed itself.

Most of the windows were cracked or scratched and the frames were half-rotten. No one dared rap on one very hard for fear it would fall out. The sill under the front of the house was all rotted away and the floor had fallen away from the bottom of the door-joint. The floor of the porch had fallen down so that the pillars were no longer holding the roof·and both of the two sets of steps leading onto it were either broken or loose.

My mother was always yelling, "Don't jump in the house or we'll end up down cellar!" Whenever anyone even so much as walked extra heavily, the floor would sag and rise under the strain and relaxation which are produced by walking.

I would keep telling myself that this is no place fit for anybody half-human to live in and that as soon as I was able to I would get out and go live where there were the comforts of electricity and automatic heat. I would go someplace where I could do what I wanted to do, rather than be stuck with barn chores every day and have almost no fun at all. I would get out of this rathole and go where there is something else.

But I would always come to and realize that the only way that I would ever get out without ruining my reputation by running away or by committing some serious crime would be just to go along with everything. So I did just that and I am now slowly breaking away from that unknown source that held me captive in this gloomy and depressing environment for so long. I am slowly becoming a free man to be able to choose what I want to, rather than have the environment force me to do things. It is now my choice whether I want to accomplish anything worthwhile or not. I now no longer have to shovel manure or carry water. I no longer have to wait for the school bus on cold winter mornings. I am now my own man.

❋   ❋   ❋   ❋

The *structure* of Ken Hinkley's essay is simple: a chronological sequence beginning with awakening and ending with a resolve to escape the grim trap the house represents. When one realizes, however, that the original "essay" (of which I do not, sadly, have a copy) consisted of a single brief paragraph which described the house very generally, one grasps the meaning of *development*. The process can be understood more clearly by my recreating part of a conversation I had with Ken

Hinkley several summers ago. Ken had mentioned "the chores," but had not expanded into their detail.

"What were they?" I asked.

He told me and I told him to develop his essay at that point. A few days later he returned. His essay included the sentence about the 10-quart buckets of water, but nothing more about that specific chore.

"That sounds easy enough," I said, "compared to getting the logs or feeding the animals."

"It was, except in winter and on washing days."

"Why?"

"In winter the well froze over."

"What did you do then?"

"I had to chip the ice away."

And so on, as the essay gradually incorporated the details of a day in this environment. The exploration of each moment gives us the feeling of that life, particularly its contact with the rough edges of nature—the frigid house, frozen well, tattered mittens. The description tells us as much about rural poverty in Maine than would all the statistics we could gather, just as *The Diary of Anne Frank* makes us feel the horror of Nazi genocide with far more impact than the figure "6 million Jews"; and just as *A Day in the Life of Ivan Denisovich* allows us to know about political prisoners in Siberia with our senses and emotions, not merely through our understanding of statistics. By moving from the original general statements like "Before I left for school, I had to do the chores" into a detailed description of those chores, Ken moves us into the world he inhabited and gradually allows us to experience the imperative to escape that place.

The method of question and answers that Ken and I used can be employed by the writer himself. Many young writers rush right past significance by covering it with a muffling generalization. In the original draft of "Barn," David Irish said merely, "On the way to the barn, we saw signs of many animals." The paragraph he developed, however, becomes a description of David's father, talking to his son about the out-of-doors and of the out-of-doors per se. The paragraph captures character and density of detail, showing us in several ways how it was on the way to the barn. A reference to "many animals" provides a scene uninformed by the development that "information" must undergo to create imaginative writing. For many young writers, then, good writing depends on development, a moving *into* experience, the writer pausing to ask himself what it was really like, what was really there, and than recreating that reality in the different reality of words. The process can be discerned in many of the pieces in this book. The effect of development can be discovered by going back and providing a general statement in place of the details the writer provides. What would be lost, for example, if Donna Van Tassell said merely, "Before the divorce there was carefreeness," and did not include the next two sentences, which create the specifics of carefreeness? The reader would receive information; but without the translation of that information into imagery, he would not experience that carefree past with the narrator and could not contrast that past against the narrower, darker world where the narrator now finds herself.

A story usually means more than just the scenes it describes, the characters it develops, or the events it narrates. Many of the stories in this book are *stories of initiation*—stories about growing up, whatever growing up may mean. "The Life of Harry Nelson" depicts a young man living by a superficial code of fashion, falling in love, and being projected to a zone where no ready-made formula applies. "The Man" shows a boy making a mistake and, as a result, being expelled from the childhood represented by that "sacred lawn." In "Riding High," an overconfident teenager moves into a harsh confrontation largely of her own making; then, however, she refuses to disturb the suppertime routines of that proper house. Many of the stories in this book— "Barn," "The Dolphin," "Vacation Bible School," "Home Thoughts" —involve initiation: the movement from the state described at the beginning of the story, through a complication or conflict, toward a different state by the end of the story. Most stories, then, tend to imitate the curve of actual experience. Almost any narrative about growing up automatically becomes a story because it incorporates the traditional components of prose fiction: a *beginning*, or exposition (the person before the experience); a *middle*, complication or conflict (the person moving through the experience); and an *end*, or resolution (the person at the end of the experience).

These considerations subsume both structure and development. The three-part structure demands the development of each component. A 14-year-old girl, who believes she has been fully tested by life, thumbs herself overconfidently toward trouble. Her attitude is reflected through her encounter with the cop. If she can handle him, she thinks, she can handle anyone. But she cannot. At the end, although she can anticipate a sympathetic reception at that Victorian house, she decides not to use the manipulative mastery that has now been so shattered. Even as she sticks out her thumb again, we infer that she has learned something. The basic structure of the story pursues the careful development of the stages of the character—from over confidence to panic and rage to a new toughness, an attitude chastened by the "experience" she thought had *already* forged her into a mature woman. In many stories, those who feel they have already passed the test discover that it has yet to come. In *The Red Badge of Courage*, Henry Fleming congratulates himself on having stood his ground during the first Confederate charge. He doesn't realize that the real test will be the second charge. When that comes, he panics and runs. Thus, what a character may see as a conclusion may be, for the writer, merely the beginning. The same generalization applies to Shakespeare's great drama of initiation, *King Lear*.

Examine the following student-written combination of prose and poetry from the standpoint of both structure and development.

✹ KILLING CATS

Chris Gahran

"Slimy-fucking-meerow......sssssss! damn. Shit! Missed the bastard."
Dogs were cool. You didn't get dogs because they were good for
hunting and stuff. But Dino hated cats.
    "Here kitty. Here pussy."
Lyonaise always ruined it.
He always had to laugh when he said pussy.
But Rosalie Kendall always laughed too.
    Cats were for summer. Late summer, when the nights just
turned cool after the stores closed, and the streetlight at the far corner
from Dino's house was heavy on us and gold. And the circling night
and the chrome on the parked cars was a quiet knife collection on black
velvet. We'd spread across the street, Dino and Laerson in the middle,
Rosalie and Kim on the sidewalks, and Pat Kendall and me on the
overgrown lawns of sooty houses that were always old and tan or white.
Dino and Laerson would screw around; tell jokes and comb their hair.
Sometimes one of them would flash his blade and kind of polish it on
his jeans, or lazily practice flicking it open. Most times it was Kendall
that found the cat.
    Sometimes it was me.
    You had to be easy with them; move really slow, like when you're
sick and it hurts to move. "Here kitty," you had to say, "Here kitty,
nice kitty," and Dino and Laerson would freeze and you could feel
their eyes. You got as close to it as you could (it was worse with kittens,
they'd just walk right up to you), then kick it fast and hard; break a leg
or a rib so it couldn't run away. Sometimes you could manage to miss.
Sometimes not.
    They were soft on your boot. The bones made a wet sound when
they broke, like twigs in the rain. Then Dino and Laerson would come
over. They'd smile and rub your head. Call you a real mean dude. Then

Rosalie would get to kick first, and after a while, sometimes after a long while, Dino or Laerson would crush its skull, or cut its throat. One time Laerson cut open its stomach to see what was inside. It made a funny sound when he did that. Like an old lady coughing.

Dino

Dino's hands
were twice as big as anyone's.
Could bend
some of the iron parts
on school desks.
Laerson used to be able to pound anybody
til Dino came,
Laerson was mean
had been to the Home in Chehalis
twice.
When they fought it took
almost an hour,
after Dino pounded me
i ran
and cried.
After that he liked me
took me to his house
showed me his blade
sometimes i even called him
by his real name
Rienaldo.

The Retards

The house the Retards lived in was the worst one around. The porch had fallen off, and you had to jump about four feet from their front door. In back there were homemade steps. There was a lilac hedge around it, and the flowers always seemed to be brown and rotten, even after a rain in spring. That was because of the garbage in it: plain tin cans with government writing on them, old trikes, old clothes that people gave them sometimes. The Retards' mother collected junk. She wore dresses with dingy flowers on them, that came down to her ankles. There were several broken cars and an old housetrailer in her backyard. Her husband worked at picking and in the sawmills. Sometimes he wouldn't be around for a couple months. She ran a foster home for the State and usually had five or six kids. They were all dumb and one was retarded, so we called them the Retards. Laerson said that one of the older girls had let him feel her up because he let her ride his bike.

Laerson and Kendall
one time
in class
Sister asked Kendall
why he was holding his armpit.
Kendall said it itched.
At recess
Kendall went to the
boy's lav
and pulled
the pencil
out of his armpit
and wiped the blood off
and gave it back to Laerson
when he came in
told him
about this gearshift
knob
he'd kyped off a truck.

Dino and the Scoutmeeting
Dino's patrol
made their own badges
only ones in the scouttroop
you went
to a hockshop
downtown
and bought a patch
like for a jacket
a black silk cobra
with white plastic fangs
on a red silk sun
and
glued in a green glass jewel
for his eye.
Jack Riggins
was fat
and an undertaker
had a little eye that rolled
and made its point
when Denney Wites mother
killed both of them
in a car wreck

Jack Riggins
made us stand in the flowers
behind the coffins
with our scoutuniforms on
Jack Riggins got mad
when Dino and Laerson
started cutting farts.
But Jack was a fine guy
drove an El Camino
drank beer with the dads
that paid
for the uniforms
and the summer camp
so
when the dads decided
that Ritchie
(nigger!)
had been scoutmaster
too long
for his own good
Jack got the job
and made a speech
scouts means work
doing orders
clean neckerchiefs
just like in the army
anybody don't like it can leave.
Dino left.
Last summer
at the scoutcamp
Dino and i'd
found
a dead hawk
nailed to a fence
crucified
Dino'd laughed
but he ripped it down
and threw it under some brush
so
when Jack turned his back to me
to tell the other side of the room
how he was sorry
Dino felt that way
but he was the boss

and that's the way it was
i walked out
and the hotness
and the tightness
in my stomach
lasted almost all the way home.
If you turned the cobra
inside out
the glass jewel
would be his body
and the black thread
would be his eye.

The Home at Chehalis

The first time Laerson came back from the State Boy's Home at
Chehalis he talked about it. The second time he didn't. He talked to
Kendall mostly. While they were breaking windows or ski jogging cars.
He said you got put in a big room with about 20 other guys. Which was
alright until they turned the lights out at night. Then the other guys
came over and pounded the crap out of you all at once, because you
were new. That was only the first couple nights though. After that you
got a friend and they left you alone.

Sometimes when Laerson was smoking with us behind the school.
He'd talk about the really hard guys he knew up there. Guys who
knocked over gas stations with real guns. Guys who knew how to
break all kinds of coin boxes—how to hang paper. Sometimes at the
laundromat on the way to school Laerson would show us what he
knew. One time he said that the guys up at Chehalis were the real
dudes. That kids like Dino were nothing to them. But everybody knew
they were all a bunch of queers up at Chehalis anyway.

One time Kendall and Laerson took one of the Retard boys into
Laerson's garage. The Retard was crying when he came out. Laerson
told him to shut up about it or he'd kill him.

Rosalie Kendall

Rosalie Kendall
would have made a better boy
her voice
sounded like she should just be starting to shave
she had short hair
and no tits til much later
she could do anything we could
—like fight better than me
she got to be a girl

in the eighth grade
when Dino and Laerson
fucked her
one night
behind the laundromat
Dino said he used a penny balloon
Laerson got a real rubber from someplace
he saved it
and showed it around
next day at school
after that
Rosalie started to wear dresses
and quit smoking
and Dino even took her to a movie once
the only thing
she liked to do with us
after that
was kill cats.

The Chain Fight

We lived on the north side of downtown. The rich kids lived on the south side and went to public school. They called us greasers. We called them soshes. Sometimes we fought. After Dino came and after Laerson came back from Chehalis the second time it got worse. There wasn't anything to do that summer, so Dino finally told one of their main guys to meet us in the vacant lot by the tracks and to bring chains. The night of the fight i was the first one to Dino's house and we sat in his basement and smoked. Dino was talking big how he was going to pound the crap out of two or three of their guys that he knew. "C'mon," he told me, "even you can take one of these dips." His cigarette made orange shadows on his face as he rubbed my hair. After a while the rest showed up and we went to the lot. There was a wind that night, and you could smell the coal piled around the tracks on it, and the wetness from the river.

There were ten of them.

Laerson ran first. Then Lyonaise and Kendall, then Dino. i was on the ground getting pounded by one of them and didn't see what happened until they were circled around me and their guy on the ground.

They were pretty chicken really. All they did was cut my forehead and kick me in the crotch a few times. The chain i was supposed to be using was Dino's. They took it when they went away. Dino never asked me about it.

❋   ❋   ❋   ❋

The following selections, by William Gibson and Anne Moody, demonstrate different approaches to the questions of structure and development. Anne Moody's narrative is straightforwardly chronological, a movement toward a kind of knowledge that becomes more and more confusing for the young woman of the story. Gibson's piece is far more complicated, a superbly orchestrated movement back and forth in place and time, invoking suggestions of that timelessness when, according to myth, Eden existed. Gibson's narrative is long, but I felt I could not delete a word, so subtle and so vital are the links within the fabric of his prose. Nor could I find any way to cut Moody's essay, so important to her young narrator's final question are the episodes she explores so completely.

✽ THE PLOT WHERE THE GARDEN LIVED

William Gibson

The neighborhood to which we had gone back was a part of the city not easily come to, moated by the Harlem River along the west and unentered by the el to the east; between them it rose like some backward green garden of hills, original rocks, grass, trees, small cornfields. It was known as Highbridge, after a footbridge high over the sewery river. In its midst was a broad barren of hill, which went rollicking down to a tar road under a rank of old trees, and in their shade stood a handful of narrow wooden houses yoked together, three families high, each house with its grace note of picket fence. In one of these we had the middle floor of five rooms, and it was from this flat that my father was soon to claim at the city morgue the body of his other brother.

I had been born on this street six years before in a better tenement with steam heat, from which my mother's quest for justice had unhoused us; she was dissatisfied in the four rooms with the el, they shrank as my sister grew, and my parents were eager to move back to the old neighborhood into "any kind of a dump" with a fifth room. The postwar pinch in housing had brought my mother low; she was gratified that the landlord charged nothing to let her rehabilitate this flat with her own hands. She, my father, and his brother Will worked nights on it together, peeling off eight layers of wallpaper, scrubbing floors, patching plaster, painting; only the ceilings cowed them, so a cousin-in-law who was a fireman painted the five ceilings, earning twenty-five dollars and a familial acknowledgment from Will, who called him a "cheap sonofabitch."

Family and craft both mattered to my namesake uncle, who had little of one and a good deal of the other. Will was the child begotten a few nights before the death of his father, and not until weeks after the funeral did his mother, Katherine Gollan, widowed at twenty-three with two girls and her little hunchback, discover she was pregnant; though she swallowed irritants and jumped from the bureau to bring on a miscarriage, the boy clung to his twig of life, and would eat his portion. Helped by her mother, Katherine kept the family together, but the hunchback died, and the mother died, and Katherine then boarded the children out so she could work, the girls in one institution and Will in another. Her second marriage reunited them, and Pop Gibson taught the boy his trade of cratemaking. Will grew into an excellent cabinetmaker, and it was about the time he was reclaiming our flat that he studied with a craftsman's eye the disappearing feats of an international celebrity, Houdini, who allowed several carpenters to erect a massive box around him onstage and then materialized in the theatre aisle; Will wrote Houdini a letter promising to build him singlehandedly on any stage a box he would never get out of, meaning never, and understandably received no reply; it was a famous if somewhat unclimactic incident in the family. But the furniture Will fashioned as gifts for every relative was still in daily use half a century later, and the white table at which I ate ten thousand meals survived in my mother's kitchen after her death, unshakable as iron.

So in the new flat I think it was not his plastering but the boy that was imperfect: I soon had an excavation in a wall which was my "telephone" to a crony in the next house, and privacy was insured by a cushion. We had no other telephone, but in time several other holes, debouches for squads of cockroaches that my mother drove back with squirts of green powder and rats in for potluck whom my father pursued around the furniture with a broom, until he packed every crevice in the flat with broken glass; and one day my crony and I overturned all the rocks in the fields roundabout, loaded two cigarboxes to the brim with petite snakes, and stored them in the earthen cellar, whence they vanished, only to reappear peeking spitefully out of rotted floorboards and riding up and down in the dumbwaiter. "Snakes now," my mother said brightly, but nervous, "rats, roaches, snakes, my goodness, this house is a regular menagerie." It had no electricity, we read by gaslight, but its chief lack was heat; with the first huff of cold weather we set out the kerosene heaters to taint the air of the flat, sealed off its front half with newspaper wads around the doors, and saw we had enlarged our lot down to three rooms. In these we huddled each winter for the next three years, burgeoning into the front rooms every spring. It was low point in the climb to our middle-class lodestar, we never again lived in so primitive or infested a house, and thirty years later my mother still spoke of "the old days in Highbridge, when we were all so happy."

The garden was not of local earth, of course, the clemency of its climate was off the flesh of my parents; some loving touch of their courtship was upon them always. Afternoons when my father left the flat for work my mother would be half out the window to watch him walk down the road to the corner rocks, where before disappearing he waved back and cried, "I, L, Y!" and she waved out and cried to him, "I, L, Y!"—their unbreakable code for the three bedrock words in the language—and the climate between them filled the block. It was more than figurative. At Christmas my father would bring home a bonus, a sum varying with the bank's profits but usually a couple of hundred dollars; he spent it to the last penny on gifts, and a generation later I was reminded by a girl who "never forgot it, there wasn't a kid on the block who didn't get a present." Children not his would run to meet him when he came home from work. In the summer nights half the block would gather under our streetlight while upstairs my father, having pushed the piano to the bay window, banged out tune after tune for the roadful to sing and dance to. The neighborhood was itself a family, a skein of friendships that tied school, church, street games, holidays, into one knot of living.

It was here my mother first led me to school by the hand, two blocks around the hilltop and across a cobblestone street, where the iron-barred yard and graystone walls engulfed me instantly in a slumber; I see no detail of three years within it except a classroom storybook and a twisted ear, two hypnotizing pities. My parents lurk in both. The twisted ear was on a boy otherwise hale and hearty whom I saw only in the schoolyard, but at each encounter I delivered to him like an automaton whatever I had on me, pennies, candies, my lunch, a little ape of my father. The fat print of the storybook told the adventures of the gingerbread boy, run, run, you can't catch me, a gleeful rebel whose tragic end, to be eaten up, was inexorable once he had run away from his matronly maker, who wished only to eat him up. I had no outer eye then for the small tyrannies of my matron, and I did her proud in school; I was twice "skipped" into higher grades of slumber.

It was a public school because my mother was convinced, by ample evidence in the Dore family, that Catholic schooling resulted in illiteracy. On weekdays she ascribed this to "too much time spent on religion," though her folk were not notable for saintliness either; on the

Sabbath however she pointed me forth through hailstorms to nine
o'clock mass and Sundayschool. Here with gummy eye I sat in a
candle-lit dungeon through years of total gibberish. The priest
wandered before the altar muttering in Latin to himself, now and then
turning to lift a bored hand in blessing, and at long last ascended the
pulpit to announce in unmistakable English that my stingy offerings
had caused a shortage of coal in the church; two altarboys in skirts
rang bells, genuflected, and decanted wine for the priest, a pair of
angels, tarnished only by my knowing I would soon be shooting immies
with them and hearing of their struggle to free the decanter from the
priest's inebriated clutch; I sat, stood, knelt each time enough of the
congregation sat, stood, knelt, all of us erratic and at the mercy of some
confident soul in the front pew, until that late moment when it was not
quite sinful to leave—perceived by all with infallible unison—and
whatever prayers remained were drowned out by hundreds of hasty
feet, mine among the first. The interlude of fact in the daylight was
shortlived. A herd of children soon trudged up the cobbled alley that
led to the Sundayschool shed of corrugated tin that sat dark green on
the rocks above our backyard; inside a multitude of folding wooden
chairs was grouped for buttocks according to age, but even the youngest
now much the worse for wear, under the tutelage of unmarried ladies
of the parish with no duties in their kitchens; they drilled us for another
hour in our catechism, and rewarded the diligent with picturecards of
the saints in sepia. The hailstorms were real enough, cackling on the
tin overhead, and it seemed a fit setting for the odd chant with which
we concluded, "Hail, Mary, full of grapes"; it was the grapes that
seemed irrelevant.

Every seventh day my head was stuffed to the ears with this quaint
cosmology, and my mother was happy. Its reward was not in the
hereafter, but in the here: I was at one in tedium with the neighborhood
gang, all named Murphy and O'Brien, and every grown-up I knew on
our block I saw in the church, except my mother and father. Home at
last, I would find them still living in sin, with my sister at her doll
cut-outs, my father at ease behind the sports page in his pajama tops
and the pants he had worn downstairs to buy the newspaper, while my
mother in a crisp housedress darted about the kitchen in the midst of
the roast with four vegetables which was her Sunday act of devotion.
And instantly I was on my belly with the gaudy funny-pages, for my
delight in which that particular newspaper was chosen by my father,
and I would inveigle him into joining heads with me over the "red
magic"—tricks with matchsticks and cards and tumblers of water, all
printed in diabolic red—which never quite worked, but cleared my
brain of other devils until the next Sunday.

My father's indifference to the deity was a male prerogative in his family; the womenfolk were all strict churchgoers, but Pop Gibson had preferred saloons. And Will in his youth was "full of fun" with his pious sisters. Much embarrassed by their stepfather, they were dismayed one night to overhear Will stagger in muttering to himself, and spied upon him trying to hang his clothes on a non-existent nail in the wall; after he was snoring Milly stole in to smell his breath, but in the dark her nose inhaled only his whisper of glee, "Go to bed, you nut." Ada's churchgoing was a profession, which presently took her off to Africa as a missionary, and always she sat discoursing of the word in a rapture, with gestures; when Will put a book in her hand it would end unnoticed in her lap, and she preached on while Will in passing handed her a towel, a sewing basket, a pipe and pouch, a shoe, until coming out of her sermon with a broom in her glorifying hands, her broad lap brimful of junk, Ada cried in exasperation, "Will, you fool!" At his jauntiest twenty my father was the recipient of a Bible inscribed to *George Irv Gibson from Sister Ada,* not with love, only an admonitory *John* 3:16 if he wished not to perish, but he steered a steady course between church and saloon behind the Sunday sports page. The one time I provoked him to a statement of faith was on the question of where all our rats came from; I said they came "from the Protestant church" on the hill, and he said irritatedly, "What's Protestant got to do with it? I'm a Protestant myself!"

In fact the Catholic church was nearer, its green shed almost touchable from our kitchen window, and much in our family life was implicated with it. Once a year the tin hall blossomed into a weeklong bazaar, whereby the church augmented its coalpile. Here, at a booth with a variety of prizes and a wheel of chance, my sister fell in love with a china doll as big as herself; it was not for sale, but all that week my father led us up the path among the rocks to the shed, where night after night he played against the wheel for the doll and never won, dollar after dollar coming out of his pocket, the week dwindling, the coalpile growing, the doll paid for several times over out of my father's three-o'clock-in-the-morning labors; on the last night he put his money down until they dismantled the booth, and then sought out the priest, laid upon him the tale of his tot's love, waited while the arrangements committee dug among invoices for the cost of the doll, paid it, and brought the doll home to my sister. The day came when she dropped it, and half the night lay moaning—"Daddy: I broke my dollie, Daddy: I broke my dollie: Daddy, I broke my dollie"—while my parents in their bed listened in that grief for a child's grief which the child cannot suspect; love like water tumbles downhill between generations.

It was this tin hall which also bred the minstrel show, a yearly venture by parishioners, at which my father played piano for any neighbor with a voice or a delusion. When my sister was a plump four my parents rehearsed her in the words and gestures of a song about a little red schoolhouse, my mother attired her in a brief red frock and hair ribbon, and with my father at the piano our sprite topped the show; I had promised her a dime if she sang without mistakes, but on our arrival home I presented her with my entire bank, and was also applauded. My parents had made a point subtler than they knew, that generosity was the gayest conqueror of envy. And it was from this tin shed that I took home as a Sundayschool prize the first book I owned, its jacket overcome by a young daredevil in goggles riding a motorcycle straight at me; I thought it a dud of a prize, books having no value in our house, but I gave the motorcycle a try and on it rode into all literature, and out of my family's arms.

But most haunting was a summer afternoon, queer as a twisted mirror, in the parish house. It was a weekday tea of the Sundayschool teachers, with my mother and me prim in our good clothes, and hovering at a piano a favorite male countenance, my uncle Will, out of work for reasons of health and brought along because he had dropped in on us in the midst of a lonely walk. A fine tenor, he seated one of the teachers at the keyboard and entertained the tea party with a ballad, which all the ladies enjoyed, so he sang another, his eyes closed in his good face with its pitted chin and boyish spill of gray hair, and all praised his third song, so he sang a fifth, and the ladies were more than satisfied, so he sang a seventh, and his grim hand would not let the lady pianist escape, and they rollicked into a ninth, and the tea broke up in a scurry of purse gathering and bobs of terrified hats with Will chanting at the top of his voice and "talking queer"; and my mother, though mortified, waited to guide him home. This was the summer I first spied the snake in the garden—when on my belly beneath a communal oak I feasted upon a bared inch of knee, the property of an adolescent girl who sat above me in a nest of baby carriages and mothers, and I lay all the idle afternoon adoring it, bland under my mother's distrustful eye—and unknown to me its venom was then writhing in the limbs of my uncle, forking into his skull.

In happier days he and his wife would stand singing to my father's jangbangling piano, two of the dozens of relatives, friends, neighbors who "loved to visit," as one recalled, because my parents were "so cheerful." My mother had a gift for hospitality which was radiantly semisuicidal. She had entered upon marriage able to cook only toast—which went unnoticed for a while, since my father's invariable meal was a charred slab of round steak—and the first dinner they gave saw her in a panic in the kitchen, beset by mutinous potfuls of unknown matter, until one husband venturing in hastily donned an apron, asked only that she "keep the guys out of here," and subdued the entire meal for her. But panic was an old acquaintance, the motor of my mother's

soul, and her genius was for turning it into useful activity; she soon
became an extraordinary housekeeper, studying the households of my
father's sisters, and so outdoing them that he said teasingly he expected
her next to "wash the coal before using it." It was literally so that
visitors could have dined off her kitchen floor, and their numbers made
it imminent, anyone dropping in at once found himself captive at the
table to too much good food, and Sunday nights were festive with
gossip and music in a resurrection of Mary Dore's parties, with ten or
twelve in for an improvised supper. The wives helped clean up and put
away the dishes, each couple left the flat feeling like the choice light of
our world, and my mother and father sat in exhaustion, pondering how
to keep from being eaten out of house and home.

All dead, the faces of those grown-ups return to me quite unlike
ghosts, laughing and boisterous, full of news of my parents, but under
the fixative of time, deaf to my questions. The neighbors ambled in
from upstairs, downstairs, adjoining houses—lettercarrier, printer, el
gateman, each with his missus—into friendships that were joined for
life; their aging faces reappeared at my father's wake. Other friends
were inseparables out of his youth, my mock uncles and aunts, all with
their troubles. The most successful was a man who had entered the
postoffice with my father a dozen years earlier; authoritative as a
hammer, he rose in his official career to the postmastership of the city,
but his unofficial career was wandering indecisively with his household
from neighborhood to neighborhood, some thirty moves in a decade;
his wife was so sickly my mother would routinely visit her to do her
housework. Two of my father's buddies were musicmakers like him, a
pair of bricklayers, one a dapper johnny with fingers so nimble on the
keyboard my father acknowledged him as "a star," the other a giant
with a baritone roar that he loosed at the ceiling, one hand cupped for
amplification behind his ear; in picnic snapshots the three stand with
interlocked arms, their straw-hatted faces majestic with cigars,
captioned by my father as "we smoke but we don't buy," and again with
their young wives, six grinning heads together, "married but happy";
one buried his wife and took to drink, the other lost his life-savings in a
lapidary shop he bought into a day before the great depression. My
mother's own pal from schooldays—"my oldest and dearest friend,
Nellie"—was a placid spinster in an auburn wig worn since a childhood
fever, who dwelt at her elbow, loyalty incarnate, and outlived her like a
severed shadow. I brought her my questions, but in old age she had no
memories other than my mother's, eerily echoed in my mother's very
words, so vicarious her life; she summoned up the young Flo as
vaguely—though emphatically—"lovely, like she always was"; then I
asked if among the seventeen brothers she had any recollection of
Alfred, dead at twenty-six, dead for more than half a century, and she

said, "I was engaged to Alfred." Others from the old postoffice gang
straggled into the flat, on shore leave from the navy or back from
drifting in the west, wistful fellows who had also missed the turn into
family life. And we had a breadline of unmarried clerks from the bank,
the most memorable of them a piano-playing cockney, a tippler who
composed hundreds of popular songs, though not popular enough; he
spent much of his week at the heels of music publishers and
songpluggers, his life going to seed for the "break" that was never to
come, while over the years he appeared with each fresh manuscript to
sing it at our piano for his only public, my father, who admired him.
My mother admired his accent, she thought it English and refined. My
parents' capacity for friendliness was exhausted only by one avuncular
character who, together with his wife, was banished from our flat. A
curly-haired runt with a missing finger, he was an heirloom from my
father's bachelor days and that rarest of souls, a person my mother
disliked, though he was widely travelled, shipping out as a strikebreaker
to scattered cities, and clever, talking compensation boards out of sum
after sum for his finger lost in honest labor ten different times, and
devoted as a tick to my father, who in periods between strikes and
prestidigital amputations kept him in handouts; my mother tolerated
him for the sake of his wife, a fruity woman, childless, who was
genuinely fond of my sister and me and often cared for us when my
mother was sick in bed, at which times the household money, in saucer
and pennybank, showed an odd tendency to evaporate. But it was not
until the winter that Will's widow after one gathering reclaimed her
purse from the bedroom where coats were heaped and missed sixty
dollars out of it that heads were put together, and tales, of other
shortages graced by the presence of the couple. My father that week
led a few complainants to a shabby flat in Harlem, where his
unemployed pal, coming home warm at last in a new overcoat, and his
wife, pale in the cheer of a new floorlamp, said their purchases were
nobody's business; and my father invited them not to visit us again.
Thirty years later the woman, dying in a county hospital where a cousin
of ours worked, still asked how my sister and I had fared. Dead with
her, all dead, that phantasmagoria of grown-ups whom I could not wait
to be like, rich, wise, lucky, they seem so to me yet; they lie coffined in
possession of a treasure I can never come by, in their earfuls of the
small talk of my parents, and their eyefuls of those two ordinary faces
in the years when I was too busy with my tops and marbles to look at
them.

Yet even around our street games the figures of all the parents,
looked at or not, lent a benevolence to the neighborhood. Its heart was
the hill, and our games came up with its seasonal changes from
outbreak of weed grass to burial drifts of snow; but it was one

changeless flock of families upon the hillside in summer and winter, and time hardly moved, the children grew no older, the parents were as durable as the big trees of the street.

In spring, when we were digging dirtholes with our heels for immies—marbles, imitations—our fathers were in view digging with spades, until the field next to the end house was a crazy quilt of little vegetable gardens; here in the evenings the grown-ups would cluster in twos and threes, the mothers in aprons talking, the men on their knees in old pants coaxing along their tomatoes and stringbeans. In the untended afternoons these garden squares, staked and roped off, made ideal sites for their sons to stage mock prizefights in, a sport which resulted in some baffling failures. The true sport was baseball on the plateau of our hill, a trodden diamond in the rough, alive all day with a scatter of players, the gang I was in and the teen-age giants who chased us off and after supper the young fathers in collarless shirts, home from the bondage of offices. At a bottom corner of the hill was a dell with the communal oak, where in late spring the "strawberry festival" with its free ice cream was sponsored by our wardheelers for a pandemonium of neighborhood children and our mothers, who had recently received the vote; their purity was expected to redeem the world, a hope which was not quite realized, it succumbed under my eyes to free strawberry ice cream.

Summer opened officially the day my mother let me out barefoot—my soles gingerly among the fallen catkins of the poplars, so like the caterpillars of her terror—and was a long contentment of dirty toes. Out of our parents' eyes we cavorted on imaginary steeds over the hillside, vying in death leaps from its ledgerocks, elevation three feet; we bellycrawled to its far side in high weeds, to spy on the walrus-faced caretaker of the Protestant church, and sprang in the air with cries of "Kaiser Bill! Kaiser Bill!" until in frenzy he lumbered after us halfway down to our road; we scavenged for the stubs of holy candles dumped back of the true church, and bore them away to the hut of slats and cardboard which was our unfinished lifework; we watched the iceman stagger under his load into our cellars, and then clambered over his horse-drawn wagon to pilfer ice for sucking, cautious not to swallow the cloudy "pneumonia" it was made with; we trekked down to the sunken Harlem, and watched the older boys dive bare-assed among a drift of feces and mystifying number of white balloons, and charged up to the footbridge above, climbing outside its iron railings to execute skips which, elevation one hundred feet, would have given my mother a heart attack to witness; we knuckled our immies along miles of gutter, and gambled on curbstone and stoop with picturecards of leaping ballplayers and menacing prizefighters that came one with each

penny's worth of gum; and gum lacking, we waited by the fire barrel of
the roadworkers and chewed the ebony nuggets of tar leavings, which
were "good for" the teeth they did not pull out. And under my father's
eye I feasted on hot dogs and sodapop in the grandstand at the
big-league ballgames he took me to. Once he instructed me to "never
forget" I had seen a no-hitter, so I never did, and another time at the
players' gate I shook hands with a second baseman beloved by him for
sliding into base head first, a practice I thereafter followed, luckily
without serious brain damage, and one dawn we stood together in line
for half the day to get into a World Series game, which canonized me in
the gang.

But that was in autumn, when my mother had shod me again for
school. To the sill outside our kitchen window my father now wired the
orange crate that was to be our winter icebox, and my mother encased
it prettily in figured oilcloth, which would keep the snow out. All along
the block the front rooms were abandoned, and children slept in
kitchens, dining rooms, parental beds. Up from the cellar bin came our
kerosene heaters, stovepipes on squat legs, glowing in the dark with
sizzly pans of water set on top to replenish the oxygen; and when in the
morning I scrambled from the sofa I found my schoolclothes on a chair
at the lively coalstove in the kitchen, hung there by my mother to make
them inhabitable.

It was the season for fire. On the hill each night the kids with
permission to "sneak out" congregated at cookfires of scrap boards
borrowed from buildings in construction, and crammed a few brands
into tin cans punched with nail holes and reined with wire, to whip
them round and round as personal ovens. In them we roasted
mickies—potatoes, stolen on the gallop past the sidewalk displays of
grocery stores—until they were as inedible as charcoal, when we ate
them. Potato thieving was only an exercise of neighborly rights, but one
night I and another fire worshipper climbed a fence into a "dago"
contractor's backyard, toted bundle after bundle of his laths over the
hill, and cooked our two mickies in a ten-foot conflagration of the
neatest firewood ever. The irate contractor next day tracked our fathers
down; mine, the other being needier, paid for all the laths, and
punished me only by convoying me to apologize to the foreigner and
advising me next time to "use my head," at which I felt more stupid
than piratical. And each fall there was a towering bonfire which
belonged to the grown-ups. For a week the neighborhood contributed
to it, piling on the hillside the unwanted articles from every household,
bundles of newspapers, cartons and crates, seatless chairs, wobbly tables
and bureaus, disgraceful mattresses, until on Election Day night two or
three of the fathers climbing over the edifice sprinkled it with

kerosene; when they touched a match to it, every family on the block
was present to cheer this gotterdammerung in honor of our brand-new
leaders with the same old strawberry ice cream.

Winter came with the first snow in the night that stuck—the trolley
cars stuck on the bridges with it, and in one blizzard my father labored
home with me in his arms for better than an hour—until in the sunlit
morning the hill was transubstantiated. It was heaven, a whiteness of
packed slope trafficked by hollering boys, girls, young parents, and a
host of sleds tugged by figures uphill, tots on wee sleds inching down,
youngsters streaking past on slim racers, big sleds loaded with families
spilling into the road, and battles of snowballs flying between the igloo
forts. Here I charged with my racer in a bellywhopping delight while
below a moving-van rolled toward us, and I shot out into the white
road; a fingersnap earlier and my sled would have been under its
doublewheel, but I struck the tire and was thrown back into my life,
and tugged my sled uphill again into a company of merrymakers intact
in our magic skins.

And the earth emerged as always, into Easter; another year of
holidays was begun. Holidays were the hinges of the seasons, remote
from their origins, and Easter signified only the terminus of the
six-week lenten fast during which, for some adult kink of reason, we
had survived without candy. It collapsed in an orgy of jellybeans and
chocolate bunnies, hidden by my mother in odd nooks of the flat,
where after church my sister and I hunted them out; they baptized
gummily the pockets of our new "good" apparel, good for nothing but
to stand around in on our sidewalk all the holy afternoon like awkward
manikins in a storewindow, stuffed with jellybeans.

The holy day of summer was the Fourth of July. Miniature
explosives had been accumulating throughout the week in every
household, but none to equal ours; my father would bear home from a
store downtown some twenty or twenty-five dollars' worth, half a
week's pay, which bought a great deal of noise. It took me from
breakfast to dusk, and fifty trips up and down our stairs after fresh
pocketfuls, to exhaust this arsenal. There were baby firecrackers, wads
of a hundred fused together, which were detached and lit singly by me,
though in a royal gesture my father would set a wad off in one wild
spitting mass; and torpedoes, which exploded when hurled onto the
sidewalk, preferably at somebody's heel; and pellets called snakes,
which if touched with a match gave birth to a writhing gray serpent that
strove along the ground and perished at last in a crumble of ash; and
sulfuric patties which were ground underheel till they crackled away to
a smoking scab; and the larger firecrackers, the two-inchers I lit with
my stick of punk and fled from, and the six-inchers I was not allowed to
play with alone, but watched my father ignite under tin cans, which

flew up over our heads; and pinwheels, nailed to a tree in twilight to whiz their colorful life away, and sparklers, the dipped wires that hissed a thousand white sparks, desirable only after dark came to the hill; and into the night my father launched our showering rocket, price one dollar, the climax of the day. Only our sparklers then, glittering in all hands, were left to star the hillside with constellations of families, until at the last quarter-inch we slung them skywards to die out like falling souls.

Autumn came with two holidays, minor and major. Though decorum was her staff, my mother was a gay participant in disorder that was institutional, and on Halloween she prepared for my sister and me the socks full of flour with which the neighborhood smallfry belabored one another, until by suppertime we ourselves looked ready for the oven; and in the evening her laugh shrilled like a bird above the shenanigans in our flat, where neighbors and their offspring joined us with hands behind backs to tongue pennies out of her platterfuls of flour, spewing, and over a washtub we stalked with dribbling noses the apples my father had turned into treasure islands, tipsy with buried silver. And on Thanksgiving Day it was my mother who with a burnt bottlecork dirtied up my sister's face and mine, and sent us downstairs in rags. Our lives that day were inverted like the jackets we wore inside out, whites turned black, boys in their mothers' skirts and girls in their fathers' pants, cherubs in false-faces with depraved noses, and all, in a travesty of that poverty our families were two jumps ahead of, begging alms, swarming in threes and fours like a plague of mad dwarfs through the houses to every doorbell—"Anything for Thanksgiving, mister?"— and choiring in the courtyards until the coins in newspaper twists came plummeting through the clotheslines, and voices pled with us to sing no more. Late in the day my sister and I would straggle home, our pockets burdened down with the neighbors' fruit, candies, and loose change, to find my father at the door handing out to the neighbors' kids a countersupply of fruit, candies, and loose change, the flat made aromatic by the pipe of my uncle Will and genial with other relatives, my mother in command of too many cooks in the kitchen, and her silverware impeccably laid out for the turkey dinner all had come to share.

And at last the earth turned toward the holiday for which the year existed. The month that intervened was somehow lived through, with its character-building threats in Santa's name, its letters mailed confidently to the North Pole, its visits to the lanky geezers with slack beards in department stores and my suspicion that something was much amiss, perhaps with my mother's eyes; and one evening my father took us all to pick our Christmas tree out of the mass on a sidewalk rope at the grocery. I helped him lug it home, and it slept that

week on our fire escape. It was not set up till the night before
Christmas, after my sister and I were tucked in but hardly asleep, and
that Santa himself ornamented it was the first fact to crumble, for we
could hear our parents long at it in the frigid parlor, wrapped in their
overcoats, hissing instructions at each other. Quiet then took over the
darkened flat, and my sister and I lay awake with all our senses alert for
Santa's entry through our coalstove. It was an endless night, when
every rat scratching in the walls promised to be him, and we started up
fearful that we had missed him or he us, calling was it time to get up,
and our parents fumbling for the alarm clock groaned it was two
o'clock, go back to sleep, and so with every half-hour as the night wore
miserably on; and before dawn they staggered out of bed, my father to
light the gas mantles and plant a kerosene heater in the parlor, my
mother to bundle us up in sweaters and bathrobes and bring hot cocoa
to us all where, in a tiny cheap cold room, we sat again under the tree of
paradise. It was broken out in a winter bloom of jubilant fruits, angels,
birds, stars, and around the cotton snowscape under its branches all the
floor was a windfall of riches that dizzied our eyes, the big gifts
standing bare amid a mob of brilliant packages that we tore apart,
crawling and yelping and backtracking from tricycle to doll carriage,
from trains to scooter, from baseball mitt and toy house to sewing
machine and soldiers, to sled, to dolls, to trucks, to games, to books, all
of my father's bonus lavished in an unthinking lesson that, in its wink
of light, the time of man was a horn of plenty.

But in the new year the tree was stripped of its miracle. My father
forced it out the bay window to drop into the tiny snowyard, and I
dragged it across the road to the hill, where in time some hand set fire
to it; half out of the snow, its charred skeleton pointed to something.
High above it the misshapen snowman with coal hunks for eyes saw
nothing of his drippage in the raids of the sun, time and the hill melting
away. For now, like the clock that ticked in the night at my parents'
skulls, the charm was running down; in the new year my uncle Will lay
dying, and I was sprouting into myself.

It was evident the summer I pondered not only a girl's knee, but
two lessons about money. I sold a half-dollar's worth of my fireworks
to another boy for a penny or two, and sat on the curbstone happy with
myself as an enterprising fellow; my father said nothing, but when my
mother told me how I had hurt his feelings an utter desolation overtook
me, I was an eight-year-old miser, I had violated his work, his code, his
love, and that two-cent transaction would always seem one of the worst
mistakes of my life. My father observed that when he was dead they
might say he "spent a lot of money, but he had a heck of a good time,"
and the pursuit of this ideal took me into the second lesson. When his
own uncle slipped a dollar into my palm I treated myself to some

penny candy, and, with a vision of buying up the world, hid my
handful of change on the darksome sill of a window high in our hallway
which let neither light nor air into our bathroom; I had to leap to it
from the banister, it was out of reach of all normal life, but my mother
was led by her angel of cleanliness even to that altitude, with chair and
dustrag, to discover my crime; and my vision and coins ended up
permanently out of reach in my piggybank. The first lesson taught me
not to live for money, and the second to put it in a safer hiding-place.

The crime was secretiveness. It is the first evidence I see that I
was finding my mother's hand steely upon me; in my father's laxities of
live and let live the chores of disciplining us fell to her, though in any
circumstances she could not but invite them; matter not in her control
made her nervous. It was by reflex that, when my sister in her baby
carriage had bitten somebody's finger, my mother bit hers back. I came
home sooty-faced from a mickie roast on the hill and my father said I
"looked like a real boy," but my mother flew for the soap, her amulet
against the devil. One afternoon a pubescent boy from upstairs backed
me against our picket fence and fed me nonsense syllables; he said,
"Say shit," and I obliged, and he said, "Say fuck," and I obliged,
and he then stopped in to tell my mother the words his devout ear had
been shocked to hear me utter; that evening I came home for
supper and found my mouth being scrubbed out with soap instead,
frothing with human justice. Much of my mother's energy was devoted
to contesting nature on the battlefield of my scalp. My hair grew
forward, but she soused and combed it back in a pompadour which,
though it brought out a certain bulgy-browned idiocy in her child, she
was fond of and determined to "train it" to; for years her hands drove
at it pistonlike, with water, brushes, vaseline, combs, lard, nightcaps,
until when I was graduated from elementary school not a hair in that
pompadour was rebellious; she could not see my soul.

It sprouted, though the days in the garden were growing chill; it
was that autumn my father's brother disappeared. Much of Will—his
humor, his skill with his hands—had in any case been fading into
his past, and his renewal in the flesh of four children had disappeared
more than a decade before. The twins his wife conceived first had
died in the womb, and were removed surgically; in her second
pregnancy she bore a daughter who a few hours later died; the
following year she gave Will a son, christened after him, and in his
fifth autumn the boy died of a brain infection. It was not mischance,
the children could not survive the inheritance of the syphilis that
commingled in their parents' flesh.

When it was contracted, nobody knew. But Will was little more
than twenty when he began marriage, on his fourteen dollars a
week in that room furnished with hope, and before he was thirty the

four children were dead. Much later the surgeon who excised the twins
told Will's mother the disease was "of long standing" in the girl,
but misdoer or dupe, it hardly mattered, two creatures were caught in
the coils of the snake, and wherever his finger of lust had appointed him,
to whorehouse or peccant bride, Will held his tongue; though he and
his wife were to separate more than once, he "never said a word
against her." Will was something of the family intellectual, a voting
socialist, reading man, owner of a few operatic records. His tenor joined
with my father's piano at many a church or bank supper, and the
two half-brothers were "very close"; the married sisters had moved out
into New Jersey towns, taking the old folks along, and with only the
brothers left in the Bronx our flat often echoed with my uncle's,
voice. The lonely walk that brought him to our door the afternoon of
the parish-house tea was not unusual, after a quarrel at home, but his
breakup of the tea was the flare of disaster: the illness exploded in
him that summer.

Taken in by his mother and half-sister Ethel in Jersey, he found
work as a carpenter on rooftops. The sun beating on his head was "the
worst thing for him," he was moody and would not join company at
the table, but chiefly his head was "burning," and he bent by the
quarter-hour soaking it under the coldwater tap; when the fright of
an imminent "spell" was on him he would ask his mother to pray with
him, and they knelt in a locked bedroom together, my whitehaired
grandmother of sixty-five and her son with the boyish spill of gray hair,
praying for the help that could not stay the microscopic worms now
festive in the brain. Its signallings were awry, he "made the screens
wrong" that he planned as a gift for Ethel's new house, and they were
left unfinished. One autumnal morning he climbed down from his roof,
and at noon turned up at his flat in the Bronx looking for his wife,
who was not at home, and he distractedly made his way on foot north
to Mt. Vernon, where he arrived by evening at the house of an uncle
dishevelled and wild with inarticulate talk "about everybody, not
like him"; the next day he was taken in custody to the penal hospital in
the East River then known as Blackwells Island.

My father visiting him there would come home shaken with the
sight of his brother in a straitjacket. It was not long since I had bought
myself a pencilbox for school, my father with one glance at its
underside said, "There'll be nothing in this house made in Germany,"
and escorted me and it down to the store to get my money back; now
the death of a brother was in his nostrils again. He was ravaged by
the bruises he saw on Will's face, which the burly guards blamed on
falls, but in our kitchen my father demanded of my mother, "Why did
he flinch? He flinched from me!" All winter in the violent ward Will
lay in the bonds of worse than death, but before the first leaf of

spring he was unsouled of that straitjacket of flesh, his lungs filled with
pneumonia and he died. His body, delivered to the city morgue,
was spoken for by my father and removed to a mortuary in Harlem; in
a coffin it reposed in familiar clothes again and a new necktie of dark
blue with white dots, his favorite pattern; my father had hunted the city
for it and said to a sister, "I bought the tie, and I tried it on him."
The body was buried in a grave with the children, the one-day-old girl,
the five-year-old boy, the forty-two-year-old man.

So went out that light, unwanted in birth and in death, the boy
who never knew his father's face, grew in no garden, and for half
his years had lived with the taste of himself as his children's killer. His
sister Milly was haunted by one memory of him, peering from behind
a fence along the road on which she and Ada, eleven and nine,
trotted from school to lunch at the home where they were boarded out;
the fence was around the other institution that held Will, then four,
and each noontime without fail the diminutive boy was there, waiting
in silence, his face between the white slats, to see his sisters come
and go; that face through the fence peered after her for seventy-five
years.

In the summer after his death we moved out of the flat that his
hands had helped make livable. My mother's goiter again was
thickening in her throat, the doctor told my father she must have rest,
and the throngs of company that dropped in for a cheerful evening with
my parents drove us half into bankruptcy and altogether out of the
state; we followed the van filled with our furniture across the river into
Jersey. We were the last of the family to leave the Bronx, and though
we were to come back to it, my childhood was no longer there.

We could not find the garden again. In better neighborhoods our
life was enriched by radiators, electricity, radio, telephone, refrigerator,
car: but we had no hill. And of all the sounds in the world, none
was to fill any other room so plangently as the music I ignored in that
parlor, evenings, when I lay on the floor teaching my sister the rules of
parchesi, at which she cheated, while my mother in the scrollwork
chair with her mandolin and my father in his collarless shirt at
the piano, both playing, gaily sang out "their" song of first encounter,
"Oh by the Golden Gate, that's where I first met Kate, she stole
my heart away: on San Francisco, oh you Frisco, San Francisco Baaay—"
Even in manhood, when I stood again before the house and saw it
ugly, cramped, defeated, and the rollicking green country gone,
carted away with the poplars and the hill, and everything around me
bronxed over with cement sidewalks and brick apartment houses,
it could not touch my image of a half-wild garden in which I still spied
the bay-window house as it was, the bellybutton of a world to come,
and its tar road under a hanging mercy of trees, and its hill populous

with knots of kids and parents, seated, standing, in the calm of
the summer evenings: we were happy as the day was long.

That time, that neighborhood, thousands of miles ago and
thirty-odd years behind me, scattered with its folk, was to live only in
me, a green haven I could never find my way home to, until by the grace
which is in our bowels I crossed a threshold, in the night around me
all the house again was safe, and slept, and checking the beds of my
unwitting boys I perceived I was back in the garden.

✿ THEN WHAT WAS IT?

Anne Moody

Now that school was out and there was no one for us to stay with, we
would sit on the porch and rock in the rocking chair most of
the day. We were scared to go out and play because of the snakes.
Often as we sat on the porch we saw them coming up the hill from the
swamp. Sometimes they would just go to the other side of the swamp.
But other times they went under the house and we didn't see them
come out. When this happened, we wouldn't eat all day because we
were scared to go inside. The snakes often came into the house.
Once as I was putting wood in the stove for Mama, I almost put my
hands on one curled up under the wood. I never touched the woodpile
again.

One day we heard Mrs. Cook's dog barking down beside the
swamp at the base of the cornfield. We ran out to see what had
happened. When we got there, the dog was standing still with his tail
straight up in the air barking hysterically. There, lying beside a log,
was a big old snake with fishy scales all over his body. Adline, Junior, and
I stood there in a trance looking at it, too scared to move. We had
never seen one like this. It was so big it didn't even look like a snake. It
looked like it was big enough to swallow us whole. Finally the snake
slowly made its way back into the swamp, leaving a trail of mashed-down
grass behind it.

When Mama came home that evening from the café, we told her
all about the snake. At first, she didn't believe us, but we were
shaking so that she had us go out back and show her where we had
seen it. After she saw the place next to the log where it had been

SOURCE: Excerpted from *Coming of Age in Mississippi* by Anne Moody.
Copyright © 1968 by Anne Moody. Used with permission of The Dial Press.

lying and the trail it left going to the swamp, she went and got
Mr. Cook. For days Mr. Cook and some other men looked in the swamp
for that snake, but they never did find it. After that Mama was
scared for us to stay at home alone, and she began looking for a house
in town closer to where she worked. "Shit, snakes that damn big
might come up here and eat y'all up while I'm at work," she said.

In the meantime, she got our Uncle Ed, whom we liked so much,
to come over and look after us every day. Sometimes he would take
us hunting. Then we wouldn't have to sit on the porch and watch those
snakes in that boiling hot summer sun. Ed made us a "niggershooter"
each. This was a little slingshot made out of a piece of leather
connected to a forked stick by a thin slab of rubber. We would take
rocks and shoot them at birds and anything else we saw. Ed was
the only one who ever killed anything. He always carried salt and
matches in his pockets and whenever he'd kill a bird he'd pick and roast
it right there in the woods. Sometimes Ed took us fishing too. He
knew every creek in the whole area and we'd roam for miles. Whenever
we caught fish we'd scrape and cook them right on the bank of the
creek. On those days we didn't have to eat that hard cold pone of
bread Mama left for us.

Sometimes Ed would keep us in the woods all day, and we wouldn't
hunt birds or fish or anything. We just walked, listening to the birds
and watching the squirrels leap from tree to tree and the rabbits
jumping behind the little stumps. Ed had a way of making you feel
so much a part of everything about the woods. He used to point out
all the trees to us, telling us which was an oak, and which was a pine
and which bore fruit. He'd even give us quizzes to see if we could
remember one tree from another. I thought he was the smartest person
in the whole world.

One day Ed was late coming and we had resigned ourselves to spending
the whole day on the porch. We rocked for hours in the sun and
finally fell asleep. Eventually Ed came. He locked the house up
immediately and rushed us off the porch. He told us he was going to
surprise us. I thought we were going to a new creek or something so I
begged him to tell me. He saw that I was upset so finally he told me
that he was taking us home with him.

As we were walking down the rock road, it occurred to me that I
had never been home with Ed and I was dying to see where he lived. I
could only remember seeing Grandma Winnie once, when she came
to our house just after Junior was born. Mama never visited Grandma
because they didn't get along that well. Grandma had talked Mama
into marrying my Daddy when Mama wanted to marry someone

else. Now that Mama and Daddy had separated, she didn't want anything to do with Grandma, especially when she learned that her old boyfriend was married and living in Chicago.

Ed told us that he didn't live very far from us, but walking barefooted on the rock road in the boiling hot sun, I began to wonder how far was "not very far."

"Ed, how much more longer we gotta go? These rocks is burning my foots," I said.

"Ain't much further. Just right around that bend," Ed yelled back at me. "Why didn't you put them shoes on? I told you them rocks was hot." He waited on me now. "Oughter make you go all the way back to that house and put them shoes on. You gonna be laggin' behind comin' back and we ain't never gonna make it 'fore Toosweet get off o'work!"

"Mama told us we ain't supposed to wear our shoes out around the house. You know we ain't got but one pair and them my school shoes."

"Here it is, right here," Ed said at last. "Essie Mae, run up front and open that gate." By this time he was carrying Junior on his back and Adline half asleep on his hip.

I ran to the gate and opened it and rode on it as it swung open. We entered a green pasture with lots of cows.

"Is that where you stay?" I asked Ed as I pointed to an old wooden house on the side of a hill.

"Is any more houses down there?" Ed said, laughing at me. "See that pond over there, Essie Mae!" he called as I ran down the hill. "I'm gonna bring y'all fishing over here one day. Boy, they got some big fishes in there! You shoulda seen what Sam and Walter caught yesterday."

I glanced at the pond but ran right past it. I didn't have my mind on fishing at all. I was dying to see Grandma Winnie's house and Sam and Walter, Ed's younger brothers, and his sister Alberta whom I had never met. Ed had told me that George Lee was now living with his daddy and stepmother. I was glad because I didn't want to run into him there.

Alberta was standing in the yard at the side of the house feeding the big fire around the washpot with kindling. Two white boys about my size stood at her side. I looked around for Sam and Walter. But I didn't see them.

"Ed, what took you so long? I oughta made you tote that water fo' you left here," Alberta shouted at Ed as she turned and saw us.

"I had to tote Adline and Junior all the way here. You must think um superman or something," Ed answered angrily.

"I ain't asked you what you is! You just git that bucket and fill that rinse tub up fulla water!" Alberta shouted. "Sam, yo'n Essie Mae help Ed with that water. And, Walter, take Adline and Junior on that porch outta the way."

I stood dead in my tracks with my mouth wide open as the two white boys jumped when Alberta yelled Sam's and Walter's names. One boy ran to the wash bench against the house and got a bucket and the other picked up Junior, took Adline by the hand, and carried them on the porch.

"Essie Mae! Didn't I tell you to help Sam and Ed with that water?" Alberta yelled at me.

"Where is Sam and Walter?" I asked with my eyes focused on the white boy on the porch with Adline and Junior.

"Is you blind or somethin'? Get that bucket and help tote that water," Alberta yelled.

I turned my head to look for Ed. He was headed for the pond in front of the house with a bucket in his hand. "Ed!" I shouted, still in a state of shock. He turned and looked at me. I stood there looking from Ed to the white boys and back to Ed again, without saying anything. Ed opened his mouth to speak but no words came. A deep expression of hurt crossed his face. For a second he dropped his head to avoid my eyes. Then he walked toward me. He picked up another bucket and handed it to me. Then he took me by the hand and led me to the pond.

As we walked toward the pond, one of the white boys ran ahead of us. He climbed through the barbed-wire fence right below the levee of the pond. Then he turned and pushed the bottom strand of the wire down to the ground with his foot and held the middle strand up with his hands, so Ed and I could walk through. I began to pull back from Ed but he clutched my hand even harder and led me toward the fence. As we ducked under, I brushed against the white boy. Jerking back, I caught my hair in the barbed-wire overhead.

"Essie Mae, watch yo' head 'fore you git cut! Wait, wait, you got your hair caught," the white boy said as he quickly and gently untangled my hair from the wire. Then he picked up the bucket I had dropped and handed it to me. Ed didn't say one word as he stood beside the fence watching us.

The white boy caught me by the hand and attempted to pull me up the levee of the pond. I pulled back. Still holding my hand, he stopped and stared at me puzzled. "Come on, Essie Mae!" yelled Ed, giving me an "it's O.K., stupid" look as he ran up the levee past us. Then the white boy and I followed Ed up the hill holding hands.

As we toted water from the pond, I kept watching the white boys and listening to Alberta and Ed call them Sam and Walter. I noticed that they treated them just like they treated me, and the white boy called Sam was nice to me just like Ed. He kept telling me about

the fish he and Walter had caught and that I should come and fish with
them sometimes.

After we finished toting the water, we went on the porch where
Adline, Junior, and Walter sat. Adline had a funny look on her
face. I could tell that she was thinking about Sam and Walter too.
Before the evening was over, I finally realized that the two boys actually
were Ed's brothers. But how Ed got two white brothers worried me.

On our way back home, Ed carried us through the woods. As we
walked, he talked and talked about the birds, the trees, and
everything else he could think of, without letting me say a word. I
knew he didn't want to talk about Sam and Walter, so I didn't
say anything. I just walked and listened.

I thought about Sam and Walter so much that night, it gave me a
headache. Then I finally asked Mama:

"Mama, them two boys over at Winnie's. Ed say they is his
brothers. Is they your brothers?"

"What boys?" Mama asked.

"Over at Winnie's. They got two boys living with her about my
size and they is the same color as Miss Cook. . . ."

"What did y'all do over at Winnie's today? Was Winnie home?"
Mama asked as if she hadn't heard me.

"No, she was at work. Wasn't nobody there but Alberta and
those two boys. . . ."

"What was Alberta doing?" Mama asked.

"She was washing and we toted water from the pond for her. Them
boys is some nice and they say they is kin to us. Ain't they your
brothers, Mama?"

"Look, don't you be so stupid! If they's Winnie's children and
I'm Winnie's too, don't that make us sisters and brothers?" Mama
shouted at me.

"But how come they look like Miss Cook and Winnie ain't that
color and Alberta ain't that color and you . . ."

" 'Cause us daddy ain't that color! Now you shut up! Why you
gotta know so much all the time? I told Ed not to take y'all to
Winnie's," she shouted.

Mama was so mad that I was scared if I asked her anything else she
might hit me, so I shut up. But she hadn't nearly satisfied my
curiosity at all.

While Mama was working at the café in town, she began to get fat.
She often told us how much she could eat while she was working. So I
didn't think anything of her slowly growing "little pot." But one day
after taking a good look, I noticed it wasn't a little pot any more.
And I knew she was going to have a baby. She cried just about every

night, then she would get up sick every morning. She didn't stop working until a week before the baby was born, and she was out of work only three weeks. She went right back to the café.

Mama called the baby James. His daddy was a soldier. One day the soldier and his mother came to get him. They were real yellow people. The only Negro near their color I had ever seen was Florence, the lady my daddy was now living with. The soldier's mother was a stout lady with long thin straight black hair and very thin lips. She looked like a slightly tanned white woman. Mama called her "Miss Pearl." All the time they were in our house, Mama acted as though she was scared of them. She smiled a couple of times when they made general comments about the baby. But I could tell she didn't mean it.

Just before the soldier and Miss Pearl left, Miss Pearl turned to Mama and said, "You can't work and feed them other children and keep this baby too." I guess Mama did want to keep the little boy. She looked so sad I thought she was going to cry, but she didn't say anything. Miss Pearl must have seen how Mama looked too. "You can stop in to see the baby when you are in town sometimes," she said. Then she and the soldier took him and drove away in their car. Mama cried all night. And she kept saying bad things about some Raymond. I figured that was the name of the soldier who gave her the baby.

At the end of that summer Mama found it necessary for us to move into town, in Centreville, where she worked. This time we moved into a two-room house that was twice the size of the other one. It was next to where a very poor white family lived in a large green frame house. It was also located on one of the main roads branching off Highway 24 running into Centreville. We were now a little less than a mile from the school that I was to attend, which was on the same road as our house. Here we had a sidewalk for the first time. It extended from town all the way to school where it ended. I was glad we lived on the sidewalk side of the road. Between the sidewalk and our house the top soil was sand about two feet deep. We were the only ones with clean white sand in our yard and it seemed beautiful and special. There was even more sand for us to play in in a large vacant lot on the other side of our house. The white people living next to us only had green grass in their yard just like everybody else.

A few weeks after we moved there, I was in school again. I was now six years old and in the second grade. At first, it was like being in heaven to have less than a mile to walk to school. And having a sidewalk from our house all the way there made things even better.

I was going to Willis High, the only Negro school in Centreville. It was named for Mr. C. H. Willis, its principal and founder, and had only been expanded into a high school the year before I started there. Before Mr. Willis came to town, the eighth grade had been the limit of schooling for Negro children in Centreville.

For the first month that I was in school a Negro family across the street kept Adline and Junior. But after that Mama had them stay at home alone and, every hour or so until I came home, the lady across the street would come down and look in on them. One day when I came home from school, Adline and Junior were naked playing in the sand in front of our house. All the children who lived in town used that sidewalk that passed our house. When they saw Adline and Junior sitting in the sand naked they started laughing and making fun of them. I was ashamed to go in the house or recognize Adline and Junior as my little sister and brother. I had never felt that way before. I got mad at Mama because she had to work and couldn't take care of Adline and Junior herself. Every day after that I hated the sand in front of the house.

Before school was out we moved again and I was glad. It seemed as though we were always moving. Every time it was to a house on some white man's place and every time it was a room and a kitchen. The new place was much smaller than the last one, but it was nicer. Here we had a large pasture to play in that was dry, flat, and always closely cropped because of the cattle. Mama still worked at the café. But now she had someone to keep Adline and Junior until I came home from school.

One day shortly after Christmas, Junior set the house on fire. He was playing in the front room. We had a small round tin heater in there and Junior raked red-hot coals out of it onto the floor and pushed them against the wall. I was washing dishes in the kitchen when I looked up and saw flames leaping toward the ceiling. I ran to get Junior. The house had loose newspaper tacked to the walls and was built out of old dry lumber. It was burning fast.

After I had carried Junior outside, I took him and Adline up on a hill a little distance away. The whole house was blazing now. I stood there with Junior on my hip and holding Adline by the hand and suddenly I thought about the new clothes Mama had bought us for Christmas. These were the first she had ever bought us. All our other clothes had been given to us. I had to get them. I left Adline and Junior on the hill and ran back to the house. I opened the kitchen door and was about to crawl into the flames and smoke when a neighbor grabbed me and jerked me out. Just as she pulled me away, the roof fell in. I stood there beside her with tears running down my

face and watched the house burn to the ground. All our new
Christmas clothes were gone, burned to ashes.

We had only lived there for a few months and now we moved
again to another two-room house off a long rock road. This time Mama
quit the job at the café to do domestic work for a white family. We
lived in their maid's quarters. Since Mama made only five dollars
a week, the white woman she worked for let us live in the house free.
Mama's job was now close to home and she could watch Adline and
Junior herself.

Sometimes Mama would bring us the white family's leftovers. It
was the best food I had ever eaten. That was when I discovered
that white folks ate different from us. They had all kinds of different
food with meat and all. We always had just beans and bread. One
Saturday the white lady let Mama bring us to her house. We sat on
the back porch until the white family finished eating. Then Mama
brought us in the house and sat us at the table and we finished up the
food. It was the first time I had seen the inside of a white family's
kitchen. That kitchen was pretty, all white and shiny. Mama had
cooked that food we were eating too. "If Mama only had a kitchen like
this of her own," I thought, "she would cook better food for us."

Mama was still seeing Raymond, the soldier she had the baby for. Now
we were living right up the road, about a mile from Miss Pearl.
Raymond started coming to our house every weekend. Often he would
bring us candy or something to eat when he came. Some Sundays,
Mama would take us out to his house to see the baby, James, who was
now two years old and looked a lot like his daddy. Mama seemed
to like the baby very much. But she was always so uncomfortable
around Miss Pearl and the rest of Raymond's people. They didn't like
Mama at all. Sometimes when Mama was there she looked as if she
would cry any minute. After we had come home from their place, she
would cry and fuss all evening. She would say things like, "They
can't keep me from seeing my baby. They must be crazy. If I can't go
see him there I'll bring him home." But she only said those things. She
knew she couldn't possibly take the baby home and work and take
care of the four of us. Once when we went out there to see the baby,
he was filthy from head to toe. Mama gave him a bath and washed all
of his clothes. Then every Sunday after that Mama would go there
just to wash his clothes and bathe him.

Raymond was going with a yellow woman at the same time he was
going with Mama. All of his people wanted him to marry her. They
didn't want him to marry Mama, who wasn't yellow and who was stuck
with the three of us. Things began to get so tense when we would
go to see the baby that we'd only stay long enough for Mama to give

him a bath. Then one day Raymond went back to the service and
that ended some of the tension. But Mama got scared to go to Miss
Pearl's without Raymond there, so she stopped going and we didn't
see the baby for a long time.

That white lady Mama was working for worked her so hard that she
always came home griping about backaches. Every night she'd
have to put a red rubber bottle filled with hot water under her back.
It got so bad that she finally quit. The white lady was so mad she
couldn't get Mama to stay that the next day she told Mama to leave
to make room for the new maid.

This time we moved two miles up the same road. Mama had
another domestic job. Now she worked from breakfast to supper and
still made five dollars a week. But these people didn't work Mama
too hard and she wasn't as tired as before when she came home. The
people she worked for were nice to us. Mrs. Johnson was a schoolteacher.
Mr. Johnson was a rancher who bought and sold cattle. Mr.
Johnson's mother, an old lady named Miss Ola, lived with them.

Our house, which was separated from the Johnsons' by a field of
clover, was the best two-room house we had been in yet. It was
made out of big new planks and it even had a new toilet. We were
also once again on paved streets. We just did make those paved streets,
though. A few yards past the Johnsons' house was the beginning of
the old rock road we had just moved off.

We were the only Negroes in that section, which seemed like
some sort of honor. All the whites living around there were well-to-do.
They ranged from schoolteachers to doctors and prosperous
businessmen. The white family living across the street from us owned
a funeral home and the only furniture store in Centreville. They had
two children, a boy and a girl. There was another white family living
about a quarter of a mile in back of the Johnsons who also had a
boy and a girl. The two white girls were about my age and the boys a
bit younger. They often rode their bikes or skated down the little
hill just in front of our house. Adline, Junior and I would sit and
watch them. How we wished Mama could buy us a bike or even
a pair of skates to share.

There was a wide trench running from the street alongside our
house. It separated our house and the Johnsons' place from a big
two-story house up on the hill. A big pecan tree grew on our side of the
trench, and we made our playhouse under it so we could sit in the
trench and watch those white children without their knowing we were
actually out there staring at them. Our playhouse consisted of two
apple crates and a tin can that we sat on.

One day when the white children were riding up and down the street on their bikes, we were sitting on the apple crates making Indian noises and beating the tin can with sticks. We sounded so much like Indians that they came over to ask if that was what we were. This was the beginning of our friendship. We taught them how to make sounds and dance like Indians and they showed us how to ride their bikes and skate. Actually, I was the only one who learned. Adline and Junior were too small and too scared, although they got a kick out of watching us. I was seven, Adline five, and Junior three, and this was the first time we had ever had other children to play with. Sometimes, they would take us over to their playhouse. Katie and Bill, the children of the whites that owned the furniture store, had a model playhouse at the side of their parents' house. That little house was just like the big house, painted snow white on the outside, with real furniture in it. I envied their playhouse more than I did their bikes and skates. Here they were playing in a house that was nicer than any house I could have dreamed of living in. They had all this to offer me and I had nothing to offer them but the field of clover in summer and the apple crates under the pecan tree.

The Christmas after we moved there, I thought sure Mama would get us some skates. But she didn't. We didn't get anything but a couple of apples and oranges. I cried a week for those skates, I remember.

Every Saturday evening Mama would take us to the movies. The Negroes sat upstairs in the balcony and the whites sat downstairs. One Saturday we arrived at the movies at the same time as the white children. When we saw each other, we ran and met. Katie walked straight into the downstairs lobby and Adline, Junior, and I followed. Mama was talking to one of the white women and didn't notice that we had walked into the white lobby. I think she thought we were at the side entrance we had always used which led to the balcony. We were standing in the white lobby with our friends, when Mama came in and saw us. "C'mon! C'mon!" she yelled, pushing Adline's face on into the door. "Essie Mae, um gonna try my best to kill you when I get you home. I told you 'bout running up in these stores and things like you own 'em!" she shouted, dragging me through the door. When we got outside, we stood there crying, and we could hear the white children crying inside the white lobby. After that, Mama didn't even let us stay at the movies. She carried us right home.

All the way back to our house, Mama kept telling us that we couldn't sit downstairs, we couldn't do this or that with white children. Up until that time I had never really thought about it. After all, we were playing together. I knew that we were going to separate schools and all, but I never knew why.

After the movie incident, the white children stopped playing in front of our house. For about two weeks we didn't see them at all. Then one day they were there again and we started playing. But things were not the same. I had never really thought of them as white before. Now all of a sudden they were white, and their whiteness made them better than me. I now realized that not only were they better than me because they were white, but everything they owned and everything connected with them was better than what was available to me. I hadn't realized before that downstairs in the movies was any better than upstairs. But now I saw that it was. Their whiteness provided them with a pass to downstairs in that nice section and my blackness sent me to the balcony.

Now that I was thinking about it, their schools, homes, and streets were better than mine. They had a large red brick school with nice sidewalks connecting the buildings. Their homes were large and beautiful with indoor toilets and every other convenience that I knew of at the time. Every house I had ever lived in was a one- or two-room shack with an outdoor toilet. It really bothered me that they had all these nice things and we had nothing. "There is a secret to it besides being white," I thought. Then my mind got all wrapped up in trying to uncover that secret.

One day when we were all playing in our playhouse in the ditch under the pecan tree, I got a crazy idea. I thought the secret was their "privates." I had seen everything they had but their privates, and it wasn't any different than mine. So I made up a game called "The Doctor." I had never been to a doctor myself. However, Mama had told us that a doctor was the only person that could look at children's naked bodies besides their parents. Then I remembered the time my Grandma Winnie was sick. When I asked her what the doctor had done to her she said, "He examined me." Then I asked her about "examined" and she told me he looked at her teeth, in her ears, checked her heart, blood and privates. Now I was going to be the doctor. I had all of them, Katie, Bill, Sandra, and Paul plus Adline and Junior take off their clothes and stand in line as I sat on one of the apple crates and examined them. I looked in their mouths and ears, put my ear to their hearts to listen for their heartbeats. Then I had them lie down on the leaves and I looked at their privates. I examined each of them about three times, but I didn't see any differences. I still hadn't found that secret.

That night when I was taking my bath, soaping myself all over, I thought about it again. I remembered the day I had seen my two uncles Sam and Walter. They were just as white as Katie then. But Grandma Winnie was darker than Mama, so how could Sam and Walter be white? I must have been thinking about it for a long

Structure and Development   155

time because Mama finally called out, "Essie Mae! Stop using up all
that soap! And hurry up so Adline and Junior can bathe 'fore that water
gits cold."

"Mama," I said, "why ain't Sam and Walter white?"

" 'Cause they mama ain't white," she answered.

"But you say a long time ago they daddy is white."

"If the daddy is white and the mama is colored, then that don't
make the children white."

"But they got the same hair and color like Bill and Katie them
got," I said.

"That still don't make them white! Now git out of that tub!" she
snapped.

Every time I tried to talk to Mama about white people she got mad.
Now I was more confused than before. If it wasn't the straight hair
and the white skin that made you white, then what was it?

✻   ✻   ✻   ✻

SUMMARY

Structure involves the way a writer chooses to shape his materials. He
may stay with a chronological sequence, which, like most human experiences, finds its beginning, middle, and end within the movement of
time. Even so, the writer cannot merely.tell what happened next. He
must shape his narrative to project experience to the senses and emotions of his reader. He may, then, realign the actual time sequence for
greater narrative effect, pausing just before a crucial moment to fill in
background and build suspense, as demonstrated in "Whale Hunt."
A writer is not bound by any strict rules of structure and form. Many
modern poets, dramatists, and writers of fiction, in fact, consciously defy
traditional conventions, as writers have done throughout the history of
literature. Such breaking away from inherited forms can succeed, however, only if the writer knows those forms. This is also true of music
and painting. The most successful revolutionaries in the realm of the
imagination are usually the ones with the greatest mastery of the rules
against which they rebel. The suggestions made in this chapter on
structure are quite traditional, but they emerge from a conviction that
they must be mastered before they can be successfully discarded.

Development involves the fullest possible exploration of those
elements the writer discovers in the experience he will shape into a
structure. Development is akin to the use of supporting evidence to
validate a general statement. Too many beginning writers muffle the
details of experience in an unsupported generalization. It happens to
be a beautiful day as I write this, in early May in Maine. But that

beauty is composed of a cool edge to the air, the shimmer of buds around the oak, maple, and elms, and a few fair-weather clouds that remind me of the five days of rain we have just experienced. Part of the beauty of the day lies in its contrast to the damp misery of the weekend just past. The "evidence" of imaginative writing is the sensory appeal that goes beyond mere information. "It was an old house" does not provide the reader with the sense of lived experience. "Whenever anyone even so much as walked extra heavily, the floor would sag and rise under the strain and relaxation which are produced by walking" does.

The intimate relationship between structure and development can be glimpsed by comparing "Gurry Bot 'Er" and "Whale Hunt." The former begins with a single fish, the latter with a boy on the mast. Each moves from that specific object to a description of the total experience responsible for the presence of the fish under the lilac bush and the boy on the masthead, a description of an alewife run and a whale hunt. Then each narrator returns to the point of its beginning, Rick Spear to that solitary fish, Mike Leonard to himself as crew member. Each narrative, after its careful development of the details of its experience, returns to touch briefly on the single entity with which it began. Each entity becomes, then, the focal point of the narrative, and the return to it provides the reader with a satisfying sense of completeness, both of structure and of development.

EXERCISE

Look again at what you have written. What is your structure? Can you discern a beginning, a middle, and an end to your narrative? Can the events you treat be reordered for greater effect? Try switching the paragraphs around remembering, that new transitions between paragraphs will have to be made. You may decide, of course, that your original structure is the most valid for your material.

Are there places in your narrative that can be more completely developed, where you shroud descriptive detail beneath a blanket of generalization (e.g., "It was a beautiful day," "I gradually became frightened," "He was very angry," "It was an ugly house")? If so, move into the details and images of the experience. Develop the experience. Make it *our* experience as well as yours.

Reread the professional pieces at the ends of previous chapters in the context of this chapter's discussion of structure and development.

FIVE

Meaning
and
Metaphor

A narrative of initiation not only conveys its own deeper meaning by recreating a pattern basic to all human experience, but it also creates an immediate link between the character in the story and the reader. The reader, too, has struggled through his own initiations. They may have been very different than those he reads about, but the pattern built into him allows him to respond to a narrative which pursues that pattern, even though it be with radically different events and with a different time, place, or social climate. His response to the *metaphor* of growing up, the implied comparison between one life and another, is similar to his response to the images the writer uses. His response to imagery is primarily sensual. His response to the shared elements of human experience, that profound metaphor also known as *archetype*, is emotional and psychological, deeper than the senses. The primary means of activating that response, of course, is through the senses. All the archetypes in the world are irrelevant unless a reader responds on the level of his senses.

Metaphor works in two ways: (1) The writer, consciously or unconsciously, compares his experience to a configuration of experience common to all people. (2) The reader, perhaps unconsciously, feels the strength of the comparison between the events of the narrative and his own similar pattern of experience. All of us, for example, have at some time felt a security that we no longer know, whether we agree with Freud that the feeling is a product of the comfort and ease of the womb and early childhood; with Jung and the cultural anthropologists that we retain a racial memory of that time when our ancestors lived as part of, rather than apart from, nature; or with the Bible story of Adam and Eve in Eden. Thus, when Joe Dane uses a "sacred lawn" as a place of security and innocence violated by arrogance and misunderstanding, he uses an explicit metaphor of Eden. We, too, have had such an experience in the past, no matter what its specific details. We can guess, perhaps, why Joe Dane calls the owner of the lawn "The Man" and not, say, Mr. Simmons.

The following story was written by a college freshman.

❄ THE DRIFTWOOD STICK

John M. MacKenzie

It wasn't hard to see why he was disgusted. When it's summer vacation no boy likes to spend the morning cleaning up the mess left over from the party his parents have thrown the night before. Even though he had almost finished, the cottage still reeked of spilled beer and stale cigarettes, and he could hardly wait to get out and go fishing.

Cleaning up had taken about two and a half hours, and now all he had to do was empty the garbage. He didn't mind this part of the job, though. For as long as his family had been coming down to Maine in the summer, it had always been his job to empty the garbage every morning in front of the cottage. The cottage itself jutted out over the edge of a small hill which dropped steeply into the ocean. The boy always made a game of how fast he could run down to the waterfront without spilling any of the garbage. With no brothers or sisters, he made a solitary game out of almost everything he did.

Separating the hill and the water was a chunk of rocky Maine Coast from which the boy always emptied the garbage. At high tide the Coast is a powerful, almost frightening sight. The water comes up high on the rocks, and as one stands just above the water, he cannot be sure that the next wave will not engulf him. Yet the boy was glad that it was not high tide that morning because he had a game to play—a game more interesting to the twelve year old than any aspect of natural beauty.

The low tide exposed a large patch of seaweed where the boy normally threw the garbage. Just to his left as he faced the water, a six-inch sewage pipe ran down from the cottage and ended about two feet above the lowest level of rock, now exposed and overgrown with thick, ugly seaweed. Every time someone flushed the toilet in the cottage, the waste gushed out the end of the pipe into a shallow yellow pool filled with dead snails and live starfish. To the boy's right and slightly above him sat the rotted remains of a dock that had been taken out of the water for winter many years ago and never used since. Now it lay high on the rocks; unpainted, useless, spotted with the white droppings of seagulls. As he walked towards his dumping spot, the boy had to be careful to avoid the pieces of broken glass scattered among the rocks.

After throwing out the garbage, he stepped back from the edge of the seaweed for about two minutes. Then, from among the rocks, he chose a small stone and stood above the dumping area now being ravaged by black and white seagulls, heeding the yodeling call of their leader. He cocked his arm and flung the rock into the swarm of gulls. No matter how hard the boy threw the rock, the gulls always felt it coming and scattered safely in all directions. As usual, this throw found the only hole in the target and buried itself in the seaweed with a muffled thud. He had come to expect this result and simply stepped back, waiting for the gulls to return.

After a few minutes he again stood above the gulls with another rock. But just as he was about to throw into the pack of gulls, he spotted an old piece of driftwood wedged between the rocks beneath him. He pulled the stick from the rocks. About twenty feet below him, the gulls, obviously unconcerned with the boy's presence, dug, fought, and scratched for every orange peel, bread crust, or clam shell that could be stolen from their fellow scavengers. As he drew his arm back, most of the gulls scrambled away, leaving only two birds fighting over a piece of pork chop from last night's dinner. He spotted this target and flung the stick. Just as one of the birds had pulled the prize from his opponent, the stick plummeted into its full white breast.

At the moment of contact, the gull shrieked a hollow "caw." With its wings fluttering unevenly, the bird landed in the water with an uncoordinated splash. For several minutes it floated on its side with one wing extended out full into the water and the other tucked neatly at its side. At short intervals the gull stretched a paddlelike foot away from his body and strained to pull the water back under him. His efforts, however, failed to counteract the push of the outgoing tide, and he began to groan in a way that sounded strangely human to the boy.

The boy edged his way down to the lowest level of seaweed and extended his arm over the water to the seagull, now only about five feet from the shore. Feeling as helpless as the gull, the boy searched for some way to help the bird—how, he did not know; but there was always a chance. He felt only a need to aid the bird, now motionless and drifting slowly away from him. He looked around for something to help him reach the bird, but could find only his driftwood weapon, lying in the seaweed. With one hand he reached the stick out towards the bobbing gull, and with the other he grabbed a clump of seaweed behind him to keep himself from falling forward.

"Come here, come on," he pleaded aloud to the bird, "we can make it." It did not help. The bird tried as hard as possible to swim away from the stick. "Don't be afraid, come here. We can make it." In spite of the boy's pleading, the frightened bird merely dragged himself towards deeper water. The boy saw he had little chance to help the bird. Each new wave washed completely over the gull, which bobbed to the surface only after the wave passed.

The youth climbed back up off the seaweed in search of a long stick. As he scrambled from rock to rock during his search, he stopped several times and looked up at his own cottage and those around it to make sure no one was watching. When he could nòt find a stick of proper length he headed back across the rocks and over the sewage pipes to the spot from which he had thrown the garbage . . . and the stick.

For several minutes the bird made a final effort to save itself in the water—knowing that it could not go onto the land. In his hand the boy still held the stick. Another wave covered the bird and the boy stared at the spot where it should have reappeared. But the bird was gone. The boy continued staring at the spot for many minutes. Finally, he hurled the stick as far out into the empty water as he could. Before the stick landed, the young man turned away from the water, scooped up the empty garbage pails and scrambled up the hill towards the safety of the cottage.

❊   ❊   ❊   ❊

John MacKenzie's story invokes a neat irony of situation. A boy about his chores suddenly becomes a murderer. His efforts to rectify his deed only confirm his crime, and he moves back up the hill a different person, burdened with a knowledge and a guilt he did not have before. He has made the transition from the singer of a song of innocence to the more somber songs of experience. His experience of guilt is one we have all shared, in different ways, of course, whether in kicking an animal, slapping a child, or in some other way denying our own part in the "one life" Coleridge suggests we all share. While the action of the young narrator seems to resemble that of Coleridge's ancient mariner, the mariner *means* to kill that albatross, whatever his motivation. The boy did not mean to kill the seagull. The driftwood stick becomes a metaphor for the seemingly harmless object that our own impulses translate into a killer, the atom which is morally neutral until man releases its power and chooses to use that power to destroy. John MacKenzie writes a story of something that happened to him, but, by extension, it has happened to all of us. The boy anticipates fishing. Instead, his plans are interrupted by an emergency that erases all previous intentions.

The narrative is enhanced by imagery that operates, finally, to do more than merely activate our senses. Only a writer who had observed coastal Maine and the activities of seagulls could provide the setting within which the event occurs and upon which it depends. The unpleasantness of the cottage's interior is echoed—although the narrator scarcely notices it—by the sewerlike area near the ocean, which, in turn, attracts the seagulls. The stick with which the boy strikes the bird becomes, ironically, the instrument whereby the boy attempts to save the bird. Finally, the boy flees the scene of his murder to the "safety" of the cottage. We know, however, that the cottage, described as reeking at the outset, will contain the guilt the now "young man" carries back with him from the shore. The story begins with his innocence contrasted to the corruption of the adult world. By the end of the story, he shares that corruption.

Metaphor in its broadest sense becomes a bridge between lives, specifically between a writer's experiences and a reader's emotions. In a more restrictive but equally vital context, metaphor is at the service of the writer in a way that imagery is not. Imagery appeals to the senses. Metaphor can appeal to a world of likenesses waiting across the bridge it represents. In Paul Ross's "The Stillness and the Fury," for example, a variety of comparisons between actual things and the sea provide a basic metaphor that threads throughout the narrative. To compare a crowd to a sea is, of course, hardly unique. But notice that, as the narrator has to immobilize himself, he experiences a "sea within" himself. As he rises that sea calms itself, and he merges with the "churning crowd." Not only is the conventional metaphor internalized in a neat ironic twist, but, structurally, we move back to the original situation—"the moving life of the street." Again, we feel the narrative's completeness, an effect assisted by a metaphor skillfully manipulated to provide pattern and vocabulary for the narrative.

In Donna Van Tassell's "Home Thoughts," the narrator suddenly quotes some lines from a play:

. . . *either boredom or some particular words within my book made me drift off into some distant memory.*
"*My Lord, I think I saw him yesternight.*"
"*Saw? Who?*"
"*My Lord, the King your father.*"
Where was my father, I wondered.

The narrator has been reading *Hamlet,* when suddenly Horatio's conversation with Hamlet about the Ghost's appearance on the parapets of Elsinore reminds her of her own father. Her mind drifts from the reading into memory—as often happens. While Donna is hardly comparing her young narrator to Prince Hamlet, each has a "father lost," and each operates within the context of that sorrow. The allusion to *Hamlet* expands the narrator's individual pain toward a more universal dimension, a metaphor of loss that includes within it both a Prince of Denmark and a lonely girl in Milo, Maine.

Consider the following brief student-written essay.

❧ JONAH AND THE WHALE

Phyllis Jalbert

"Phyllis, don't go over there."

"Why not?"

"There's a deep hole over there. You know you can't swim."

"Hah. Baloney. I can swim as well as you can."

Mark had always been sarcastic about my swimming and I knew he was a much better swimmer than I was, even though he was younger than I. He was 10 and I was 12.

Just as he had called to me, I'd been planning to go back to shore to rest because my dog paddling was getting slower and my body was sinking slowly into the cold St. John River. But I wasn't going to take anything from my little brother.

"Ha, ha. Look at Phyllis trying to swim. I dare you to let yourself go, see."

I decided to see if Mark was right about the hole. So I stopped paddling and began to sink down in the river, feeling with my toes for the rocky bottom. But I couldn't feel any bottom and I swallowed some water which tasted like fish and had an overpowering desire to reach for clean fresh air. I thrashed to the surface and tried to call for help but the water choked me and I tried to get air in my lungs, like a fish out of water dying of too much air, and I sank a second time. My body soon became helpless. Down, down I sank, surrendering my body to this natural force. As it engulfed me, my body receded from reality and I saw my sisters and brothers and the trees and rocks and the island ascending from me—these things that I loved, that were my life.

My lungs were bursting with enormous gulps of water and my stinging eyes could see the percolating bubbles.

My black hair was streaming wildly as though it were trying to reach the surface. The hole seemed indefinitely deep and my first visions were of Jonah and the whale that I had seen in the children's bible a day earlier. It was like sinking through a green crystal world towards the mouth of a whale.

Some unknown force began to move my arms and legs and I fought against the power, the gravity of the river, that was pulling me down. My head broke the surface and my mouth groped for air to feed my pounding chest.

I still couldn't call for help but there was Mark's hand. Gratefully, I clenched to his hand, almost pulling him under. "Easy Phyllis, I've got you now." The water flowed past me as he towed me towards the shore until my feet could feel the rock bottom. I could breathe again and thanked God for delivering me from that whale.

✳   ✳   ✳   ✳

The story is a vivid account that extends itself into a further dimension through its allusion to Jonah. The imagery of the Jonah story was obviously in Phyllis's mind as she sank into the river. Ordered by God to preach against Nineveh, chief city of the Assyrians, Jonah disobeys and boards a ship bound to Tarshish. God raises a great tempest. To allay the storm, the mariners cast Jonah overboard. He is swallowed by a "great fish." He prays to God: "The waters compassed me about unto the soul: the depth closed me round about, and the weeds were wrapped about my head." But he is saved: "Thou has delivered me from the belly of the fish, and all these dangers, as it were raising me from death to life." He goes to Nineveh, where his preaching causes its king and its people to repent.

Phyllis hardly pretends to be a prophet of the Old Testament, who falls from God and is restored. But her story neatly parallels that of Jonah—the ignoring of her own best judgment, the punishment for her lack of discretion, and her deliverance from the mouth of that metaphoric whale, death, which her imagination conjures up. The basic metaphor of the story itself, of course, finds us where we live. We, too, have denied our best instincts in the face of fear or temptation and we, too, have courted the consequences. Phyllis's specific reference to Jonah expands the reach of her basic metaphor of experience into an area seemingly far removed from the twentieth century, but, as it turns out, consistent with our own lives. Metaphor can make such seemingly impossible leaps across time and space.

Other elements of the story worthy of comment include the smaller metaphor in which Phyllis compares sinking to a kind of "gravity." Often, we can help our reader share our experience by comparing it to something within *his* experience. Few of us have come this close to drowning, but all of us, at some point, have been arrested by the law of gravity.

The structure is straightforward, a chronological account that moves from beginning, as the narrator is about to paddle back to shore; to middle, the near-drowning; to end, as Phyllis's brother holds out a helping hand. The brother, a catalyst of her near-disaster, returns at the end; he not only provides an essential assist to the narrator, but also gives the story its sense of completeness. He, too, seems to have changed during the story, from the mocking younger brother to the concerned attitude expressed in "Easy, Phyllis, I've got you now."

The following story was written by a college student.

❊ WHITEY

Steve Sylvester

Perhaps I should start with me; if I hadn't been a lonely, messed-up ten-year-old, things might have happened differently. Or not at all. If I hadn't been in need of a friend, if I hadn't felt that here was a kindred spirit, I would never have come to "know" Whitey. But I'm jumping ahead already—as I said, perhaps I should start with me:

I first suspected that I wouldn't achieve my dream of becoming the Handsome All-American Super-Athlete Movie Star when I couldn't see the "two" on the clock; it got all fuzzy, and a couple of days later the seven did the same thing. Since I was only in the first grade I was scared to tell anyone, because I knew what it meant and I didn't want it to happen. But it did—the rest of the clock went, and so did the blackboard, until two weeks later I had to ask Mrs. Howe what the second spelling word was, and she looked at me kinda funny and wrote a note to Mom that said I needed an eye examination.

So I went to Dr. Jacobson's office and nervously waited in a little green room. There were no comic books or anything to read, but I remember being fascinated by some pictures on the wall of some cutesy-wootsy baby cannibals guarding a missionary in a stew-pot; they had big brown eyes, thick pink lips, curly black hair, and bones in their noses. After awhile, I was led into another room where I had to try to read a chart, and the only thing I could see was the Big E at the top. And two weeks after that, I came to school wearing what I'd feared ever since the two on the clock got fuzzy—Glasses; the first kid in my class to have to get them.

"Well, look at Sylvester the Cat today! Hey . . . I gutta new name for him! Owl Eyes! Hey, Owl Eyes, whatcha gut on your face? Isn't he cute? Haw, haw, haw!" Etc. Sylvester the Cat had been an obnoxious enough nickname, but Owl Eyes was unbearable. I bore it all through the rest of that year and most of the second grade, until other kids started getting glasses too. Then I became Sylvester the Cat again.

The summer after second grade, I was eligible to try out for Little League, so I hopefully trudged out to the field with my playmates and my new glove. Everybody had a favorite team that he hoped to make; the "Knights of Columbus" were the best that year, so none of us figured we'd be good enough for them. But the "Elks" were good, and there were some real neat guys on the "Bath Iron Works."—"Hoy Puddy-Tat, think you'll make the South-End P.T.A. [The worst team]?" "I don't know . . . I think there was a coach from the 'Jaycees' [another bad one] kinda interested in me."

When the results appeared in the paper I started at the top and worked my way down, just to keep my hope up. ("I gotta at least make P.T.A. They'll take anybody!") But my name was nowhere on the page. I thought maybe I'd missed it, so I went back over the list; no luck. All the other kids had made it, but they told me that since I was small for my age, and still had another year of eligibility, I'd make it next year for sure. I believed them.

During third grade I did indeed grow . . . very fat. I also grew very religious; the two were connected, really, because the latter gave me strength to accept the former. I'd started Sunday School the year before at the insistence of my parents; they were atheists, but they figured exposure to religion would be good for me, and I could decide for myself whether or not to believe in God.

So every Sunday morning I waddled to the nearest church, which happened to be Baptist. It was pretty boring, until one Sunday when I was particularly depressed, I heard the minister read, "Blessed are the persecuted . . ." and lots of other things that made me realize I was just the kind of person God loved the most.

Sunday School got really interesting after that; I learned all the secrets of salvation until I was quite convinced that all the other kids would some day roast in Hell while I enjoyed Eternal Bliss. One day a new secret was revealed to me—that I should love my enemies and turn the other cheek. In the past, whenever a gang of kids had beaten me up, I had fought back; I was anxious to try this new technique. I soon got a chance; the next day after school, three big guys accosted me—one held me, another took my glasses off (point of honor), and the third began to punch. When I made no attempt to struggle, they stopped in amazement. "It works!" I thought happily. The next day they brought some friends along and pounded the shit out of me. "Forgive them, Lord, for they know not what they do," I prayed, but after that I either fought back or ran like hell. I figured God would understand my not turning the other cheek, just as long as I continued to love my enemies.

The most important thing that happened that year, however, was neither my conversion to Christianity nor my increased weight; it was the arrival of my two front teeth. At first I was pleased that the gap in my mouth would finally be filled—until I saw what it would be filled with: tusks. They stuck out at nearly a 45 degree angle, had a space between them of a quarter-inch, and weighed about a pound each. And thus I acquired another nickname—Bucky Beaver, which later was changed to Goofy, after the similarly endowed Walt Disney character.

The following summer, I trudged once more to the Little League tryouts, equipped with glove, bat, glasses, fat, and teeth. The head coach made a speech about the fostering of good sportsmanship, and how the most important thing was desire, not talent. I knew I'd get a position after that, and I did: they let me sell popcorn at the Tuesday and Thursday night games. (I was also substitute batboy, but no one got sick that summer.)

Thus passeth Childhood. By age ten and the fifth grade, I had no friends at all. I can't really blame the other kids—as a substitute for athletic prowess, I got straight A's and stupidly bragged about it; I learned to play the piano and constantly "showed off." These particular talents were not high on the prestige list for ten-year-old boys, anyway, and my obnoxious displays of them didn't exactly win friends and influence people.

The only admirable quality I had was compassion; having suffered so much myself, I was quick to recognize injustice and defend the underdog. I never laughed at retarded kids, or stared at cripples. And I felt particularly enraged by the "Negro Problem" in the South, because I knew that they were suffering for their appearance just as I was. I'd never met one before, but I knew if I got the chance, I'd be especially kind to him.

One day I heard the laughter I had come to associate with heckling and persecution, and walked over to investigate. A group of boys had encircled a crow and were kicking at him, while he frantically tried to fly out. "Cut it out you guys! Leave the poor thing alone," I said, but they refused to listen until I added, "Or I'll tell the teacher!" "Fuck you, Goofy," retorted one particularly wicked lad, but the group grudgingly dispersed. The crow, however, instead of immediately flying away, stood straightening his feathers before leisurely strolling off.

The word soon spread that an old man who lived near the school had a pet crow named Whitey; that explained his lack of fear when the boys left—he was tame. (I've never learned whether the name was intentionally ironic, or whether, as popular legend asserted, he had actually been white as a baby.) Boy, was I excited! I had never seen or heard of a tame crow before, and I thought I might be able to make friends with him. Maybe he'd let me feed him! The next day I got my chance. Sitting alone (as usual) in a corner of the playground at lunch I spied his black, brooding figure nearby.

I broke off a piece of my sandwich and held it tentatively out—"Here, Whitey! Hey crow, you want somethin' to eat? Look what I've got . . . Mmmm, really good! C'mon, Whitey. Aw, you stupid crow, you're probably not tame at all." And I threw the tidbit on the ground. Whitey raised a suspicious eyebrow (so to speak) as if to say, "Hey, didn't I see you yesterday when those dudes were beatin' on me?" and then gobbled up the food.

After a few such meetings, Whitey began to draw closer until
he was eating from my hand. I had a sense of great accomplishment.
Tame though he may have been, he didn't trust the other kids
enough to do that with them. Gee, what a great guy I was! Nobody
else was nice to Whitey; they all laughed at him and threw things. But
I was nice to him, I gave him food and protected him.

Soon Whitey arrived regularly at the school each day around
noon, to wait for me and get his lunch. And after awhile, I decided that
I might be able to teach him tricks, sort of make him work for his
food. I began by holding out the bread and snatching it away as he
grabbed for it; gradually he learned to plunge as he grabbed.
After that, I started pulling it farther and farther away until I rose
from my crouched position to a straight standing one, and thus Whitey
learned to fly up for his food. "Fantastic! Why, I can probably train
him to do all kinds of neat things," I thought, and began to develop
more elaborate schemes, making it increasingly difficult for him to eat.

But there seemed to be a limit to Whitey's talents. Try
though I might, I couldn't teach him anything more. (Of course, I
was too young to realize that a combination of my training techniques
and his limitations was responsible for the failure—I blamed
everything on him.) In frustration, I began to insult him, "You stupid,
lazy, good-for-nothing crow. You don't want to try, that's all. You'd
rather sit back and let me serve you on a silver platter. Well, I
won't! You don't get any more food until you prove to me that you're
willing to earn your lunch. (How he was supposed to do that, I
don't know. I didn't consider that it might be impossible for him to
earn his food unless I gave him a chance. I sort of expected him
to miraculously come up with a plan of his own.) I've been good to
you, Whitey, and this is how you treat me. Well, forget it buddy!
From now on, you get your food some place else."

The next day Whitey was waiting for me at our usual place, but
I didn't go over. I had hoped that he'd spot me and come to where I
was, but of course he didn't. On the second day, I decided that I'd
better lure him, or he wouldn't come anymore at all. I wiggled
uncomfortably in my seat until noontime, wondering if he'd be waiting
for me again; when I stepped outside, I spotted him. I stood several
yards away and called, "C'mere, Whitey. C'mere if you want your
food."

What happened next was so surprising that I couldn't quite
comprehend it until it was over. I didn't even see Whitey fly;
suddenly he just pounced on top of my head, viciously pecking at me
with his sharp beak, pounding me with his wings, scratching me
with his claws. In the distance I heard someone scream—unlike the
literary cliché, it was not myself. I only stood where I was, trying

to protect myself with my arms, transfixed with terror, too surprised to call out. A group of kids had come to my aid, and the next thing I knew, the flapping had suddenly ceased, my ears began to burn with pain, and I saw that my hands were covered with blood. "I—I'm all right," I stammered, and went to the nurse's office for first aid.

The next morning as I approached school thinking about the previous day, the nightmare struck again. One moment I was walking on the sidewalk, the next I was cowering on it, arms over my head, claws digging into my scalp and hands, wings furiously beating against me. Once again the terror ended abruptly and the pain began as Whitey was frightened away; once again the school nurse bathed my hand and ears with antiseptic in the places where the beak and claws had bloodied me.

I stayed inside during lunch and cautiously crept home after school, jumping at every noise, constantly watching the sky and trees. It is impossible to convey how I felt that afternoon; a large bird like a crow is extremely powerful, and the thought of another attack was terrifying. When I recall the incidents today, my strongest memories are of the gouging and tugging of the evil beak as it pulled flesh from me like a robin pulling worms from the ground. Worse than that was the godawful silence—there was never a warning until suddenly the air around my head started pounding, whipped into a frenzy by the thrashing wings, never a cry of victory or hate from the bird's throat. And then he was gone, as swiftly and silently as he had come.

When I arrived safely home, I remembered thankfully that it was Friday and that I would not have to face the ordeal again the next day. I didn't know what I'd do on Monday, but I hoped that Whitey would give up over the weekend. Saturday mornings I took piano lessons, but I wasn't worried about a confrontation then, because the route to my teacher's house was nowhere near the one I took to school.

Next morning after the lesson, I saw something that stopped me dead in my tracks and made my stomach feel like it had been hit by a cannonball. There, sitting on a snowbank, patiently, composedly waiting, was the sinister black figure of the crow. His beady, cold eyes fastened on me as if to say, "I still exist on weekends; I won't let you forget me." This time he attacked my legs, as I stood paralyzed, afraid of running and provoking him further. He held me prisoner there for fifteen minutes, standing on my foot and taking an occasional peck at my leather boots, until he became bored and flew off (gleefully, it seemed to me).

I ran home and told my parents what had happened. "That's the last straw," said my mother. "It's not even safe for you to walk on the streets anymore. I'm going to call his owner." "Mom, look . . . don't

try to get him put to sleep or anything. Just make them lock him up so
he won't bother me anymore. I don't want him killed; it's not his
fault."

She called the old man, and he was very sympathetic, "Look,
son," he said to me, "just don't take no sassiness from him. He's
probably playin' some kinda game. Belt him a good one and he'll learn.
That's what I done when he gut uppity with me." Sunday night
I lay in bed, shivering as I thought of what I'd do if he attacked again.

Monday arrived, a chilly, grey March morning with a damp
mist in the air. I headed for school, listening and watching. As I
passed a secluded spot, I sensed that Whitey was near, and seconds
later he struck. I began to flail my arms, hitting him hard, tearing him
from my head and screaming, "Get away from me, you black
bastard! Get away!" All my hate and rage and fear poured out until
he flew off. I was safe, but rather than feeling victorious, I had a sense
of irreplaceable loss.

Thursday night the phone rang; it was the old man. "Hey, you
seen Whitey lately?" "Not since Monday, no. I uh, I did what you told
me . . . I hit him and stuff." "Jesus, you didn't kill 'im or nawthin'
didja?" "No. He just flew towards the woods." "Ah, that's it. Well,
I guess we won't see him no more. He's gone back where he b'longs.
Didn't like bein' shut up with us; gone off with his own kind,
prob'ly. Spoze it's for the best."

I always kept a lookout for Whitey after that, but as far as I
know, no one ever saw him again. It did seem like there were a lot of
crows around, though. They'd all sit together on the trees, cawing
and screaming and laughing loudly, staring down at me scornfully.
I didn't exactly develop a phobia about them, or even hate them in any
way . . . but I was very aware of their presence. And whenever I
saw or heard them, I felt sad and . . . I don't know, ashamed, I guess.
I felt as if I should be doing something to make up for the past;
but I knew there was really nothing I could do. And the crows
continued to band together. To watch. And to wait.

❊   ❊   ❊   ❊

The style of Steve Sylvester's story is colloquial, as if the story were
being told at the moment you read it, or, more accurately, listen to it.
The casual, conversational tone, however, should not be allowed to
conceal the story's careful craftsmanship. Whitey is introduced early,
but incompletely. We do not know immediately that he is a crow.
The boy's fear of glasses is built up until he is actually wearing them.
The sequence of the glasses parallels nicely the later and more profound buildup of fear within the narrator and, more immediately, de-

fines him as a misfit within the norms of his society. Unlike Harry Nelson, this younger narrator cannot fit himself within the codes that allow people to be fashionable. He notices the cute cannibals on the doctor's walls—pictures to find their significance later in the context of "Whitey." The Little League episode increases our sense of the boy as "reject," an episode seemingly unrelated to the Whitey sequence but actually another crucial aspect of the story's development. The narrator's desperate groping toward religion and his pragmatic application of religion to his own life reminds us of the more cynical approach of the narrator of "Who Was Really Responsible?" The cruel nicknames change as the boy grows teeth, a triumph for some but for him the invitation for another of those epithets whereby he measures his "growth." The narrator's evolving sympathy for the similarly persecuted leads to his meeting with Whitey.

When he meets Whitey, the narrator finds himself part of an allegory, a series of events with a single deeper meaning. Allegory is a type of metaphor. In this one, the benevolent white boy befriends the persecuted black, the brooding figure who becomes a central figure in the narrative. The boy's impatience with the crow grows. The boy is unwilling to admit that Whitey is, after all, a crow. Like the narrator of "The Driftwood Stick," this narrator cannot accept the bird *as* bird. And, again, the results are disastrous. In each story the boy is lonely. In "Whitey," however, the boy substitutes the crow for a human companion, and, when the crow fails to behave as the boy feels it should, the boy withdraws his food. And the crow attacks. The allegory involves paternalism with its latent arrogance and the development of a seemingly inevitable hatred and fear. The story of the boy and the crow becomes the story of a society, or of two societies isolated from each other, but ominously aware that each exists. Steve Sylvester's story would seem to have its origins in such diverse works as Poe's *The Raven*, Alfred Hitchcock's *The Birds*, and Ted Hughes's *Crow*; but the story is true. Steve was inspired to write it by *The Autobiography of Malcolm X*, which suggests that Steve perceived the allegory latent in his own experience. He did not, however, see the deeper meaning until after he had written the narrative. Does that mean that the story is not allegorical? Would the story be as effective had Steve set out to write an allegory rather than merely to recreate a vivid experience from his past?

The answer to the first question is no. As we have seen, the deeper meaning of a story, its metaphor, need not be the writer's conscious product. The writer's job is to tell his story as vividly and as effectively as possible: to make us feel the frustrations of a fat kid wearing glasses yet still trying to play baseball, to show us the crow nonchalantly straightening his feathers, to endow a seemingly innocent phrase ("like a robin pulling worms from the ground") with horror. That is the answer to the second question. Had Steve set out to write an allegory he might well have allowed his story to be controlled by the single meaning under the narrative surface; his characters and events might· have become puppets pulled by the strings of a predetermined format. The story would then have been drained of the reality that captures us, whether *we* perceive the allegory or not. If a story has a deeper meaning, that meaning emerges from the vividness of the details and from the pace of the narrative. If a writer imposes meaning upon his materials. or allows his story to be controlled by what he wants it to mean, the story invariably loses its meaning.

Stories of initiation often describe disillusionment as a concomitant of the difficult process of growing up, as suggested by the following story, written by a college student.

❀ THE DAY OF MY BIRTH

Aubrey Haffiz

It was a pleasant day, the intensity of the hot tropical sun dampened by a cool breeze blowing in from the sea. He sat on the back stairs, feeling the pleasant tingling of the afternoon sun on his skin, watching, on the ground in front of him, the dancing shadows from the swaying branches of the mango tree, while listening to the soft rustling of the leaves overhead. It had rained the day before, still obvious from the tiny shoots of bright green grass around the yard, and the fresh smell of damp earth that permeated the air. He had always liked the smell of freshly turned earth; it reminded him of the days he spent each year with his grandparents in the country.

"Also," he thought, as he became aware of the next door neighbor singing at the top of her voice, accompanied by the splash of her left-over lunch hitting the back alley, "where there are no Mrs. Gonzaleses throwing garbage in the alley ways, and the houses aren't so damn close."

But even that didn't bother him too much today.

His gaze wandered lazily around the yard, from the familiar mango tree, to the sewage pipe that he used to imagine was a horse, to Mrs. Gonzales' kitchen window, and finally rested at the foot of the stairs. He noticed a fat green caterpillar crawling slowly up the concrete pillar that, with its seven companions, held the house off the ground. Picking up a stout piece of stick, he reached for the insect, and then changed his mind.

"Naw, let'em live. Stupid worm!"

He was happy; it was his birthday. He didn't know why, but he was supposed to be happy, cause it was his birthday, so he was happy.

He watched his father come through the gate, wheeling his bicycle, which he put on its stand, and walked toward the stairs.

"Good afternoon."

"Hey kid, how d'ya feel? Had a good day?"

He smelled the arid stink of alcohol as his father leaned over and grabbed his shoulder in the manner that had become his habit, resting his hands firmly between the boy's shoulder blades and shaking him back and forth.

"No package. He didn't have a package. Why couldn't he just rub my head or something," he thought irritably, "the way normal fathers do."

He felt disappointed, and was about to squash the green worm when his father dropped a ring of keys into .his lap. Then he saw it, the bicycle, it was brand new, shining brand new. He watched, fascinated, as the rays of sunlight glinted off the chrome parts, tinting them rainbowlike reds and blues, and he could almost smell the new rubber of the tires.

"Is that . . . mine . . . ?"

"All yours, son. Bought it just for you. Happy Birthday. Here, take a ride. What'd your mother give you?"

"Wow, thanks a lot, ah . . . nothing . . . yet."

He leaped off the stairs, raced up to the bicycle and then stopped abruptly a few feet away from it, and advanced slowly. His father laughed and started up the stairs, swaying momentarily.

Later that night he lay on his top bunk, staring out the window at the great old star-apple tree outside, its branches and leaves bathed in the glow of silvery moonlight. The dinner had been good; for once he hadn't been forced to eat anything he didn't want. True, the old man had been too loud, as usual, but even that was excusable today. Now, with his arms folded behind his head, he lay on his back and watched the outline of the full moon through the canopy of leaves, trying to make shapes of the clouds that floated slowly by, each momentarily illuminated as it crossed the moon's path. His people had an old saying about "prophesy in the shapes of the clouds," and the boy wondered if it was all on the other side, to be seen only by the green guy and his dog. He sure couldn't make head nor tail of those clouds.

The curtain began to billow, and without changing his position he raised his right leg and pulled the window down, for it was almost midnight, the time when jumbies (spirits of the dead) of all types were most active, especially on a moonlit night. He was glad that he had shined his new bike and locked it in the shed behind the chicken coop before going to bed. He couldn't sleep, and as his thoughts turned to the bicycle, his hand crept under the pillow for the thousandth time to touch the keys. His fingers felt the soft richness of the new leather keyholder, and he thanked his old man silently.

"Well, what the hell did you give him, eh?"

He listened to the voices coming from his parents' room.

"Well, answer, huh. What did you give him? A shirt! A cheap shirt on his birthday."

He looked over to the corner where the shirt was hanging, but couldn't see it. Well, he hadn't expected any more, he was quite content with the shirt, but the bicycle was something else. He heard his mother's voice raised in anger.

"Oh yeah, Mr. Big Shot, so you bought your son a brand new bicycle and come home drunk."

"Aw shaddup, it's the boy's birthday, I had to celebrate."

He wished they wouldn't argue so much. As far back as he could remember, they were always arguing, often about him. Here he was, the center of another argument. ". . . but Harold, did you have to use the house money? Did you have to spend most of your salary on a new bike? What're we going to eat with?"

"Aah, shut the hell up woman. Why you always nagging at me? For Christ's sake it's my son's birthday, lemme alone, huh!"

The boy arose slowly, blinded by the sudden rush of tears. He reached under the pillow, took out the bunch of shiny metal keys, and walked, half-stumbling, over to the dinner table. Carefully, very carefully, he placed the keys in the center of the table and went back to bed.

❊   ❊   ❊   ❊

In Aubrey Haffiz's story, the birthday becomes an example of irony of situation. The young man is born into the enmity of his parents, the swaggering, big-shot father, and the practical mother, whose own attitude could be read as a reason behind the father's arrogant efforts to play a role inconsistent with his paycheck. As this story suggests, birthdays often make good subjects for narratives. On such days our experiences seem to coalesce and past moments take on a sudden focus that can capture with new clarity our own attitudes and the personalities of those on whom our birth depended. An individual metaphor worthy of consideration is the "fat green caterpillar." In what way does the caterpillar help reflect some of the story's meanings?

Here is another student-written story, to be analyzed for meaning and metaphor.

❀ LET'S TAKE A RIDE INTO TOMORROW

David Olmstead

I am just a poor boy
People look at my clothes
And say what trash he must be
As I walk along the road of life
Nobody walks with me
Because I am just a poor boy
Yet they don't look into my mind
Just my house, not into my soul
Just into my wallet
I am just a poor boy
But my heart is filled with love
Love for people who call me
Poor white trash.

At home there is a place where most of us guys hang out. It's a dirty place, where not much really happens; but if anything does happen it starts from there. This place is a gas station and mixed up among the normal business of the station there is the guys. Now most of us don't have anything else to do but just hang around and wait for something to happen. It may take hours for something to happen, or minutes, but we always wait, for there isn't anything else to do.

Before the gas station we used to jump the freight trains, but the train goes through too fast now, so we just let it go on by without us. Also, a long time ago, we used to have a movie theater, but that is a thing of the past. Somewhere in between the time of the movie theater and the gas station, there was a small diner where we used to go, but it also has left us. But we still have the gas station, at least for a while.

In the station there is John. John is a dropout who works at the gas station. He is the one who starts most things happening. John has all of the contacts, so if we want any beer, John is the one to see. During the day I see John at least three different times, but the conversation is basically the same—we talk about drinking, cars, and women—in that order.

As I walk into the station John says, "How's Dave?"

"All right."

"How's John?"

"All right."

"What's doing?"

"Nothing."

"What did you do last night, John?"

"Not much."

"What did you do?"

"Sat on the bridge and counted cars."

"How high did you get?"

"Ten."

"Great!"

"Where's everybody?"

"Around. There was an accident last night."

"That right?"

"Yeah."

"I think I'll take a look. See you later."

"All right."

I walked down the street and looked at the car, then I went back to the station.

"How's Dave?"

"All right."

"How's John?"

"All right."

※   ※   ※   ※

The following selections, by Lillian Smith and Frank Conroy, illustrate in different ways this chapter's assertion that good writing often goes beyond itself. Lillian Smith's experience—strangely similar to that of Anne Moody—stands for more than just itself. As she intended to do, she has captured part of the South at a moment in its history. Conroy's essay relies on his intense exploration of himself and his surroundings as metaphors for a fear that builds to terror.

❁ WHEN I WAS A CHILD

Lillian Smith

Even its children know that the South is in trouble. No one has to tell them; no words said aloud. To them, it is a vague thing weaving in and out of their play, like a ghost haunting an old graveyard or whispers after the household sleeps—fleeting mystery, vague menace, to which each responds in his own way. Some learn to screen out all

SOURCE: Reprinted from *Killers of the Dream* by Lillian Smith. By permission of W. W. Norton & Company, Inc. Copyright 1949, © 1961 by Lillian Smith.

except the soft and the soothing; others deny even as they see plainly, and hear. But all know that under quiet words and warmth and laughter, under the slow ease and tender concern about small matters, there is a heavy burden on all of us and as heavy a refusal to confess it. The children know this "trouble" is bigger than they, bigger than their family, bigger than their church, so big that people turn away from its size. They have seen it flash out like lightning and shatter a town's peace, have felt it tear up all they believe in. They have measured its giant strength and they feel weak when they remember.

This haunted childhood belongs to every southerner. Many of us run away from it but we come back like a hurt animal to its wound, or a murderer to the scene of his sin. The human heart dares not stay away too long from that which hurt it most. There is a return journey to anguish that few of us are released from making.

We who were born in the South call this mesh of feeling and memory "loyalty." We think of it sometimes as "love." We identify with the South's trouble as if we, individually, were responsible for all of it. We defend the sins and sorrows of three hundred years as if each sin had been committed by us alone and each sorrow had cut across our heart. We are as hurt at criticism of our region as if our own name were called aloud by the critic. We have known guilt without understanding it, and there is no tie that binds men closer to the past and each other than that.

It is a strange thing, this umbilical cord uncut. In times of ease, we do not feel its pull, but when we are threatened with change, suddenly it draws the whole white South together in a collective fear and fury that wipe our minds clear of reason and we are blocked off from sensible contact with the world we live in.

To keep this resistance strong, wall after wall has been thrown up in the southern mind against criticism from without and within. Imaginations close tight against the hurt of others; a regional armoring takes place to keep out the "enemies" who would make our trouble different—or maybe rid us of it completely. For it is a trouble that we do not want to give up. We are as involved with it as a child who cannot be happy at home and cannot bear to tear himself away, or as a grown-up who has fallen in love with his own disease. We southerners have identified with the long sorrowful past on such deep levels of love and hate and guilt that we do not know how to break old bonds without pulling our lives down. *Change* is the evil word, a shrill clanking that makes us know too well our servitude. *Change* means leaving one's memories, one's sins, one's ancient prison, the room where one was born. How can we do this when we are tied fast!

The white man's burden is his own childhood. Every southerner knows this. Though he may deny it even to himself, yet he drags

through life with him the heavy weight of a past that never eases and
is rarely understood, of desire never appeased, of dreams that died
in his heart.

In this South I was born and now live. Here it was that I began to
grow, seeking my way, as do all children, through the honeycomb cells
of our life to the bright reality outside. Sometimes it was as if all
doors opened inward. . . . Sometimes we children lost even the desire
to get outside and tried only to make a comfortable home of the
trap of swinging doors that history and religion and a war, man's
greed and his guilt had placed us in at birth.

It is not easy to pick out of such a life those strands that have to
do only with color, only with Negro-white relationships, only with
religion or sex, for they are knit of the same fibers that have gone into
the making of the whole fabric, woven into its basic patterns and
designs. Religion . . . sex . . . race . . . money . . . avoidance
rites . . . malnutrition . . . dreams—no part of these can be looked at
and clearly seen without looking at the whole of them. For, as a
painter mixes colors and makes of them new colors, so religion is turned
into something different by race, and segregation is colored as much
by sex as by skin pigment, and money is no longer a coin but a lost
wish wandering through a man's whole life.

A child's lessons are blended of these strands however dissonant a
design they make. The mother who taught me what I know of
tenderness and love and compassion taught me also the bleak rituals of
keeping Negroes in their place. The father who rebuked me for an
air of superiority toward schoolmates from the mill and rounded out
his rebuke by gravely reminding me that "all men are brothers," trained
me in the steel-rigid decorums I must demand of every colored male.
They who so gravely taught me to split my body from my feelings
and both from my "soul," taught me also to split my conscience from
my acts and Christianity from southern tradition.

Neither the Negro nor sex was often discussed at length in our
home. We were given no formal instruction in these difficult matters but
we learned our lessons well. We learned the intricate system of taboos,
of renunciations and compensations, of manners, voice modulations,
words, feelings, along with our prayers, our toilet habits, and our
games. I do not remember how or when, but by the time I had
learned that God is love, that Jesus is His Son and came to give us more
abundant life, that all men are brothers with a common Father, I
also knew that I was better than a Negro, that all black folks have their
place and must be kept in it, that sex has its place and must be
kept in it, that a terrifying disaster would befall the South if ever I
treated a Negro as my social equal and as terrifying a disaster would

befall my family if ever I were to have a baby outside of marriage. I
had learned that God so loved the world that He gave His only
begotten Son so that we might have segregated churches in which it
was my duty to worship each Sunday and on Wednesday at evening
prayers. I had learned that white southerners are a hospitable,
courteous, tactful people who treat those of their own group with
consideration and who as carefully segregate from all the richness of
life "for their own good and welfare" thirteen million people whose skin
is colored a little differently from my own.

I knew by the time I was twelve that a member of my family
would always shake hands with old Negro friends, would speak gently
and graciously to members of the Negro race unless they forgot
their place, in which event icy peremptory tones would draw lines
beyond which only the desperate would dare take one step. I
knew that to use the word "nigger" was unpardonable and no well-bred
southerner was quite so crude as to do so; nor would a well-bred
southerner call a Negro "mister" or invite him into the living room or
eat with him or sit by him in public places.

I knew that my old nurse who had patiently cared for me through
long months of illness, who had given me refuge when a little sister
took my place as the baby of the family, who comforted me, soothed,
fed me, delighted me with her stories and games, let me fall asleep
on her deep warm breast, was not worthy of the passionate love I felt for
her but must be given instead a half-smiled-at affection similar
to that which one feels for one's dog. I knew but I never believed it,
that the deep respect I felt for her, the tenderness, the love, was a
childish thing which every normal child outgrows, that such love begins
with one's toys and is discarded with them, and that somehow—though
it seemed impossible to my agonized heart—I too, must outgrow
these feelings. I learned to give presents to this woman I loved, instead
of esteem and honor. I learned to use a soft voice to oil my words of
superiority. I learned to cheapen with tears and sentimental talk of "my
old mammy" one of the profound relationships of my life. I learned
the bitterest thing a child can learn: that the human relations I
valued most were held cheap by the world I lived in.

From the day I was born, I began to learn my lessons. I was put in
a rigid frame too intricate, too complex, too twisting to describe here
so briefly, but I learned to conform to its slide-rule measurements.
I learned that it is possible to be a Christian and a white southerner
simultaneously; to be a gentlewoman and an arrogant callous creature in
the same moment; to pray at night and ride a Jim Crow car the next
morning and to feel comfortable in doing both. I learned to
believe in freedom, to glow when the word *democracy* is used, and to
practice slavery from morning to night. I learned it the way all of

my southern people learn it: by closing door after door until one's mind and heart and conscience are blocked off from each other and from reality.

I closed the doors. Or perhaps they were closed for me. Then one day they began to open again. Why I had the desire or the strength to open them or what strange accident or circumstance opened them for me would require in the answering an account too long, too particular, too stark to make here. And perhaps I should not have the insight or wisdom that such an analysis would demand of me, nor the will to make it. I know only that the doors opened, a little; that somewhere along that iron corridor we travel from babyhood to maturity, doors swinging inward began to swing outward, showing glimpses of the world beyond, of that clear bright thing we call "reality."

I believe there is one experience in my childhood which pushed these doors open, a little. And I am going to tell it here, although I know well that to excerpt from a life and family background one incident and name it as a "cause" of a change in one's life direction is a distortion and often an irrelevance. The profound hungers of a child and how they are filled have too much to do with the way in which experiences are assimilated to tear an incident out of a life and look at it in isolation. Yet, with these reservations, I shall tell it, not because it was in itself so severe a trauma, but because it became for me a symbol of buried experiences that I did not have access to. It is an incident that has rarely happened to other southern children. In a sense, it is unique. But it was an acting-out, a special private production of a little script that is written on the lives of most southern children before they know words. Though they may not have seen it staged this way, each southerner has had his own dramatization of the theme.

I should like to preface the account by giving a brief glimpse of my family and background, hoping that the reader, entering my home with me, will be able to blend the ragged edges of this isolated experience into a more full life picture and in doing so will see that it is, in a sense, everybody's story.

I was born and reared in a small Deep South town whose population was about equally Negro and white. There were nine of us who grew up freely in a rambling house of many rooms, surrounded by big lawn, back yard, gardens, fields, and barn. It was the kind of home that gathers memories like dust, a place filled with laughter and play and pain and hurt and ghosts and games. We were given such advantages of schooling, music, and art as were available in the South, and our world was not limited to the South, for travel to far places

seemed a simple, natural thing to us, and usually there was one of
the family in a remote part of the earth.

We knew we were a respected and important family of this small
town but beyond this knowledge we gave little thought to status.
Our father made money in lumber and naval stores for the excitement
of making and losing it—not for what money can buy nor the security
which it sometimes gives. I do not remember at any time wanting "to be
rich" nor do I remember that thrift and saving were ideals which our
parents considered important enough to urge upon us. Always in
the family there was an acceptance of risk, a mild delight even in
burning bridges, an expectant "what will happen now!" We were not
irresponsible; living according to the pleasure principle was by no
means our way of life. On the contrary we were trained to think that
each of us should do something that would be of genuine usefulness to
the world, and the family thought it right to make sacrifices if
necessary, to give each child adequate preparation for this life's work.
We were also trained to think learning important, and books, but 'bad"
books our mother burned. We valued music and art and craftsmanship
but it was people and their welfare and religion that were the foci
around which our lives seemed naturally to move. Above all else, the
important thing was what we "planned to do with our lives." That
each of us must do something was as inevitable as breathing for
we owed a "debt to society which must be paid." This was a family
commandment.

While many of our neighbors spent their energies in counting
limbs on the family tree and grafting some on now and then to
give symmetry to it, or in reliving the old bitter days of Reconstruction
licking scars to cure their vague malaise, or in fighting each battle and
turn of battle of that Civil War which has haunted the southern
conscience so long, my father was pushing his nine children straight into
the future. "You have your heritage," he used to say, "some of it
good, some not so good; and as far as I know you had the usual number
of grandmothers and grandfathers. Yes, there were slaves, far too
many of them in the family, but that was your grandfather's mistake,
not yours. The past has been lived. It is gone. The future is yours. What
are you going to do with it?" Always he asked this question of his
children and sometimes one knew it was but an echo of the old
question he had spent his life trying to answer for himself. For always
the future held my father's dreams; always there, not in the past,
did he expect to find what he had spent his life searching for.

We lived the same segregated life as did other southerners but
our parents talked in excessively Christian and democratic terms. We
were told ten thousand times that status and money are unimportant
(though we were well supplied with both); we were told that "all

men are brothers," that we are part of a democracy and must act like
democrats. We were told that the teachings of Jesus are real and
important and could be practiced if we tried. We were told also that
to be "radical" is bad, silly too; and that one must always conform to the
"best behavior" of one's community and make it better if one can.
We were taught that we were superior not to people but to hate and
resentment, and that no member of the Smith family could stoop so low
as to have an enemy. No matter what injury was done us, we must not
injure ourselves further by retaliating. That was a family commandment
too.

We had family prayers once each day. All of us as children read
the Bible in its entirety each year. We memorized hundreds of Bible
verses and repeated them at breakfast, and said "sentence prayers"
around the family table. God was not someone we met on Sunday but a
permanent member of our household. It never occurred to me until I
was fourteen or fifteen years old that He did not see every act and
thought and chalk up the daily score on eternity's tablets.

Despite the strain of living so intimately with God, the nine of us
were strong, healthy, energetic youngsters who filled our days with
play and sports and music and books and managed to live much of our
lives on the careless level at which young lives should be lived. We
had our times of profound anxiety of course, for there were hard lessons
to be learned about the body and "bad things" to be learned about
sex. Sometimes I have wondered how we ever learned them with a
mother so shy with words.

She was a wistful creature who loved beautiful things like lace and
sunsets and flowers in a vague inarticulate way, and took good care of her
children. We always knew this was not her world but one she
accepted under duress. Her private world we rarely entered, though
the shadow of it lay at times heavily on our hearts.

Our father owned large business interests, employed hundreds of
colored and white laborers, paid them the prevailing low wages, worked
them the prevailing long hours, built for them mill towns (Negro
and white), built for each group a church, saw to it that religion was
supplied free, saw to it that a commissary supplied commodities at
a high price, and in general managed his affairs much as ten thousand
other southern businessmen manage theirs.

Even now, I can hear him chuckling as he told my mother how he
won his fight for Prohibition. The high point of the campaign was
election afternoon, when he lined up the entire mill force of several
hundred (white and black), passed out a shining silver dollar to
each one of them, marched them in and voted liquor out of our county.
It was a great day in his life. He had won the Big Game, a game he
was always playing with himself against all kinds of evil. It did not

occur to him to scrutinize the methods he used. Evil was a word written in capitals; the devil was smart; if you wanted to win you outsmarted him. It was as simple as that.

He was a practical, hardheaded, warmhearted, high-spirited man born during the Civil War, earning his living at twelve, struggling through bitter decades of Reconstruction and post-Reconstruction, through populist movement, through the panic of 1893, the panic of 1907, on into the twentieth century accepting his region as he found it, accepting its morals and its mores as he accepted its climate, with only scorn for those who held grudges against the North or pitied themselves or the South; scheming, dreaming, expanding his business, making and losing money, making friends whom he did not lose, with never a doubt that God was always by his side whispering hunches as to how to pull off successful deals. When he lost, it was his own fault. When he won, God had helped him.

Once while we were kneeling at family prayers the fire siren at the mill sounded the alarm that the mill was on fire. My father did not falter from his prayer. The alarm sounded again and again—which signified that the fire was big. With quiet dignity he continued his talk with God while his children sweated and wriggled and hearts beat out of their chests in excitement. He was talking to God—how could he hurry out of the presence of the Most High to save his mills! When he finished his prayer, he quietly stood up, laid the Bible carefully on the table. Then, and only then, did he show an interest in what was happening in Mill Town. . . . When the telegram was placed in his hands telling of the death of his beloved favorite son, he gathered his children together, knelt down, and in a steady voice which contained no hint of his shattered heart, loyally repeated, "God is our refuge and strength, a very present help in trouble. Therefore will we not fear, though the earth be removed, and though the mountains be carried into the midst of the sea." On his deathbed, he whispered to his old Business Partner in Heaven: "I have fought the fight; I have kept the faith."

Against this backdrop the drama of the South was played out one day in my life:

A little white girl was found in the colored section of our town, living with a Negro family in a broken-down shack. This family had moved in only a few weeks before and little was known of them. One of the ladies in my mother's club, while driving over to her washerwoman's, saw the child swinging on a grate. The shack, as she said, was hardly more than a pigsty and this white child was living with ignorant and dirty and sick-looking colored folks. "They must have kidnapped her," she told her friends. Genuinely shocked, the clubwomen busied themselves in an attempt to do something, for the child was very white indeed. The strange Negroes were subjected to a grueling questioning and finally grew frightened and evasive and refused to talk at all. This only increased the suspicion of the white group, and the next day the clubwomen, escorted by the town marshal, took the child from her adopted family despite their tears.

She was brought to our home. I do not know why my mother consented to this plan. Perhaps because she loved children and always showed tenderness and concern for them. It was easy for one more to fit into our ample household and Janie was soon at home there. She roomed with me, sat next to me at the table; I found Bible verses for her to say at breakfast; she wore my clothes, played with my dolls and followed me around from morning to night. She was dazed by her new comforts and by the interesting activities of this big lively family; and I was as happily dazed, for her adoration was a new thing to me; and as time passed a quick, childish, and deeply felt bond grew up between us.

But a day came when a telephone message was received from a colored orphanage. There was a meeting at our home, whispers, shocked exclamations. All afternoon the ladies went in and out of our house talking to Mother in tones too low for children to hear. And as they passed us at play, most of them looked quickly at Janie and quickly looked away again, though a few stopped and stared at her as if they could not tear their eyes from her face. When my father came home in the evening Mother closed her door against our young ears and talked a long time with him. I heard him laugh, heard Mother say, "But Papa, this is no laughing matter!" And then they were back in the living room with us and mother was pale and my father was saying, "Well, work it out, honey, as best you can. After all, now that you know, it is pretty simple."

In a little while my mother called my sister and me into her bedroom and told us that in the morning Janie would return to Colored Town. She said Janie was to have the dresses the ladies had given her and a few of my own, and the toys we had shared with her. She asked me if I would like to give Janie one of my dolls. She seemed hurried, though Janie was not to leave until next day. She said, "Why not select it now?" And in dreamlike stiffness I brought in my dolls and chose one for Janie. And then I found it possible to say, "Why? Why is she leaving? She likes us, she hardly knows them. She told me she had been with them only a month."

"Because," Mother said gently, "Janie is a little colored girl."

"But she can't be. She's white!"

"We were mistaken. She is colored."

"But she looks——"

"She is colored. Please don't argue!"

"What does it mean?" I whispered.

"It means," Mother said slowly, "that she has to live in Colored Town with colored people."

"But why? She lived here three weeks and she doesn't belong to them, she told me she didn't."

"She is a little colored girl."

"But you said yourself that she has nice manners. You said that," I persisted.

"Yes, she is a nice child. But a colored child cannot live in our home."

"Why?"

"You know, dear! You have always known that white and colored people do not live together."

"Can she come over to play?"

"No."

"I don't understand."

"I don't either," my young sister quavered.

"You're too young to understand. And don't ask me again, ever again, about this!" Mother's voice was sharp but her face was sad and there was no certainty left there. She hurried out and busied herself in the kitchen and I wandered through that room where I had been born, touching the old familiar things in it, looking at them, trying to find the answer to a question that moaned in my mind like a hurt thing. . . .

And then I went out to Janie, who was waiting, knowing things were happening that concerned her but waiting until they were spoken aloud.

I do not know quite how the words were said but I told her that she was to return in the morning to the little place where she had lived because she was colored and colored children could not live with white children.

"Are you white?" she said.

"I'm white," I replied, "and my sister is white. And you're colored. And white and colored can't live together because my mother says so."

"Why?" Janie whispered.

"Because they can't," I said. But I knew, though I said it firmly, that something was wrong. I knew my father and mother whom I passionately admired had done that which did not fit in with their teachings. I knew they had betrayed something which they held dear. And I was shamed by their failure and frightened, for I felt that they were no longer as powerful as I had thought. There was something Out There that was stronger than they and I could not bear to believe it. I could not confess that my father, who had always solved the

family dilemmas easily and with laughter, could not solve this. I knew
that my mother who was so good to children did not believe in her
heart that she was being good to this child. There was not a word in my
mind that said it but my body knew and my glands, and I was filled
with anxiety.

But I felt compelled to believe they were right. It was the only
way my world could be held together. And, like a slow poison, it began
to seep through me: *I was white. She was colored. We must not be
together. It was bad to be together. Though you ate with your nurse
when you were little, it was bad to eat with any colored person
after that. It was bad just as other things were bad that your mother
had told you. It was bad that she was to sleep in the room with me that
night. It was bad. . . .*

I was suddenly full of guilt. For three weeks I had done things that
white children are not supposed to do. And now I knew these things
had been wrong.

I went to the piano and began to play, as I had always done
when I was in trouble. I tried to play Paderewski's *Minuet* and as I
stumbled through it, the little girl came over and sat on the bench
with me. Feeling lonely, lost in these deep currents that were sweeping
through our house that night, she crept closer and put her arms
around me and I shrank away as if my body had been uncovered. I had
not said a word, I did not say one, but she knew, and tears slowly
rolled down her little white face. . . .

And then I forgot it. For more than thirty years the experience was
wiped out of my memory. But that night, and the weeks it was tried
to, worked its way like a splinter, bit by bit down to the hurt places in
my memory and festered there. And as I grew older, as more experiences
collected around that faithless time, as memories of earlier, more
profound hurts crept closer and closer drawn to that night as if to a
magnet, I began to know that people who talked of love and Christianity
and democracy did not mean it. That is a hard thing for a child to
learn. I still admired my parents, there was so much that was strong and
vital and sane and good about them and I never forgot this; I
stubbornly believed in their sincerity, as I do to this day, and I loved
them. Yet in my heart they were under suspicion. Something was
wrong.

Something was wrong with a world that tells you that love is good
and people are important and then forces you to deny love and to
humiliate people. I knew, though I would not for years confess it
aloud, that in trying to shut the Negro race away from us, we have shut
ourselves away from so many good, creative, honest, deeply human
things in life. I began to understand so slowly at first but more and
more clearly as the years passed, that the warped, distorted frame we

have put around every Negro child from birth is around every white child also. Each is on a different side of the frame but each is pinioned there. And I knew that what cruelly shapes and cripples the personality of one is as cruelly shaping and crippling the personality of the other. I began to see that though we may, as we acquire new knowledge, live through new experiences, examine old memories, gain the strength to tear the frame from us, yet we are stunted and warped and in our lifetime cannot grow straight again any more than can a tree, put in a steel-like twisting frame when young, grow tall and straight when the frame is torn away at maturity.

As I sit here writing, I can almost touch that little town, so close is the memory of it. There it lies, its main street lined with great oaks, heavy with matted moss that swings softly even now as I remember. A little white town rimmed with Negroes, making a deep shadow on the whiteness. There it lies, broken in two by one strange idea. Minds broken in two. Hearts broken. Conscience torn from acts. A culture split in a thousand pieces. That is segregation. I am remembering: a woman in a mental hospital walking four steps out, four steps in, unable to go further because she has drawn an invisible line around her small world and is terrified to take one step beyond it. . . . A man in a Disturbed Ward assigning "places" to the other patients and violently insisting that each stay in his place. . . . A Negro woman saying to me so quietly, "We cannot ride together on the bus, you know. It is not legal to be human in Georgia."

Memory, walking the streets of one's childhood . . . of the town where one was born.

❀ WHITE DAYS AND RED NIGHTS

Frank Conroy

Jean and my mother had weekend jobs as wardens at the Southbury Training School, a Connecticut state institution for the feeble-minded. Every Friday afternoon we drove out deep in the hills to an old cabin they had bought for a few hundred dollars on the installment plan.

The first dirt road was always plowed for the milk truck, but never the second, and in the snow you could see the tracks of wagon wheels

SOURCE: From *Stop-Time* by Frank Conroy. Copyright © 1965 by Frank Conroy. Reprinted by permission of The Viking Press, Inc.

and two narrow trails where the horses had walked. A mile down
the road was the Green's farm. Every morning they hauled milk to the
pick-up station, a full silent load up to the hill, and then back, the empty
returns from the previous day clanging raucously behind the horses
as if in melancholic celebration. No one else ever used the road. If it
was passable we drove to the cabin, if not, we walked, single file, in the
horses' tracks, our arms full of food.

Every Friday the cheap padlock was opened, every Friday I
stepped inside. A room so dim my blood turned gray, so cold I knew
no human heart had ever beaten there—every line, every article of
furniture, every scrap of paper on the floor, every burned-out match in a
saucer filling me with desolation, depopulating me. A single room,
twelve feet by eighteen. A double bed, a bureau, a round table to eat
on, and against the wall a counter with a kerosene cooker. In the exact
center of the room, a potbellied coal stove. All these objects had been
watched by me in a state of advanced terror, watched so many long
nights that even in the daytime they seemed to be whispering bad
messages.

My mother would make a quick meal out of cans. Corned-beef
hash or chili. Conversation was usually sparse.

"I have a good cottage tonight."

"I can't remember where I am. We'd better stop at the
administration building."

Outside, the lead-gray afternoon slipped almost imperceptibly into
twilight. Very gradually the earth moved toward night and as I sat
eating I noted every darkening shadow. Jean sipped his coffee and
lighted a Pall Mall. My mother arranged the kerosene lamp so she
could see to do the dishes.

"Frank, get me some water."

Through the door and into the twilight, the bucket against my
thigh. There was a path beaten through the snow, a dark line curving
through the drifts to the well. The low sky was empty, uniformly leaden.
Stands of trees spread pools of darkness, as if night came up from
their sunken roots. At the well I tied a rope to the handle of the bucket
and dropped it into the darkness upside down, holding the line.
The trick was not to hit the sides. I heard a muffled splash. Leaning
over the deep hole, with the faintest hint of warmer air rising against my
face, I hauled the bucket hand over hand until it rose suddenly
into view, the dim sky shimmering within like some luminous oil.
Back to the house with the water. Absolute silence except for the
sounds of my own movement, absolute stillness except for a wavering
line of smoke from the stovepipe.

While Mother did the dishes Jean and I sat at the table. He

sipped at his second cup of coffee. I fished a dime out of my pocket.
"Could you get me a couple of Baby Ruth bars?"

Jean sucked his teeth and reached for a wooden pick. "The stuff is
poison. It rots your teeth."

"Oh Jean, I know. It won't take you a second. There's a stand
in the administration building."

"You're so finicky about food and you go and eat that stuff. Can
you imagine the crap in those mass-produced candy bars? Dead
roaches and mouse shit and somebody's nose-pickings."

"Jean, for heaven's sake!" My mother laughed.

"Well, he won't touch a piece of perfectly good meat and then he'll
eat that junk."

"It'll only take you a second." I pushed the dime across the table.

"I know the trouble with you. You're too lazy to chew your
food. You wash everything down with milk," He glanced at the coin,
his eyes flicking away. "All right. If you want to kill yourself. Keep
the dime." He finished his coffee and cigarette slowly, savoring the
mixed flavors and the moment of rest. Since he'd stopped using the
holder his smoking style had changed. He'd take a quick drag, blow out
about a third of the smoke immediately, inhale the rest, and let
it come out as he talked. I often made it a point to sit in such a way
that a strong light source behind him showed up the smoke. It was
amazing how long it came out, a fine, almost invisible blue stream,
phrase after phrase, changing direction smoothly as he clipped off the
words. For some reason I admired this phenomenon tremendously.
I could sit watching for hours.

Jean pushed back his chair and stood up, stretching his arms and
yawning exaggeratedly. Even this he did gracefully. Like a cat, he
was incapable of making an awkward move. Looking out the window he
sucked his teeth noisily. "Well," he said slowly, "the lions and tigers
seem to be under control tonight."

I felt my face flush and quickly turned away. It was a complicated
moment. My fear of staying alone in the house had been totally ignored
for weeks. For Jean to mention it at all was somehow promising,
and I was grateful despite the unfairness of his phrasing. He knew of
course that it wasn't lions and tigers I was afraid of—by using that
image he was attempting to simplify my fear into the realm of
childishness (which he could then ignore in good conscience) as well
as to shame me out of it. Jean was telling me, with a smile, that
my behavior was irrational and therefore he could do nothing to help
me, something I would never have expected in any case. I knew
perfectly well that no one could help me. The only possible solution
would have been for me to stay in the city on weekends with Alison,

but that battle had been lost. Jean and Mother wanted me with them. Not because they felt they had to look after me but because I was useful. I drew the water. I tended the fire so the house would be warm in the morning when they returned.

"We'd better go," Mother said, lifting the last dripping dish from the plastic basin. "Frank, you dry the dishes and put them away."

I watched their preparations with a sense of remoteness. It was as if they were already gone. Mother dried her hands carefully and put on her heavy coat. Jean bent over the row of paperback books and pulled out an Erskine Caldwell. "I won't be able to read tonight but I'll take it anyway."

"All right?" Mother asked. They stood for a last moment, waiting, making sure they hadn't forgotten anything, sensing in each other the precise moment to leave. Then they were through the door and away. I followed a few moments later, stepping in their footprints to the road. I watched them walk into the darkness underneath the trees. My mother turned at the top of a rise and called back to me over the snow. "Don't forget to set the alarm!" She hurried to catch up with Jean. As they moved down the hill it was as if they sank deeper and deeper into the snow. Dimly I could make out the top halves of their bodies, then only their shoulders, their heads, and they were gone.

I went back to the house. After an initial surge of panic my mind turned itself off. Thinking was dangerous. By not thinking I attained a kind of inner invisibility. I knew that fear attracted evil, that the uncontrolled sound of my own mind would in some way delineate me to the forces threatening me, as the thrashing of a fish in shallow water draws the gull. I tried to keep still, but every now and then the fear escalated up into consciousness and my mind would stir, readjusting itself like the body of a man trying to sleep in an uncomfortable position. In those moments I felt most vulnerable, my eyes widening and my ears straining to catch the sound of approaching danger.

I dried the dishes slowly and put them away, attempting to do the whole job without making a sound. Occasionally a floorboard creaked under my weight, sending a long, lingering charge up my spine, a white thrill at once delicious and ominous. I approached the stove nervously. The coal rattled and the cast-iron grate invariably banged loudly despite my precautions. I had to do it quickly, holding my breath, or I wouldn't do it at all. Once finished I checked the window latches. There was nothing to be done about the door; it couldn't be locked from the inside and Mother refused to lock it from the outside because of the danger of my getting trapped in a fire.

By the yellow light of the kerosene lamp I sat on the edge of the bed and removed my shoes, placing them carefully on the floor. The Big Ben alarm clock ticked off the seconds on a shelf above my head, and every now and then a puff of coal gas popped in the stove as the fuel shifted. I got under the covers fully clothed and surveyed the stillness of the room, trying to slow my breathing. For an hour or more I lay motionless in a self-induced trance, my eyes open but seldom moving, my ears listening to the sounds of the house and the faint, inexplicable, continuous noises from outside. (In this state my ears seemed rather far away. I was burrowed somewhere deep in my skull, my ears advance outposts sending back reports to headquarters.) As I remember it the trance must have been close to the real thing. It was an attempt to reach an equipoise of fear, a state in which the incoming fear signals balanced with some internal process of dissimulation. At best it worked only temporarily, since fear held a slight edge. But for an hour or two I avoided what I hated most, the great noisy swings up and down. The panic and the hilarity.

At the first flashing thought of the Southbury Training School I sat up and took a book from the shelf. Escaped inmates were rare, and supposedly harmless, but I knew that a runaway had ripped the teats from one of the Greens' cows with a penknife, and that another had strangled four cats in a barnyard. I read quickly, skimming the pages for action and dialogue while most of my mind stood on guard. Book after book came down from the shelf, piling up on the bed beside me as I waited for sleep. I knew that if I left the lamp on I would stay awake most of the night, so when the pages began to go out of focus I set the alarm clock, cupped my hand over the mouth of the lamp chimney and blew myself into darkness.

Being sleepy and being scared do not cancel each other out. After hours of waiting the mind insists and slips under itself into unconsciousness. The sleeping body remains tense, the limbs bent as if poised for flight, adrenalin oozing steadily into the blood. Every few minutes the mind awakens, listens, and goes back to sleep. Fantastic dreams attempt to absorb the terror, explaining away the inexplicable with lunatic logic, twisting thought to a mad, private vision so that sleep can go on for another few seconds.

I wake up in the dark, a giant hand squeezing my heart. All around me a tremendous noise is splitting the air, exploding like a continuous chain of fireworks. The alarm clock! My God, the clock! Ringing all this time, calling, calling, bringing everything evil. I reach out and shut it off. The vibrations die out under my fingers and I listen to the silence, wondering if anything has approached under the cover of the ringing bell. (Remember a children's game called Giant Steps?)

I sit up cautiously. My body freezes. Rising before me over the foot of the bed is a bright, glowing, cherry-red circle in the darkness, a floating globe pulsating with energy, wavering in the air like the

incandescent heart of some dissected monster, dripping sparks and
blood. I throw myself backward against the wall behind the bed. Books
tumble around me from the shelves, an ashtray falls and smashes
on the floor. My hands go out, palms extended, towards the floating
apparition, my voice whispering "Please . . ." Impossibly a voice
answers, a big voice from all around me. "FRANK! FRANK!" My
knees give out and I fall off the bed to the floor. I can feel the pieces of
broken ashtray under my hands.

From the corner of my eye I see the red circle. I keep quite still,
and the circle doesn't move. If I turn my head I seem to sense a
corresponding movement, but I can't be sure. In the blackness there is
nothing to relate to. Step by step I begin to understand. My body
grows calmer and it's as if a series of veils were being whisked away
from my eyes. I see clearly that the circle is only the red-hot bottom of
the stove—a glowing bowl, its surface rippling with color changes from
draughts of cool air. The last veil lifts and reveals an image of magic
beauty, a sudden miracle in the night. I fall asleep watching it,
my shoulder against the bed.

Hours later the cold wakes me and I climb up under the covers.
When dawn comes my limbs relax. I can tell when dawn has come
even though I'm asleep.

I woke up when the wagon went by, creaking like a ship, passing
close, just on the other side of the wall by my head. Chip would be
driving, I knew, with Toad in back watching the cans. They never spoke
as they went by. Sometimes Chip would murmur to the horses, "Haw,
gee-aw." The traces rang quietly and the tall iron-rimmed wheels
splintered rocks under the snow.

It was hard to get out of bed. The air was cold. Water froze in the
bucket and the windows were coated with ice. The light was gray,
exactly the same quality as the twilight of the night before, devoid of
meaning. I cleaned out the stove, laid paper, a few sticks of kindling
and some coal, splashed kerosene over everything, and struck a match.
With a great whoosh the stove filled with flames. My teeth chattering,
I rushed back under the covers. I fell asleep waiting to get warm.

When Jean and my mother came through the door I woke up.
They seemed tremendously alive, bustling with energy, their voices
strangely loud.

"It's freezing in here. What happened to the fire?" I sat up in
bed. The fire had gone out, or more likely had never caught after the
kerosene had burned.

"You forgot to set the alarm," my mother said.

"No I didn't."

She knelt and relit the fire. Jean stood in the open doorway, knocking snow off his galoshes. He closed the door and sat on the edge of the bed, bending over to open the buckles. "My God, it's cold. We should have stayed in Florida."

"I vote for that," I said.

"Just get your ass out of that bed." He rubbed his stocking feet and twisted up his face. "How about some coffee?"

"Just a second," my mother said, still fussing with the stove.

Jean stood up and undid his belt. "Okay. Let's go." He waited till I was out of bed, took off his trousers, and climbed in. The heavy black and red flannel shirt he wore in cold weather was left on, buttoned tight over his narrow chest. He ran a finger over his mustache and waited for his cup of coffee.

Mother made if for him while I fixed myself a bowl of cornflakes.

"It's not very much to ask to keep the stove going," my mother said. "I never ask you to do anything."

I ate my cornflakes. The stove was beginning to give off a little heat and I pulled my chair closer, arranging it so my back was to the bed. I heard Mother undressing, and then the creak of rusty springs as she got in beside Jean. From that moment on I was supposed to keep quiet so they could sleep.

There was no place else to go. Outside the land was hidden under two and a half feet of snow. The wind was sharp and bitter (I found out later that locals considered it the worst winter in forty years) and in any case I didn't have the proper clothes. Even indoors, sitting in the chair with the stove going, I kept a blanket wrapped around me Indian style. The time dragged slowly. There was nothing to do. I tried to save the few books for nighttime, when my need of them was greater. I drew things with a pencil—objects in the room, my hand, imaginary scenes—but I was no good and quickly lost interest. Usually I simply sat in the chair for six or seven hours. Jean snored softly, but after the first hour or so I stopped hearing it.

Midway through the morning I remembered the candy bars. Certain Jean had forgotten them, I looked anyway, getting up from the chair carefully, tiptoeing to his clothes and searching through the pockets. Nothing. I watched him in bed, his face gray with sleep, his open mouth twitching at the top of each gentle snore. My mother turned to the wall. Jean closed his mouth and rolled over. The room was absolutely silent. I went back to the chair.

They awoke in the early afternoon and stayed in bed. Although the small stove was working it was still the warmest place. Freed from the necessity of keeping quiet, I walked around the room aimlessly, getting a drink of water, rubbing the haze off the windows to look outside. My mother raised her voice and I realized she was talking to me.

"Take some money from my purse and go down to the Greens' and get a dozen eggs."

The trip to the Greens' would take an hour each way. Outside the temperature was five or ten degrees above zero and it was windy. I didn't want to go. My heart sank because I knew I had to.

Children are in the curious position of having to do what people tell them, whether they want to or not. A child knows that he must do what he's told. It matters little whether a command is just or unjust since the child has no confidence in his ability to distinguish the difference. Justice for children is not the same as justice for adults. In effect all commands are morally neutral to a child. Yet because almost every child is consistently bullied by older people he quickly learns that if in some higher frame of reference all commands are equally just, they are not equally easy to carry out. Some fill him with joy, others, so obviously unfair that he must paralyze himself to keep from recognizing their quality, strike him instantly deaf, blind, and dumb. Faced with an order they sense is unfair children simply stall. They wait for more information, for some elaboration that will take away the seeming unfairness. It's a stupid way of defending oneself, but children are stupid compared to adults, who know how to get what they want.

"Couldn't we wait until they come up with the wagon?"

"No. The walk will do you good. You can't sit around all day, it's unhealthy."

"Oh Mother, it'll take hours."

Suddenly Jean sat up, his voice trembling with anger. "Look, this time just go. No arguments this time."

I looked at him in amazement. He'd never even raised his voice to me before. It was against the unwritten rules—my mother was the disciplinarian. I could see he was angry and I had no idea why. Even my mother was surprised. "Take it easy," she said to him softly. "He's going."

Jean's anger should have tipped me off, but it didn't. Wearing his galoshes and his overcoat I went to the Greens' without realizing why they had sent me.

❅   ❅   ❅   ❅

SUMMARY

In its broadest sense, metaphor is indistinguishable from meaning. If a narrative is basic to human experience, however unique the events depicted, it creates links to the experience of the reader. Stories about the loss of innocence or the achievement of a measure of wisdom, or both, inevitably involve the reader, but only if imagery, contrast, structure, and development and the other elements discussed in this book are effectively integrated into the narrative. The deep link with the universals of human experience can be enhanced by more specific metaphors: the "sacred lawn" that reminds us of the gardens from which we, too, have been exiled; the "driftwood stick" that reminds us of the ways we, too, have hurt or killed, consciously or unconsciously; a story that reminds us that we, too, have treated others with insensitivity or arrogance; or a story that reminds us that we, too, have had to move away from home against our will. Metaphor, then, is not only meaning, but also a way in which meaning can be transmitted. Metaphor can also be an avenue to imagery. As soon as we perceive a likeness, we can move into a different world of images; for example, we can bridge the gap between the sensation of drowning and our own more common experiences, as Phyllis Jalbert does in comparing drowning to falling. Even an abstract word like "presentiment," a feeling of coming evil or harm, can reach into our senses if a poet like Emily Dickinson compares it to "that long shadow on the lawn."

EXERCISE

Read the narratives you have written so far. Does your writing create a metaphor of human experience? Does your narrative conform to both the basic patterns of human experience and the usual patterns of narrative structure (i.e., "One day I woke up and I was this way. Then something happened. After that, I was not the same.")? Merely to recreate the pattern, of course, does not mean that you have written a good narrative.

Are there specific metaphors you can develop in your narrative, that is, comparisons between what actually happened and elements that will either help your reader to experience events (e.g., drowning is something like falling) or extend his imagination beyond what is actually happening (e.g., my experience, in its way, was like that of Hamlet's)? Seek not merely the metaphor which suggests "how" your story means, but also that metaphor which can make your story mean more without telling us "what this story means." Only your reader can really tell you what your story means, but you can guide him by controlling and developing your metaphors. The perception of the valid and illuminating metaphor is one of the chief functions of that elusive quality known as imagination. In providing metaphors, as in providing imagery, the writer makes an assumption about his reader. The reader, too, has an imagination, often awaiting excitement by the writer.

Reread the professional pieces at the ends of previous chapters in the context of this chapter's discussion of meaning and metaphor.

SIX
Criticism
and
Revision

One of the hardest things for a writer to accept is criticism of his work. Some criticism, of course, is invalid, and the writer should defend those aspects of his writing that he feels reflect his intentions accurately. These are, after all, his words, and he stands behind them and within them. To give them to us is to surrender a part of himself. If he does not feel that commitment, he has written either a perfunctory or a dishonest narrative. Writing well is an intensely personal confrontation with the self, and it is usually difficult to confront someone who does not feel that the writing has been done well. Criticism often emerges with an irritating vagueness, as the critic gropes for precise terminology: "I don't feel that this passage works," or "The dialogue doesn't sound right," or "This doesn't grab me," or "I don't understand what you are doing here." The writer has the delicate task of defending what he has done and, paradoxically, perceiving the potential value of even the most generally phrased reservations of his critics. Part of the integrity that goes into being a writer is the writer's ability to grow. He cannot grow merely by writing a lot. His writing has to be directed and informed by criticism, that of his classmates and that criticism he develops as he grows in his craft. To give up something that the writer felt initially was good is a difficult process. But it is something he must do to grow, as we all do. We throw away something that is not working for us and try to develop the more promising aspects of our being. We recognize that we are not finished products, that we are "incomplete." And often the writing we submit as finished product represents a first draft. It has yet to be explored for its meanings, to have its general statements vivified into imagery, to discover its structure, to communicate its metaphors to its audience.

The function of criticism is not, in this formulation, that of the teacher, but of the class—of which the teacher is a vital component. The most successful writing classes are often those in which the teacher says little, in which the students go back and forth among themselves. Such a class demands the willingness of the students not only to participate in dialogue, but to submit their work to the scrutiny of their classmates, to read it aloud, defend it when they can, and, above all, absorb suggestions for improvement and development. The process requires a relaxation of the ego, and there is no ego of more seeming strength and more real vulnerability than that of the writer. The process also allows the writer to develop his own faculty of self-criticism, without which no writer can grow. The comments of the class will show the writer that he writes to communicate with an audience—not to lower himself to the lowest common denominator of his audience, but to bring to them convincingly to where he is. My own experience suggests that the process I describe is not some ideal vision of the way things should be, but a valid description of the way things are when a group of students come together to help themselves learn to write. The teacher as guide, mentor, orchestrator, and, possibly, practitioner, is essential to this process.

All writers revise their work, usually after someone else—a friend or editor—has read and commented on it, and often after they have already gone through several drafts, starting from the first bangings on the typewriter, dictation into the tape recorder, or handwriting on the long yellow pad. Many writers read their work aloud to themselves. They may feel self-conscious at first, but they are able to listen to their own words and prose rhythms, noting those places where their meanings are imprecise, their sentences awkward, their rhythms rambling or choppy; they are aware that good imaginative writing should be heard or, at the very least, written so well that it will always read well. The writer who develops a good ear achieves an attribute more important by far than his knowing all the rules of grammar. The same is true of a class as it develops the ability to listen accurately and respond to what doesn't work and what does. The class will gradually exchange its earlier vague response for precision. But the individual members of the class should not come to believe that literary criticism replaces a valid gut response. The latter is still, shall we say, vital. It can, however, become increasingly articulate. If honesty is essential to the writer, it is equally absolute for the critic.

When a writing class heard Saranne Thomke read "The Dolphin" in the spring of 1972, the story was greeted enthusiastically. This was partly because Saranne, being English, handles those accents superbly, but largely because the conflict in the story is so vividly captured in the imagery. The primary objection the class raised concerned the last several sentences of the story, which do not appear in the revised version contained in Chapter 3: "Sonsie slid to the ground, her arms around the pony's neck. 'They killed him,' she sobbed. 'Oh, Eve, why are they so cruel and stupid? They killed him and I loved him." Among the comments made about the original ending were, "It's too sentimental; reminds me of the Bobbsey Twins," "We know what happens. Let it end where it should end. We can infer the rest," and "We know that she loved the dolphin and that the men are cruel and stupid. Why state at the end what the story has already established?" and, finally, "Right. Not only is the ending sentimental but it's unnecessary." Saranne had already come to pretty much the same conclusions. But she had left the ending in to see whether the class confirmed her feeling that, like many writers, she had gone a little too far, had not trusted the story she had written to convey its own meanings, and had thus "summarized" at the end. Summaries are often important at the end of expository prose in which arguments may require reiteration. But a story convinces us in a different way, through its images, characters, conflicts. A good story needs no summing up. And the best summary possible could not save a story that did not convince us of its experience.

The following is the original version of "Riding High (from Chapter 2). The italicized portions indicate where revisions were made.

❊ ORIGINAL VERSION OF *RIDING HIGH*

By the age of fourteen *I did not doubt my invulnerability.* I had witnessed the emaciating, year-long *death* of a father-idol, and emerged from the experience feeling superior to my naive peers for the agony I'd known and the intensity they'd lacked. I had survived for two days and one sea-stormed night through what everyone had assumed to be my death by drowning. I had giggled my way through countless marijuana highs, jolted my way through a dozen acid trips, and learned, even, to expertly stab that Methedrine-filled syringe into flexed veins. Other people, I knew, were forced under by the weight of their own living, *by that intensity of life experience.* But I was invulnerable; I felt my weight to be equal to that of any that might press down on me—I believed my determination to be greater.

This *particular* day in that *fourteenth* year, I was standing by the side of the road, thumb extended and trustworthy smile set, waiting to catch a ride. A highway patrol car pulled up to the curb and the patrolman, holstered hips swinging, strolled towards me.

"Why aren't you in school?"

"School! My God, do I seem that young?"

I convinced him that my driver's license had been carelessly forgotten in my bureau drawer and assured him that I, being legally adult, was capable of making my own decisions as to the advisability of climbing in and out of strangers' automobiles. I had faith in my competence and projected that faith to the Paternal Figure, who strolled back to his ornamental vehicle with an admonition to be careful and a resigned shake of his balding head.

My life had taught me that people act almost exclusively by reaction. Their response to me was dictated solely by my approach to them. I recognized that people expected certain actions under certain

circumstances, *and that by behaving in a manner inconsistent with
those expectations, their perceptions of the whole circumstance would
be altered.* I'd attended formal gatherings and, experimentally, had
behaved informally and then studied the others present *reassessing the
social climate. They'd adjust their behavior to fit what they
perceived to be a different, and now informal, circumstance.* So I
had no real fear of unfamiliar persons, of the dangerous men I'd been
warned throughout my childhood to "never get into cars with."
I believed I could control anyone's behavioral reactions, be they polite
social acquaintance or psychotic rapist. I was the supreme
manipulator. I was invulnerable.

A dingy-grey Chevy pulled up beside me. I opened the car door
and peered in at the driver, assessing his greasy black hair, middle-age,
and T-shirted, paunchy torso. Then, judging *his facial features not
attractive,* but not threatening," I stepped into the seat beside him and
with a reflexive "thank you," slammed the door.

We exchanged trivial conversation and he offered to travel
fifteen miles out of his way to deliver me straight to my destination.
I knew he expected an abashed, "Oh—you don't have to bother!" and I
gave him one. But he insisted, as I assumed he would, so I settled
back in the seat and congratulated myself once again on how aptly I'd
handled that highway patrolman. We traveled in silence for a few
minutes and the hum of the wheels, the heat of the Indian Summer,
left me drowsy. I slept.

I was woken by a change in the rhythm of that wheel humming. By the
sharp jolting of the seat beneath me, I knew we were moving over
unpaved surface. I straightened and looked out to see acres of orchard
and a twilight sky. It seemed that a moment ago it had been midday
in a city of homes, of people, of familiarity. *Our location now was
unrecognizable to me.* My thoughts, my attempts to assess and clarify
the circumstances, were too vague to be panicky. I turned to question
the driver, the car slowed, he switched off the ignition and turned
to me. My thoughts were clarified—my hand reached for the door
handle.

Instantaneously, the *quiet* that had come with the stilling of the
motor was broken, replaced by the man's tight grip on my wrist
and his incoherent, throaty soundings. I strained to recall all I'd been
taught *as to the most effective action to take* against the rapist's
attempts, but no recollection could come clear. There was no time to
consider an analysis of his psyche while I struggled against his rough,
thick arms enclosing me, his sweating, reddened, contorted face
pressing towards me.

A scream, *seeming to be formed from outside of me,* beyond

the range of my voice and the strength of my lungs, reverberated. His
hand clamped over my mouth, I heard his short breaths, tasted
the salt of his flesh, and my teeth clenched over his fingers. My cheek
was burned with the impact of his slap. His other hand groped over my
thigh and my whole body recoiled. The fear I'd known a few
seconds before vanished, replaced by only rage, hatred, hatred and rage
for the despicable hand, the sticky, urgent, fondless touch of the
aggressor.

*I did not question myself as to the most preferable course of
action to follow. My behavior bore no relation to rational calculation,
but rather sprang up from an instinctive reflex, the result of an
ancestoral, primitive past when, it is said, countless women were bashed
over the head and dragged into the cave. My whole Being reacted,
my whole Essence was of force, of struggle.* Legs knew to kick out,
arms knew to slug and strike, voice knew to wail. Mind assumed
no control over Body. Mind was not required.

I was out of his hold, out of his car. The man, sweating and
swearing profusely, not stopping to slam the car door I'd *by some means*
managed to open, sped off into the orchard leaving a wave of dust,
a row of tire tracks, and a young girl racing frantically towards some
well-traveled road, towards homes, towards people, towards anywhere
familiar. Though he'd driven out of my sight range by this time I
ran with the terror of the victim of pursuit—the hound's rabbit,
the lion's gazelle. Anticipating meeting him any moment face to face,
I turned my head constantly in every direction to lose the pursuer.

*Feeling the hot tears, the straining of my breath to support
simultaneously both sobbing chest and racing body,* I tripped over a
stone, tasted the dust, and heard my torn dress rip even wider.
The orchard path seemed *to continue on without end* and I imagined
myself, rat on a metal wheel, running forever, running towards nothing,
sobbing and sweating.

I came to a paved road. On the far side stood a staid, white Victorian
home. A familiar suppertime aroma drifted from it. The scent
brought to mind the dusks of my childhood when Mama would call
me in to set the table and I'd hurry to finish the chore in time to
greet my father as he came in from the day's work. I wanted to cross the
road, to tell the strangers there of that fear, that rage, that struggle.
But the home projected an aura of such placidity I knew my presence
would be a disruption. A single car approached from farther down
the roadway. I rearranged my twisted clothing, dabbed at the tears, and
stuck out my thumb.

❊   ❊   ❊   ❊

Most of the revisions involve condensation, the paring down of language for greater clarity and impact. Why force a reader through more words than necessary? What, after all, is the difference between "the weight of their own living" and "that intensity of lived experience"? Kris Keller is doing what we often do in first drafts: saying the same thing two ways, as if unsure which version is superior. In revising, she made the choice. The original version is vague and wordy about the way the writer conditions others at social gatherings. The rewritten passage represents a tightening of verbiage and obvious gains in clarity. The discussion is still rather general, but it now has more relevance to the specific encounter toward which her overconfidence is pressing her.

Other changes involve precision. "Dying" for "death" more clearly captures the sense of *process*. The quick question "Where was I now?" is more precise and dramatic—the breaking in on the narrator's own thought—than the awkward "Our location was now unrecognizable to me." The change is also a better prelude to panic. The long disquisition about reflex and primeval courtship is not only unnecessary, but represents a "scholarly" intrusion into a moment where such analysis, however accurate, could not occur.* As Kris says, "Mind was not required." Yet we get a dose of mind in the original version. Moments of extreme stress are very difficult for a writer to handle. They are usually best treated with understated brevity and a focus on details, not on words like "panic," "fear," or "absolute terror." This suggestion applies to the eliminated sentence about the "hot tears" and to the ending of "The Dolphin," where the oil towers, the still pony, the girl stiff on the pony's back, the shots, and the rain provide the details around which the emotional experience—sorrow, horror, anger, helplessness—is organized. In "Riding High," we can infer the "hot tears" and "sobbing chest." The eliminated sentence is nicely organized, but it represents the expected clichés of the experience, not an extension of the experience into vividly realized imagery. The class made a similar comment about the "orchard path." One person said that it reminded her of that old phrase "after what seemed like an eternity." The sentence was left in in a condensed form, because, as Kris pointed out, it provides a necessary transition from the path to the paved road. Although the sentence verges on cliché, it does lead nicely to the turn at the end of the story, where the girl refuses to intrude upon that proper house. We can imagine another ending: "Oh you poor dear! What happened? There, there, come in and sit by the fire. Here, use my handkerchief. I'll get you some nice hot tea and some bisquits." *That* is the cliché against which the ending of "Riding High" works effectively.

---

* Notice that an apparent exception to this caveat, "It is said that in situations like these . . ." in "Who Was Really Responsible?" is an intentional intrusion, ironic and tongue-in-cheek.

The changes in "Riding High" resulted from criticism from the class that involved suggestions for improvements in a promising first draft. Criticism does not have to be negative; positive criticism makes it easier for the writer to accept suggestions for alterations, to put himself or herself within the context of a group of students who are all trying to develop their own writing skills and to help others realize the same goal. The writer is critic and the critic is writer, and usually the two faculties develop simultaneously. The student who develops greater insight into the work of his classmates almost invariably achieves a stronger control over his own writing.

The following is an earlier version of "The Driftwood Stick" (Chapter 5), a version that had already undergone substantial revision. The words in parentheses were eliminated from the final version as either unnecessary or amenable to condensation.

❀ EARLIER VERSION OF *THE DRIFTWOOD STICK*

It wasn't hard to see why he (the boy) was disgusted. When it's summer vacation no boy likes to spend the morning cleaning up the mess left over from the party his parents have thrown the night before. Even though he had almost finished (cleaning up), the cottage still reeked of spilled beer and stale cigarettes, and he could hardly wait to get out and go fishing.

Cleaning up had taken about two and a half hours, and now all he had (left) to do was empty the garbage. He didn't mind this part of the job, though. For as long as his family had been coming down to Maine in the summer, it had always been his job to empty the garbage every morning in front of the cottage. The cottage itself jutted out over the edge of a small hill which dropped steeply into the ocean. The boy always made a game of how fast he could run down to the waterfront without spilling any of the garbage. With no brothers or sisters he made (it was only natural for him to make) a solitary game out of almost everything he did.

Separating the hill and the water was a chunk of rocky Maine Coast from which the boy always emptied the garbage. At high tide the Coast is a powerful, almost frightening sight. The water comes up high on the rocks, and as one stands just above the water, he cannot be sure that the next wave will not engulf him (in its foamy grasp). Yet the boy was glad that it was not high tide that morning because he had a game to play—a game more interesting to the twelve year old than any aspect of natural beauty. (In fact, on that morning the tide was at its lowest, and he decided that it was time to play the game.)

The low tide exposed a large patch of seaweed where the boy normally threw the garbage. Just to his left as he faced the water, a six-inch sewage pipe ran down from the cottage and ended about two feet above the lowest level of rock, now exposed and overgrown with thick, ugly seaweed. Every time someone flushed a toilet in the cottage, the water gushed out the end of the pipe into a shallow yellow pool filled with dead snails and live starfish. To the boy's right and slightly above him sat the rotted remains of a dock that had been taken out of the water for winter many years ago and never used since. Now it lay high on the rocks; unpainted, useless, spotted with the white droppings of seagulls. As he walked towards his dumping spot, the boy had to be careful to avoid the pieces of broken glass scattered among the rocks.

(When he threw out the garbage, it stayed on top of the seaweed, untouched by the saltwater below it.) After throwing out the garbage, he stepped back from the edge of the seaweed for about two minutes. Then, from among the rocks, he chose a small stone and stood above the dumping area now being ravaged by black and white seagulls, heeding the yodeling call of (one of) their leader(s). (Now was a perfect time for him to play his game.) He cocked (back) his arm and flung (threw) the rock into the swarm of gulls. No matter how hard the boy threw the rock, the gulls always felt it coming and scattered safely in all directions. As usual, this throw found the only hole in the target and buried itself in the seaweed with a muffled thud. He had come to expect this result and simply stepped back, waiting for the gulls to return.

After a few minutes he again stood above the gulls with another rock. But just as he was about to throw it into the pack of gulls, he spotted an old piece of driftwood wedged between the rocks beneath him. He pulled the stick from the rocks. About twenty feet below him, the gulls, obviously unconcerned with the boy's presence, dug, fought, and scratched for every orange peel, bread crust, or clam shell that could be stolen from their fellow scavengers. As he drew (cocked) his arm back, most of the gulls scrambled away, leaving only two birds fighting over a piece of pork chop from last night's dinner. He spotted this target and flung the stick. Just as one of the birds had pulled (stolen) the prize from his opponent, the stick plummeted into its full white breast.

At the moment of contact, the gull shrieked a hollow "caw." With its wings fluttering unevenly, the bird landed in the water with an uncoordinated splash. For several minutes it floated on its side with one wing extended out full into the water and the other tucked neatly at its side. At short intervals the gull stretched a paddlelike foot away from its body and strained to pull the water back under him. His efforts, however, failed to counteract the push of the outgoing tide, and he began to groan in a way that sounded strangely human to the boy.

(As if to help his stricken victim) The boy edged his way down to the lowest level of seaweed and extended his arm over the water to the seagull, now only about five feet from the shore. Feeling as helpless as the gull, the boy searched for some way to help the bird—how, he did not know; but there was always a chance. He felt (had derived no sense of superiority from his actions) only a (pressing) need to aid the bird, now motionless and drifting slowly away from him. He looked around for something to help him reach the bird, but could find only his driftwood weapon, lying in the seaweed. With one hand he reached the stick out towards the bobbing gull, and with the other he grabbed a clump of seaweed behind him to keep himself from falling forward.

"Come here, come on," he pleaded aloud to the bird, "we can make it, come on." It did not help. The bird tried as hard as possible to swim away from the stick. "Don't be afraid, come here. We can make it." In spite of the boy's pleading, the frightened bird merely dragged himself towards deeper water. The boy now saw he had little chance to help the bird. Each new wave washed completely over the gull, which bobbed to the surface only after each wave passed.

The youth climbed back up off the seaweed in search of a longer stick. As he scrambled from rock to rock during his search, he stopped several times and looked up at his own cottage and those around it to make sure no one was watching. When he could not find a stick of proper length he headed back across the rocks and over the sewage pipes to the spot from which he had thrown the garbage . . . and the stick.

For several minutes the bird made a final effort to save itself in the water—knowing that it could not go onto the land. In his hand the boy still held the stick (he had used first to injure the bird and later to try to help it). Another wave covered the bird and the boy stared at the spot where it should have reappeared. But the bird was gone. The boy continued staring at the spot for many minutes. Finally, he hurled the stick as far out into the empty water as he could. Before the stick landed, the young man turned away from the water, scooped up the empty garbage pails and scrambled up the hill towards the safety of the cottage.

❉   ❉   ❉   ❉

With the exception of the substitution of a more precise "pulled" for "stolen" and the elimination of the cliché "in its foamy grasp," almost all of the changes involve the cutting of unnecessary words and phrases. In every case, the words eliminated tell us something we already know or can easily infer from the context. They get in the way. While some writers tell us too little and must develop their work toward a full exploration of the narrative's implicit experience (as was the case with Ken Hinkley's "To Get Away"), others say too much. Perhaps the final stage of any revision occurs when the writer goes through what he considers his finished work and cuts out *all* words that do not contribute to the communication of the experience his narrative relates.

SUMMARY

Criticism is the process whereby a class discusses the work submitted, measures its effectiveness, and attempts to isolate those areas that could be (1) expanded toward a fuller treatment of experience only briefly suggested, (2) condensed for greater impact and clarity, (3) eliminated, or (4) changed in some other way. Criticism should be positive. But critics should not be supportive of writing they really feel is bad. Undeserved praise for slovenly or dishonest writing is probably far worse for the writer than honest objection. The writer whose work is condemned suffers a possibly shattering experience, but often that experience is necessary to the clearing away of cliché and verbiage and the development of writing that does convey experience validly and vividly. Some classes work effectively if their members assume the pose of magazine editors looking for work they consider publishable. And it need not be a pose. The class can, if it wishes, publish its best work, even if only in dittoed form. The production of a journal can give class members a goal that offers greater point and promise to the job of criticism.

Revision is the process whereby we develop our first draft toward a finished story. It involves our becoming aware of not only what works for us but also what works for our audience, a balance between what we want to say and how we can best communicate with others. The process of revision is greatly enhanced by the writer's ability to listen to his writing and develop the ear that tells him when his writing can be improved. Hopefully, neither his ear nor his audience will accept the easy cliché, the vague phrasing, the imprecise image, or the wordiness that muffles rather than transmits experience. Revision is often a painful process in which the writer must eliminate or alter passages he thought effective in his earlier draft. But revision is the process whereby writing reaches maturity.

Criticism and revision represent the necessary learning process that all writers must undergo. Even the finest professional writers go through the process constantly.

EXERCISE

Even though you have no doubt been receiving criticism and revising your writing as you have submitted it to the class, return to one of the earlier pieces you wrote and read it aloud. Can you hear places that require changes—patches of language that don't sound right? Does your narrative contain words and phrases you can eliminate? Can you give more specific details about the experience you are describing? Are there places where generalizations can be replaced with details and images that convey to the reader's experience what your generalizations merely state? If you are noticing places where your work can be improved and making those improvements, you are accomplishing the goals of that simultaneous process every writer undergoes: criticism and revision. The goals keep moving into the distance just ahead of the writer's reach, but as he reaches for them, his writing must improve.

Conclusion

There should be no conclusion. By now, as you read this, you should have launched into one of the most exciting processes that life affords: that of looking at aspects of your own experience—seeing them, feeling them, responding to them, understanding them not just in the mind but within the emotions—and of shaping that experience into literature. By now you should recognize that the writing of literature is within your spectrum of abilities; it is not merely something other people do to provide books that you must read. Literature, like living, is something *you* do. That does not mean that you now sit constantly before your notebook or typewriter. But it should mean that your own awarenesses have been heightened so that you can respond more sensitively to what has happened to you, to what is happening to you, and to what will happen to you. Then perhaps, you will see your life as a unique human process that evolves from its sources and moves *into* experience. You will perhaps see that your life is not merely a superficial series of events which have no contact with the special symbolism of *your* experience. A life inevitably reaches its conclusion, but the measure of the value of a life to the person living it may well be the intensity of that person's response to his experience.

I reach no conclusion here except to say that the approach this book suggests should not cease when the semester in which it is used ends. If that happens, the book has failed. If, however, the book provides a stimulus for an opening out into the world of experience that is all before us, as well as in our past, if the book encourages an opening into an individual's unique response to his or her experience, then it has succeeded. Discipline and creativity are essential components of successful writing and, more deeply, of successful life, however we choose to measure success. Unless we are about human things in this life, however, any success we may achieve must, inevitably, become ashes in our mouths. We come to ashes soon enough—"Golden lads and girls all must, / As chimney-sweepers, come to dust," from Shakespeare's *Cymbeline*.

Perhaps the only conclusion this book can offer is the hope that what it has begun cannot be concluded. The following narrative is by a writer looking back at his own life through the alter ego of his son, who inhabits the world in which the writer, too, was once young. The narrative incorporates superbly the elements of technique and imagination that this book has emphasized.

❈ ONCE MORE TO THE LAKE

E. B. White

One summer, along about 1904, my father rented a camp on a lake in Maine and took us all there for the month of August. We all got ringworm from some kittens and had to rub Pond's Extract on our arms and legs night and morning, and my father rolled over in a canoe with all his clothes on; but outside of that the vacation was a success and from then on none of us ever thought there was any place in the world like that lake in Maine. We returned summer after summer—always on August 1st for one month. I have since become a salt-water man, but sometimes in summer there are days when the restlessness of the tides and the fearful cold of the sea water and the incessant wind which blows across the afternoon and into the evening make me wish for the placidity of a lake in the woods. A few weeks ago this feeling got so strong I bought myself a couple of bass hooks and a spinner and returned to the lake where we used to go, for a week's fishing and to revisit old haunts.

I took along my son, who had never had any fresh water up his nose and who had seen lily pads only from train windows. On the journey over to the lake I began to wonder what it would be like.

SOURCE: From *One Man's Meat* by E. B. White. Copyright 1941 by E. B. White. By permission of Harper & Row, Publishers, Inc.

I wondered how time would have marred this unique, this holy spot—the
coves and streams, the hills that the sun set behind, the camps and
the paths behind the camps. I was sure that the tarred road would have
found it out and I wondered in what other ways it would be
desolated. It is strange how much you can remember about places
like that once you allow your mind to return into the grooves which
lead back. You remember one thing, and that suddenly reminds
you of another thing. I guess I remembered clearest of all the early
mornings, when the lake was cool and motionless, remembered how the
bedroom smelled of the lumber it was made of and of the wet
woods ·whose scent entered through the screen. The partitions in the
camp were thin and did not extend clear to the top of the rooms, and
as I was always the first up I would dress softly so as not to wake
the others, and sneak out into the sweet outdoors and start out in
the canoe, keeping close along the shore in the long shadows of the
pines. I remembered being very careful never to rub my paddle against
the gunwale for fear of disturbing the stillness of the cathedral.

The lake had never been what you would call a wild lake. There
were cottages sprinkled around the shores, and it was in farming
country although the shores of the lake were quite heavily wooded.
Some of the cottages were owned by nearby farmers, and you would
live at the shore and eat your meals at the farmhouse. That's what our
family did. But although it wasn't wild, it was a fairly large and
undisturbed lake and there were places in it which, to a child at least,
seemed infinitely remote and primeval.

I was right about the tar: it led to within half a mile of the shore.
But when I got back there, with my boy, and we settled into a
camp near a farmhouse and into the kind of summertime I had known,
I could tell that it was going to be pretty much the same as it had
been before—I knew it, lying in bed the first morning, smelling
the bedroom, and hearing the boy sneak quietly out and go off along
the shore in a boat. I began to sustain the illusion that he was I,
and therefore, by simple transposition, that I was my father.
This sensation persisted, kept cropping up all the time we were there.
It was not an entirely new feeling, but in this setting it grew much
stronger. I seemed to be living a dual existence. I would be in
the middle of some simple act, I would be picking up a bait box or
laying down a table fork, or I would be saying something, and suddenly
it would be not I but my father who was saying the words or making
the gesture. It gave me a creepy sensation.

We went fishing the first morning. I felt the same damp moss
covering the worms in the bait can, and saw the dragonfly alight
on the tip of my rod as it hovered a few inches from the surface of the
water. It was the arrival of this fly that convinced me beyond any

doubt that everything was as it always had been, that the years were a
mirage and there had been no years. The small waves were the
same, chunking the rowboat under the chin as we fished at anchor,
and the boat was the same boat, the same color green and the ribs
broken in the same places, and under the floor-boards the same
fresh-water leavings and débris—the dead helgramite, the wisps of moss,
the rusty discarded fishhook, the dried blood from yesterday's catch.
We stared silently at the tips of our rods, at the dragonflies that
came and went. I lowered the tip of mine into the water, tentatively,
pensively dislodging the fly, which darted two feet away, poised,
darted two feet back, and came to rest again a little farther up the rod.
There had been no years between the ducking of this dragonfly
and the other one—the one that was part of memory. I looked at the
boy, who was silently watching his fly, and it was my hands that
held his rod, my eyes watching. I felt dizzy and didn't know which rod
I was at the end of.

We caught two bass, hauling them in briskly as though they were
mackerel, pulling them over the side of the boat in a businesslike
manner without any landing net, and stunning them with a
blow on the back of the head. When we got back for a swim before
lunch, the lake was exactly where we had left it, the same number
of inches from the dock, and there was only the merest suggestion of a
breeze. This seemed an utterly enchanted sea, this lake you could
leave to its own devices for a few hours and come back to, and
find that it had not stirred, this constant and trustworthy body of
water. In the shallows, the dark, water-soaked sticks and twigs, smooth
and old, were undulating in clusters on the bottom against the
clean ribbed sand, and the track of the mussel was plain. A school of
minnows swam by, each minnow with its small individual shadow,
doubling the attendance, so clear and sharp in the sunlight. Some of the
other campers were in swimming, along the shore, one of them
with a cake of soap, and the water felt thin and clear and unsubstantial.
Over the years there had been this person with the cake of soap, this
cultist, and here he was. There had been no years.

Up to the farmhouse to dinner through the teeming, dusty field; the
road under our sneakers was only a two-track road. The middle
track was missing, the one with the marks of the hooves and the
splotches of dried, flaky manure. There had always been three tracks
to choose from in choosing which track to walk in; now the choice
was narrowed down to two. For a moment I missed terribly the middle
alternative. But the way led past the tennis court, and something
about the way it lay there in the sun reassured me; the tape had
loosened along the backline, the alleys were green with plantains and
other weeds, and the net (installed in June and removed in September)

sagged in the dry noon, and the whole place steamed with midday
heat and hunger and emptiness. There was a choice of pie for
dessert, and one was blueberry and one was apple, and the waitresses
were the same country girls, there having been no passage of
time, only the illusion of it as in a dropped curtain—the waitresses
were still fifteen; their hair had been washed, that was the only
difference—they had been to the movies and seen the pretty girls with
the clean hair.

Summertime, oh summertime, pattern of life indelible, the
fade-proof lake, the woods unshatterable, the pasture with the sweetfern
and the juniper forever and ever, summer without end; this was the
background, and the life along the shore was the design, the cottagers
with their innocent and tranquil design, their tiny docks with the
flagpole and the American flag floating against the white clouds in the
blue sky, the little paths over the roots of the trees leading from
camp to camp and the paths leading back to the outhouses and the
can of lime for sprinkling, and at the souvenir counters at
the store the miniature birch-bark canoes and the post cards that
showed things looking a little better than they looked. This was the
American family at play, escaping the city heat, wondering whether
the newcomers is the camp at the head of the cove were "common" or
"nice," wondering whether it was true that the people who drove
up for Sunday dinner at the farmhouse were turned away because there
wasn't enough chicken.

It seemed to me, as I kept remembering all this, that those times
and those summers had been infinitely precious and worth saving.
There had been jollity and peace and goodness. The arriving (at the
beginning of August) had been so big a business in itself, at the railway
station the farm wagon drawn up, the first smell of the pine-laden
air, the first glimpse of the smiling farmer, and the great importance of
the trunks and your father's enormous authority in such matters,
and the feel of the wagon under you for the long ten-mile haul, and at
the top of the last long hill catching the first view of the lake
after eleven months of not seeing this cherished body of water. The
shouts and cries of the other campers when they saw you, and the
trunks to be unpacked, to give up their rich burden. (Arriving was
less exciting nowadays, when you sneaked up in your car and parked it
under a tree near the camp and took out the bags and in five
minutes it was all over, no fuss, no loud wonderful fuss about trunks.)

Peace and goodness and jollity. The only thing that was wrong
now, really, was the sound of the place, an unfamiliar nervous
sound of the outboard motors. This was the note that jarred, the one
thing that would sometimes break the illusion and set the years
moving. In those other summertimes all motors were inboard; and

when they were at a little distance, the noise they made was a sedative, an ingredient of summer sleep. They were one-cylinder and two-cylinder engines, and some were make-and-break and some were jump-spark, but they all made a sleepy sound across the lake. The one-lungers throbbed and fluttered, and the twin cylinder ones purred, and that was a quiet sound too. But now the campers all had outboards. In the daytime, in the hot mornings, these motors made a petulant, irritable sound; at night, in the still evening when the afterglow lit the water, they whined about one's ears like mosquitoes. My boy loved our rented outboard, and his great desire was to achieve singlehanded mastery over it, and authority, and he soon learned the trick of choking it a little (but not too much), and the adjustment of the needle valve. Watching him I would remember the things you could do with the old one-cylinder engine with the heavy flywheel, how you could have it eating out of your hand if you got really close to it spiritually. Motor boats in those days didn't have clutches, and you would make a landing by shutting off the motor at the proper time and coasting in with a dead rudder. But there was a way of reversing them, if you learned the trick, by cutting the switch and putting it on again exactly on the final dying revolution of the flywheel, so that it would kick back against compression and begin reversing. Approaching a dock in a strong following breeze, it was difficult to slow up sufficiently by the ordinary coasting method, and if a boy felt he had complete mastery over his motor, he was tempted to keep it running beyond its time and then reverse it a few feet from the dock. It took a cool nerve, because if you threw the switch a twentieth of a second too soon you would catch the flywheel when it still had speed enough to go up past center, and the boat would leap ahead, charging bull-fashion at the dock.

We had a good week at the camp. The bass were biting well and the sun shone endlessly, day after day. We would be tired at night and lie down in the accumulated heat of the little bedrooms after the long hot day and the breeze would stir almost imperceptibly outside and the smell of the swamp drift in through the rusty screens. Sleep would come easily and in the morning the red squirrel would be on the roof, tapping out his gay routine. I kept remembering everything, lying in bed in the mornings—the small steamboat that had a long rounded stern like the lip of a Ubangi, and how quietly she ran on the moonlight sails, when the older boys played their mandolins and the girls sang and we ate doughnuts dipped in sugar, and how sweet the music was on the water in the shining night, and what it had felt like to think about girls then. After breakfast we would go up to the store and the things were in the same place—the minnows in a bottle, the plugs and spinners disarranged and pawed over by the youngsters from the boys' camp, the fig newtons and the Beeman's gum. Outside, the road was tarred and cars stood in front of the store. Inside, all was just as it had always been, except there was more Coca Cola and not so much Moxie and root beer and birch beer and sarsaparilla. We would walk out with a bottle of pop apiece and sometimes the pop would backfire up our noses and hurt. We explored the streams, quietly, where the turtles slid off the sunny logs and dug their way into the soft bottom; and we lay on the town wharf and fed worms to the tame bass. Everywhere we went I had trouble making out which was I, the one walking at my side, the one walking in my pants.

One afternoon while we were there at that lake a thunderstorm came up. It was like the revival of an old melodrama that I had seen long ago with childish awe. The second-act climax of the drama of the electrical disturbance over a lake in America had not changed in any important respect. This was the big scene, still the big scene. The whole thing was so familiar, the first feeling of oppression and a general air around camp of not wanting to go very far away. In midafternoon (it was all the same) a curious darkening of the sky, and a lull in everything that had made life tick; and then the way the boats suddenly swung the other way at their moorings with the coming of a breeze out of the new quarter, and the premonitory rumble. Then the kettle drum, then the snare, then the bass drum and cymbals, then crackling light against the dark, and the gods grinning and licking their chops in the hills. Afterward the calm, the rain steadily rustling in the calm lake, the return of light and hope and spirits, and the campers running out in joy and relief to go swimming in the rain, their bright cries perpetuating the deathless joke about how they were getting simply drenched, and the children screaming with delight at the new sensation of bathing in the rain, and the joke about getting drenched linking the generations in a strong indestructible chain. And the comedian who waded in carrying an umbrella.

When the others went swimming my son said he was going in too. He pulled his dripping trunks from the line where they had hung all through the shower, and wrung them out. Languidly, and with no thought of going in, I watched him, his hard little body, skinny and bare, saw him wince slightly as he pulled up around his vitals the small, soggy, icy garment. As he buckled the swollen belt suddenly my groin felt the chill of death.